Computer-Assisted Investigative Reporting
Development and Methodology

LEA's Communication Series
Jennings Bryant/Dolf Zillmann, General Editors

For a complete list of other titles in LEA's Communication Series, please contact Lawrence Erlbaum Associates, Publishers.

Computer-Assisted Investigative Reporting
Development and Methodology

Margaret H. DeFleur
Boston University

LEA LAWRENCE ERLBAUM ASSOCIATES, PUBLISHERS
1997 Mahwah, New Jersey

Lawrence Erlbaum Associates, Inc., Publishers
10 Industrial Avenue
Mahwah, New Jersey 07430

cover design by Kathryn Houghtaling

Library of Congress Cataloging-in-Publication Data

DeFleur, Margaret H.
    Computer-assisted investigative reporting : development
and methodology / by Margaret H. DeFleur.
        p. cm.
    Includes bibliographical references and index.
    ISBN 0-8058-2162-7 (cloth : alk. paper). — ISBN
0-8058-2163-5 (pbk. : alk. paper)
    1. Investigative reporting—Data processing.   I. Title.
PN4781.D39   1997   96-51568
070.4'3—dc21
                                                    CIP

Books published by Lawrence Erlbaum Associates are printed
on acid-free paper, and their bindings are chosen for strength and
durability.

Printed in the United States of America
10 9 8 7 6 5 4 3 2 1

Contents

Preface

Conducting computer analyses for the purpose of revealing information of significance to the press represents an extension of one of the most important forms of American journalism into the contemporary era of new technologies. Investigative reporting, as it has been practiced for more than a century, had its start with the establishment of the metropolitan newspaper during the early decades of the 1900s. At the time, it was a continuation of the evolving tradition of freedom of the press that had characterized American political life since colonial times. As it developed, investigative reporting stressed facts, rather than the opinions of the editor or reporter. In turn, that tradition had its own intellectual roots. The concept of freedom of the press extends back at least to the position set forth by John Milton in the late 1600s—that freedom of the press provides a "marketplace of ideas," and is essential to society.

Today, computer-assisted investigative reporting (CAIR) extends that "marketplace of ideas" into systematic examinations of the electronic records of government. In addition, computer analyses of other kinds of information systematically gathered by journalists can provide the press with insights into trends and patterns unlikely to be revealed by other means.

Although the value of information revealed by computer analyses is indeed considerable, electronic investigation does not replace the traditional strategies by which reporters uncover and disclose situations in government or elsewhere. As chapter 1 shows with a well-known example of CAIR, computer-generated data do not stand by themselves. They reveal facts that could not easily have come to light by other means; they uncover trends and patterns that must be interpreted; they provide leads that must be followed with interviews with key players or by other traditional means. Thus, the computer is a tool that can be used with great effectiveness by a reporter but it must be supplemented with a basic "shoe-leather" approach. Using a computer becomes effective only after the suspicions of journalists lead to a conclusion that a problem should be investigated. Moreover, CAIR retains the need for creative and analytical thinking about where to look for activities or situations that should be disclosed, who might be responsible, and why the outcome may be important to the public.

Computer-Assisted Investigative Reporting is not a "how-to" book in the strictest sense. That is, it will not tell its readers exactly which buttons to push on the computer to produce an analysis of data or which specific software to use, but it will help to plan and conceptualize a project. Equally important, it is also a "how it developed" book. The overall purpose of this book is to describe the historical and intellectual development of a new area of practice in journalism. It does so by showing how several trends have come together to provide contemporary journalists with an important new tool. With the assistance of prominent scholars and distinguished journalists who contributed ideas to the present work, the book develops an understanding of both the historical development and the analytical methodology of this form of analysis.

Clearly, computer-assisted investigative reporting requires an understanding of several kinds of skills and knowledge. These include not only the traditional skills of critical thinking and writing but also an understanding of computers and software, the legal structure by which reporters can (and sometimes cannot) obtain electronic records, and the logic of analytical strategies by which conclusions can be reached using procedures that others will accept as legitimate. Overall, then, the purpose of this book is to address these issues as well as to provide a number of examples of specific projects that have been developed within this framework.

In reviewing the development of computer-assisted reporting, the computer may seem like a relatively recent innovation. Prior to World War II, few Americans knew that such machines were being developed. No one could have envisioned the central place that they would occupy in society by the end of the century. Certainly few individuals in the 1950s could foresee that one day the desktop computer would be as common in newsrooms as typewriters, or that this technology would become a critical tool for investigative reporting.

As chapter 2 explains, the modern computer became a reality during the late 1940s, when the first electronic, digital, all-purpose, programmable computers were designed and built. However, this technology did not leap into existence with the famous ENIAC, the first "electronic brain" that was capable of calculation at the speed of light. The principles on which today's computers are based stretches back to an unknown point in time at which the very first devices were designed to assist in calculation. The common abacus that provides the foundation appears to have been used as far back as written history extends. In time, mechanical calculators were developed to assist in such laborious tasks as the multiplication of large numbers. Inventive individuals devised ways to "program" their hand-cranked machines, and to use electricity for counting and tabulating machines. Thus, the development of the computer resulted from a step-by-step accumulation of solutions over time. The story of this development is necessary to appreciate the incredible tool that we now have at our disposal. Finally, the chapter discusses the use of computers by reporters in the newsroom.

Chapter 3 traces the unfolding of one of the most remarkable situations in the history of government. From the earliest times, the records of rulers and their administrations were kept secret—jealously shielded from public scrutiny. Indeed, it was not all that different in the United States prior to World War II. Before that time, the agencies of federal government had no mandate to keep records or to make them available to public scrutiny. But in 1946, the U.S. Congress passed a new law—the Administrative Procedure Act—that required all federal agencies to maintain records. A very important second step was taken in the 1960s when the first Freedom of Information law (FOIA) was passed. It was a remarkable concession to democracy, opening government records to scrutiny by the public. Shortly after this, however, the medium of record-keeping changed from paper to electronic entries on magnetic tape. This transition caused a number of problems because the law was inadequate for addressing the problems of a computer age. Although the law was amended in 1974 and 1986, it failed to resolve many of the controversies that arose when citizens first tried to obtain the computerized records of government. These controversies resulted in a number of legal challenges and court rulings that have a direct impact on the development of computer-assisted reporting. Obviously, many obstacles remain and the situation continues to change. The nature and development of FOIA is a complex story and one that should be understood by any journalist who intends to conduct a computer-assisted analysis.

In chapter 4, the development of computer-assisted investigative reporting itself is described and its current status is discussed. Beginning modestly in the 1960s, this approach to reporting has become a part of the functions of many newsrooms around the country. The chapter describes the work of CAIR "pioneers" such as Phil Meyer, David Burnham, Elliot Jaspin, and others. The chapter also illustrates the great variety of stories that have been produced in the nation's newsrooms in recent years. The chapter also describes several strategies in which computer analyses of records have produced the foundations for important stories. Some of these have won significant prizes and many have made major contributions to the community and society. Others are of the kind that make up the routine stories of any daily newspaper.

Beginning with chapter 5, the book describes the techniques and procedures that often are used by journalists in computer analyses. It discusses the analytical procedures used and advocated by CAIR pioneers. It also summarizes the procedures and strategies of analysis used by a number of journalists by reviewing more than 130 computer-assisted stories. These stories probe the performance of public officials and agencies of government at all levels and focus on issues that have long been mainstays of the American press—for example, crime, politics, financial misconduct, and social inequality. The review shows the variety of topics, techniques, and strategies that have been used. The majority of these analyses employed basic, descriptive statistics and simple computer procedures. However, a significant number used complex strategies and advanced statistical procedures.

An analysis of a very large-scale database of government records is described in chapter 6. The major purpose of this chapter is to show how large bodies of records can be investigated, and to describe a number of the procedures, techniques, and problems that are central to this level of analysis. The records were obtained from the U.S. Federal Court System. The data represent more than 5 million court cases and transactions that took place over an 18-year period within the 94 federal judicial districts. In addition, more than 100 economic and social variables obtained from the U.S. Census were examined for selected districts. This analysis used a supercomputer to accommodate the huge amount of electronic information.

Some may question why the federal court data were used for an example of a large-scale project. As one reviewer for this book stated, "I would prefer to see the focus on local and state courts. Students cannot readily identify with federal courts. They are seldom exposed to them, even in entry-level jobs." The reviewer also suggested that an example using education, city hall, or other traditional beats would be more appropriate.

Although the chapter discusses some of the findings and implications of the findings for the Federal Court system, the purpose of this discussion is not to focus so much on the specific findings of the project, but rather on its procedures. The goal, then, was threefold. One purpose was to demonstrate what kinds of information can be obtained by using computer analyses to uncover trends and patterns in large assemblies of records that would not be revealed by other means. A second purpose was to identify a number of specific problems, difficulties, procedures, and strategies of analysis that may be relevant to many computer-assisted analyses.

Finally, the federal court study is an example of what David Burnham called a "performance audit." It is a broad-based review of the records developed by a major government agency over an extended period. Rather than using a computer analysis to answer a specific question or to focus on a particular aspect of an agency's performance, every transaction or record is analyzed for a complete, in-depth examination of an agency's history. Burnham, cofounder of Transactional Records Access Clearinghouse (TRAC) at Syracuse University, believes that the performance audit is one of the most powerful tools for fulfilling the watchdog role—and one neglected by journalists. And although the energies of most newspapers are devoted to regional and local issues, he believes that more resources should be directed toward an in-depth assessment at the federal level. Thus the federal court study was used in this chapter as an example of a performance audit.

Chapter 7 reviews some of the major findings of the analysis of the federal court data and discusses the ways in which the press responded to these findings. Again, it is not the actual findings that are most important here, but the lessons learned about how reporters interpreted the results and wrote news stories for the public. Because the findings had implications for a number of regions of the country, reporters in those areas prepared stories that emphasized the conclusions that were most relevant for their readers. Many journalists used the findings to question experts and key players.

In chapter 8, the relationship between social science, precision journalism, and CAIR is explored. These forms of intellectual inquiry and analyses are similar in many ways although each has distinctive attributes. The basic assumptions and characteristics of these modes of investigation are systematically examined and conceptualized. Although social science, and by extension precision journalism, has a well-established methodology, that has not been the case with CAIR.

Finally chapter 9 suggests a systematic methodology for CAIR that incorporates the concepts, strategies, techniques, and procedures described in the previous chapters. The methodology consists of a series of preliminary steps, conceptual strategies, and responsibilities for conducting computer analyses to develop news stories and present them to the public. The chapter begins by defining the term *methodology* and reviewing how that term is understood by philosophers of science and social science researchers. It shows that *methodology* refers broadly to the logic of analysis that is in use within a given field. It also shows that it is up to the practitioners in a field to determine which requirements, procedures, and rules of analysis are acceptable.

Thus, the final chapter of *Computer-Assisted Investigative Reporting* describes a methodology that builds on the experiences and efforts of many individuals mentioned in this book. This effort is intended to be just that—a beginning. Just as John Milton set forth the concept of a "marketplace of ideas" three centuries ago to describe the value of debate in print, just such a marketplace is needed now to continue to debate what should constitute a shared methodology for CAIR. The eventual outcome may be a greater consensus and understanding of how to conduct CAIR analyses.

A number of journalists, scholars, and researchers have assisted in the development of this book and their contributions are gratefully acknowledged. In particular, the author thanks David Burnham and Susan B. Long, cofounders and directors of Transactional Records Access Clearinghouse at Syracuse University for the opportunity to work with them on their projects. Their dedication and guidance is responsible for my interest in this area. In addition, I express my thanks to Phil Meyer for patiently reviewing my work and thrashing out many of the issues with me. Finally, I send a special thanks for Joan Deppa and Lynne Flocke for, among other things, convincing me and encouraging me to write this book.

1

From Bordello to Watergate and Beyond: The Changing Nature of Investigative Reporting

Representative government cannot exist and cannot even be theoretically conceived unless provision is made for the governed to know what their governors are doing, are not doing and are contemplating doing.

—*Louis W. Hodges,* Mass Communication Review, *1987*

Since a reporter was first hired by Benjamin Day in 1833 to write interesting stories about what happened in the morning police court for his *New York Sun,* the work of American journalists has continued to change. As this book discusses, reporters are changing the way in which they conduct their investigations perhaps more rapidly today than at any point during the last two centuries. In particular, the Computer Age, into which we continue to rush headlong, has brought new challenges to journalists. That has been especially true for investigative reporters, who seek to uncover objective facts about situations that are of importance and interest to the public. In their capacities as "watchdogs" of the public interest, they constantly try to exercise oversight on the functioning of government agencies, the performance of public officials, and other kinds of situations about which they feel the public has a right to know. It is a critical service to our democratic society and investigative reporters are the channel by which objective assessments of the functioning of public institutions, mismanagement, or even wrongdoing are routinely disclosed to the public.

Investigative reporting in the United States has a rich and remarkable history. It developed in ways that may have been impossible in other societies, where different values prevailed concerning the rights of those governed to have access to accurate and detailed information about the performance of their public institutions. The role of the press as a "fourth estate" was defined during the 18th century in many societies. However, as this chapter shows, the idea developed in the United States with special vigor.

Beginning in the 19th century, the investigative reporter became an important figure in the United States, admired by the public for persistence, audacity, and dedication to the cause of democracy. Indeed, by the middle of the 20th century, investigative reporting had emerged as an adventurous, even glamorous, role within the labor force of journalism. Although it was mainly a function performed by newspaper journalists, important contributions had been made by magazine writers, novelists, and, later, reporters working within the broadcast industries.

By the end of World War II, the techniques used were well understood. Investigative reporting was based on interviews with various kinds of officials and other figures, tips gained from informants, documents that were either leaked or otherwise tracked down in government files, plus a great deal of insight, inductive reasoning, and sometimes just plain luck. It was, as some have said, a "shoe leather" operation, where the investigator spent a great deal of time tracking down information in a variety of places from a variety of people.

Then, beginning in the late 1960s and accelerating during the 1970s, a significant change began to take place in the nature of investigative reporting. While traditional procedures, strategies and "shoe leather" approaches remained important, something new was added. By the late 1980s, a new approach to journalism emerged. It not only made use of traditional "shoe leather" procedures for identifying leads, finding cooperating informants, tracking down relevant paper documents, and interviewing officials, but it also required the use of new and sophisticated technologies. The new procedures required reporters to obtain electronic records on magnetic tape, to use mainframe and desktop computers, and to analyze databases of information. One name for the new approach was computer-assisted investigative reporting—referred to by the acronym CAIR in this book.

INVESTIGATIVE REPORTING IN A CHANGING TECHNOLOGICAL ENVIRONMENT

To provide an illustration of CAIR as a new frontier of investigative reporting, a brief summary of a rather dramatic project is presented in the following paragraphs. It indicates how computer technology has become important in the task of the contemporary "watchdog" of the public interest. This case history of a CAIR project also shows how the more traditional approach and the newer technologies have merged.

While working on a story about subsidized housing for the *Providence Journal,* investigative reporter Elliot Jaspin met the executive director of the Rhode Island Housing and Mortgage Finance Corporation (RIHMFC). Jaspin learned that this agency sold tax-free municipal bonds and used the proceeds to provide more than 30,000 mortgages for Rhode Island families with low and moderate incomes. The program loaned money for the mortgages at relatively low interest rates to these families of limited means so that they could purchase modest homes. At a time when conventional mortgage rates were running as high as 19%, these families had been squeezed out of the housing market. The below-market rates of the RIHMFC mortgages made them a great bargain and competition to get such a loan was intense.

During a local election campaign in 1985, Jaspin received a phone call from an anonymous tipster who suggested that something was amiss in this state agency. In addition, another *Journal* reporter, Kathy Gregg, received a phone call from an individual who claimed that one of the candidates in the election had a home financed by RIHMFC, but did not actually live in the house. If true, this would be a clear violation of the conditions for receiving the low-interest money. A short time later, Gregg heard from still another anonymous caller, who said the other candidate in the election had two RIHMFC loans, even though the rules stated that only one such loan could be obtained by a person. Furthermore, the rules stated that only first-time home buyers were eligible. Both of these provisions would rule out having two homes financed by the fund.

Jaspin and Gregg decided that if these claims were true, there just might be something "fishy" going on at RIHMFC. With the backing of their newspaper, they decided to take a closer look at the agency to try and determine just who it was that had benefited from the pool of low-interest money.[1]

The first step was to interview the executive director of the agency. He readily admitted that one of the candidates had received two mortgages, but claimed that this was not a problem because the candidate was selling the first home while moving into the second one. And, yes, the agency did sometimes give mortgages to people who were not first-time home buyers. However, because of privacy concerns, the director would not reveal who else had received a loan as a result of this unannounced "special" policy.

By this time, the reporters' suspicions were really aroused and they asked to see the agency's records. They knew, of course, that it would take an incredibly long time to go through the paper records of all of the 30,000 mortgages that the agency had approved. The reporters were aware, however, that all information about each of the low-interest mortgages was also recorded on a computer tape by RIHMFC. The reporters asked for a copy of the tape. However, their request was immediately denied. They were referred to the agency's attorney, who refused to provide the tape on the grounds that the people holding the mortgages had a right to privacy in their personal financial affairs.

At this point, the newspaper filed suit against the agency under the information access laws of Rhode Island, which gave citizens a right to examine public records. The reporters demanded a copy of the electronic records on the grounds that RIHMFC was a state agency, that the tape was a public record under the law, and that they had a right, as did any citizen, to examine what information they contained.

Meanwhile, an individual who worked in the agency claimed that the director was worried about what would show up on the tape if the newspaper won its court case. In fact, the head of the agency had ordered an employee to begin deleting certain records from the tape. When the Rhode Island Attorney General's office learned about this, the State Police were authorized to seize the records. The newspaper later won the court case and a copy of the computer tape was delivered to the newspaper.

Jaspin immediately went to work deciphering the information that the tape contained. He determined that at least 1,140 records were missing from the computer tape. He also discovered that some of the missing records were from an earlier loan program that had been kept open, even though the public had been told that it was closed. Ultimately, the reporters learned that the money from this earlier program had been used to create a secret pool of funds that was used to grant favors to a few "special" people.

Jaspin's computer analysis showed that a number of individuals with political connections had used this low-interest money to purchase expensive homes. And, although other individuals who received RIHMFC loans had to pay as much as 13.75% for a mortgage, these "special" people were given 8.5% loans from the secret pool. The list of individuals who received these loans made very interesting reading. It included the daughter of a former governor, the son of a former state treasurer, the daughter of a former state senate majority leader, bank officials, and several RIHMFC employees.

As a result of the *Journal*'s computer-based investigation and disclosures, the director of the agency was charged with fraud and later went to jail.[2] A total of 25 indictments resulted from official state investigations spurred by the newspaper's disclosures, and the scandal forced a complete overhaul of the policies of the RIHMFC agency. It was a classic case of investigative reporting that resulted in significant reform.

What are the implications of this example of CAIR? That is, how did the agency manage to conceal its illegal activities? After all, the tapes Jaspin used were public records, and the state's open records laws mandated access to this information. Jaspin wondered, then, why the agency made no attempt to hide any of the fraudulent transactions when they were originally recorded on paper and on magnetic tape. The information was there for any determined individual to find.

Jaspin finally concluded that the head of the agency had made two assumptions: The first was that no one would take the time to go through the paper documents. The second was that even if someone obtained the computer tapes, no one would know what to do with them. These assumptions were not unreasonable at the time. First, Jaspin estimated that it would take a reporter 73 weeks to go through all of the paper records, even if that reporter spent only 5 minutes on each mortgage. That would certainly prevent even the most determined individual from poring through the documents. Second, and more important for this book, in 1985 most journalists did not know much about electronic records and few had tried to use computers, other than for word processing. For one thing, analytical software was not usually available in newsrooms and the knowledge, skills, and technology necessary to make use of computerized data often seemed formidable. Even several years later, Jaspin reported that only about 30 newspapers had any kind of organized program to use computerized records.[3]

By now, however, the picture has changed. CAIR analyses and the use of computer technology by investigative and other kinds of journalists have become more common. In fact, investigative journalism has entered a new era in its historical development. To provide an understanding of where it began, and the nature of these developments, the early chapters of this book trace the events that brought together one of the most important traditions of American journalism with the electronic technology of data analysis. Out of this merging has come an important new era in the history of the press as the watchdog for society. The combination of traditional investigative journalism and the ability to look at masses of public records kept on magnetic tape have become an invaluable means whereby reporters can alert the public to unsatisfactory performance by public officials and agencies, as took place in Rhode Island.

THE EVOLUTION OF THE PRESS AS A FOURTH ESTATE

How did this combination of traditional and technological skills come about to modify the nature of journalism's watchdog function? The answer to that question requires an understanding of the development of both investigative reporting and of the technological changes that led government agencies to adopt computerized record keeping. In the sections that follow, the development of traditional investigative reporting is outlined. (The technological changes that led to computerized records are discussed in the next chapter).

Historically, investigative reporting evolved from the belief in the function of the press as a fourth estate during the earliest years of the newspaper. It was a concept that developed mainly in France, England, and the American colonies during the 18th century. During that period, the press did not engage in a watchdog function as we know it today. It was opinion-based journalism. The fourth estate concept was exercised mainly by criticizing government and its officials in print. It was not based on investigative strategies for systematically gathering factual information about unacceptable situations to be disclosed to the public in the form of news stories. That form of journalism would not appear until the 19th century.

The Foundation of Political Values

The basic political values that provide the ideological foundations of investigative journalism today were developed as a part of the great revolution in social philosophy that began in Europe during the 17th century. Those political values focus on a number of principles and concepts that provide the moral and ethical justifications—indeed the necessity—of investigative reporting as it has evolved in the United States. They include the unacceptability of censorship, the importance of freedom of the press, an acknowledgment of the "peoples' right to know," and the need for a "marketplace of ideas."[4]

Thus, the foundation of values that has been brought forward into contemporary investigative journalism was derived from general political theories that marshaled arguments against despotic government. These theories—which are as important today as they were centuries ago—incorporate and defend the ideas of protest and criticism of government as the *natural right* of citizens. At the time they were formulated, it was dangerous to express such views. For speaking out against those who ruled, individuals were regularly jailed, sometimes mutilated, and even executed. Nevertheless, a number of 17th- and 18th-century philosophers set forth the basic blueprints for democratic government, including those related to a free press, well before their theories were incorporated into the Constitutions of either France or the United States.

Although there were many writers who contributed to the great changes in political thinking that occurred in Western society during the 17th and 18th centuries, a number of specific contributions can be briefly identified: Arguments against censorship appeared in a famous pamphlet called *Areopagitica,* written by John Milton in 1644.[5] Only 7 years later, in 1651, Thomas Hobbes in his *Leviathan* published a defiant attack on traditional monarchy and an explanation of the origins of the "social contract" as a foundation of democratic government.[6] In 1690, John Locke's *Two Treatises of Government* spoke against the power of monarchs, championing individual rights and majority rule.[7] In his 1748 *Spirit of the Laws,* Charles-Louis de Montesque wrote convincingly about the virtues of democracy and set forth the rational basis for the doctrine of the separation of powers within an effective government.[8] Finally, in 1762, in his *Social Contract,* Jean Jacques Rousseau set forth the doctrine that the sovereignty (right to rule) of the people is invested in them alone, and is both inalienable and indivisible.[9]

The Significance of Print

It is clear that this body of ideas about human rights and the nature of government provided the ideological bases of the American and French Revolutions.[10] However, it was the development of printing, more than two centuries earlier, providing for the availability of books and other printed media that made possible the relatively rapid spread of ideas.[11] In 1455, after 25 years of experimentation and development, Johannes Gutenberg was able to produce multiple and identical copies of a page with the use of a press and individual letters of movable type. Although seldom emphasized by historians, it was a great turning point in human communication, replacing the laborious process of producing *manu scripti* by copying every letter, line, and page. In spite of Gutenberg's fears that the *literati* might prefer hand-copied works to his mechanically produced books, the printing press was quickly adopted in all parts of the western world. Even before Columbus sailed on his famous voyage, millions of copies of books were being produced by the presses of Europe.[12]

The availability of a means of producing large numbers of documents quickly and cheaply was at first of interest mainly to those who produced books. However, as knowledge of the printer's art spread, the press came to be seen as a means of publicizing many kinds of ideas for a variety of purposes. By the 1600s, presses were churning out not only books, but also an avalanche of political pamphlets, religious tracts, intelligence sheets for commercial use, and the earliest forms of magazines and newspapers. The Age of Print had truly arrived.

A key factor in the development of investigative reporting (that would come in the 19th century) was the fact that these early printed products were by no means universally welcomed. Many of the monarchs of Europe and religious authorities saw them as a threat. They instituted tight controls over presses, printers, and publishing. Secular rulers sought to suppress seditious ideas that challenged governmental power and authority; religious authorities guarded against assaults on approved interpretations of the supernatural and teachings that might undermine the established moral order.[13] It was, of course, this suppression in the face of the spread of philosophies defining the ultimate power to govern as vested in the people that led to the struggle for freedom of expression. Its print counterpart, of course, was freedom of the press. Without these philosophical foundations and the advances made in both communication and political systems, the concept of investigative reporting could never have emerged.

ESTABLISHING THE ROLE OF INVESTIGATIVE REPORTER

How did journalists make the change from passive reporting and complaining in print to actively gathering facts for systematic investigations and disclosures? That transition involved colorful chapters in U.S. history and it took almost a century.

When the basic protections for the press in the United States were first set forth in the initial Amendment to the Constitution, the nation was a simple agrarian society. The activities of the new federal government only rarely touched the daily lives of its citizens. During the succeeding two centuries, the United States became a huge, urban–industrial society with a massive federal government that controls, regulates, and influences virtually every aspect of the political and economic life of its citizens. Even state and municipal governments have become complex, impersonal, and increasingly difficult for the ordinary citizen to understand.

Today, in the face of this almost impenetrable complexity, the need for a vigorous press that can scrutinize the actions, policies, and performance of those who are in charge may be of greater importance than it was in earlier times. The press, in its watchdog function, is the vital communicating link between the concerned citizen who wants to assess how those who are running things are doing and the evidence that can indicate the quality of their performance. It is difficult to analyze and understand the incredible range of agencies and bureaucratic systems that have been devised for managing the problems with which society must cope. Therefore, the potential for inefficient, irresponsible, unethical, or even outrageously illegal behavior on the part of those we trust has never been higher.[14] Correspondingly, the importance of the press as the eyes and ears of the public in monitoring governmental activities has never been greater and its task has never been more difficult.

During the 1800s, as the complexity of social life and government increased, and as newspapers became widely adopted in the United States, an increasingly mature and vigorous press moved beyond its traditional function of *surveillance* and expanded the meaning of its role as the fourth estate. No longer were newspapers and magazines simply *critics* of government, or channels by which persons who opposed its policies could register their discontents. The press developed an *investigative* function, with reporters digging into and uncovering information about the operation of federal, state, and local government that those in charge did not want made public. During the 19th century, then, techniques and traditions of investigative reporting were developed that became a standard part of the functioning of American journalists. Those who pioneered these changes left an indelible mark on today's journalism and an increasing public awareness of the significance of a free and independent press.

Reporters Become Aggressive Gatherers of Facts

When popular newspapers were first established, reporters were little more than individuals authorized by an editor to observe and summarize the proceedings of what took place in official transactions. In fact, the term *reporter* was not even among the titles used by editors prior to the 1830s.[15] Up to that time, those who prepared news stories about government functions sat, along with other spectators, in a gallery where they could watch the deliberations of a legislative body, or in a court where they could observe the conduct of the proceedings. They did not investigate anything or interrogate anyone in search of news. Given the norms of the time, that would have been regarded as an unseemly intrusion. Such inquiries were left to the police or other authorities, and reporters prepared their stories mainly from information provided by official sources.[16]

The first on-the-scene interview by a journalist in search of facts for a story is usually credited to James Gordon Bennett, the colorful editor of the

New York Herald.[17] On April 11, 1836, both the *Herald* and Benjamin Day's *New York Sun* printed lengthy crime stories based on a report of an ax murder by a coroner's jury. The body of a young prostitute, Ellen Jewett, had been found dead on her bed in a house of "ill repute." She had a deep gash in her skull and her bed had been set on fire. A young man had been arrested and charged with the crime.

Bennett decided to go further. He went to the brothel to talk with Madame Townsend, the proprietress, and to look over the premises for additional facts about which to write. Using a question-and-answer procedure, he completed (and published) what is generally accepted as the first formal interview conducted for a journalist's investigation. Bennett also examined the remains of the unfortunate victim, her bed, the room, her personal possessions, and indeed the entire scene of the crime. The information he gathered was developed into a story about the affair that occupied the entire first page of the *Herald* on June 4, 1836.[18] Two additional stories followed within a short time. In other words, it was not just an exercise in reporting the facts, but a determined effort to *uncover facts*. The public loved it, and the intensely competitive journalists of New York quickly adopted the innovation.

The new role for reporters was soon to launch a more aggressive era in American journalism. The major newspapers began to send reporters out to uncover all kinds of news, rather than just waiting for it to arrive, or writing stories from observing courts and official bodies in action. News was redefined from reports based on official versions of what had taken place to accounts incorporating facts gathered by reporters themselves. Soon, reporters were regularly dispatched to cover wars, crime, elections, and a growing panoply of other events that were judged by editors to be of interest to readers.

By the time of the Civil War, reporters were active. Communication technology had improved and they were able to provide accounts by telegraph from the scenes of the great battles. Newspaper usage rose to new heights during the period as Americans were concerned about the state of the nation and the fate of their loved ones. Thus, the role of reporter was institutionalized and defined in modern terms as the last half of the 19th century began.

Investigative Reporting Begins

The period following the Civil War was an age of especially flamboyant journalism. For example, Bennett's son, James Gordon Bennett, Jr., who inherited the *Herald,* sent Henry Morton Stanley to Africa in 1869 to locate

Dr. David Livingston.[19] In 1889, Elizabeth Cochran (better known as Nellie Bly) embarked on a highly publicized 72-day around-the-world trip sponsored by her editor, Joseph Pulitzer of the *New York World*. Earlier, she made investigative history by exposing conditions in a state insane asylum on Blackwell's Island near New York City. With the cooperation of her paper and medical authorities, she posed as a mental patient without revealing her true identity. She was examined by the system's doctors, pronounced insane, and was committed to the institution. She stayed there for 10 days, seeing firsthand how patients were treated. None of the personnel at the institution suspected that she was a reporter. After being extricated she wrote stories exposing the brutal conditions she encountered. Her accounts became world famous and resulted in reforms in the treatment of the mentally ill.[20]

Thus, the late 19th century was a time in which the concept of investigative reporting developed into an aggressive and politically oriented activity. Over the decades that followed, it matured and the contemporary tradition of the watchdog of society was more firmly established. As legal scholar Timothy W. Gleason noted:

> As the commercial newspaper industry experienced rapid growth after the Civil War and the newsgathering function grew more complex and institutionalized, [newspaper publishers] described the press as "public journals" with a duty and responsibility to act as a watchdog for the public in matters of government and public importance.[21]

By the end of the century, then, both the definition of the press as an active watchdog, and aggressive reporting by individuals developed together to become significant parts of the American press.

The Muckrakers

As the 1900s began, American print media made use of a sophisticated technology that included not only complex and rapid printing, but also photoengraving, a vast network of telegraph wires and cable services, numerous syndicates providing various kinds of content, inexpensive postal services, and rapid transportation for both journalists and their products. Newspapers and magazines were widely read and were in many ways not much different than their counterparts today.[22]

During the post-Civil War period, U.S. industry expanded greatly and huge monopolies and trusts developed. Great "captains of industry" ran their empires with the assistance of the best politicians that money could buy and government rarely intervened. During this time, magazine journalists made some of the greatest contributions to investigative journalism with their relentless exposures of problems in the American society:

> Between 1903 and 1912, a small group of writers produced almost 2,000 detailed, factual articles on the national corruption and confusion. The accounts were complimented by editorials and cartoons, touted by flashy titles and glossy, beckoning covers which promised shocking revelations on the inside, and backed up by similarly sensational revelations and preachments in the local press. The subject matter was corruption. The style was accusatory. America was in crisis, somehow falling apart. Not only were the marketplace and its prime institution, the corporation, betraying America, but so were the local, state, and national governments . . . [23]

These journalists collectively came to be called *muckrakers,* a term coined by President Theodore Roosevelt.[24] He criticized them as individuals who—using imagery from Bunyan's *Pilgrim's Progress*—were stirring up the muck of American society, rather than raising their heads to see its celestial crown of great advances in business and industry. Later, he admitted that they did the nation a great service in calling attention to needed reforms.

During the first decade of the new century, the names of several investigative journalists became household words. For example, the January 1903 issue of *McClure's Magazine* contained an article by Lincoln Steffens entitled, "The Shame of Minneapolis: The Rescue and Redemption of a City that was Sold Out." It also contained a chapter on the oil war of 1872 from Ida Tarbell's lengthy analysis of the *The History of the Standard Oil Company,* and an article by Ray Stannard Baker entitled, "The Right to Work, the Story of the Non-Striking Miners" (in the coal fields of Pennsylvania). Each provided a detailed exposure of conditions in government or industry that Americans found distressing.[25] These exposures set new standards for investigative reporting. Above all, they were thorough and well documented. Each was based on extensive personal observation, numerous interviews, and reviews of public records.

Of all of the investigators of the time, it was Ida Tarbell who led in developing those standards with her *History of the Standard Oil Company,* first published as a series of 18 articles in *McClure's Magazine* between November 1902 and January 1903. Her father had been forced out of the oil business by Rockefeller's companies in Pennsylvania, and she had great sympathy for those who were ruined by his operations.

Tarbell's investigative strategies were straightforward. She tracked down the court records of dozens of suits in which the Standard Oil Company had been involved. This was difficult because they were scattered in many locations around the country. She interviewed dozens of people who had suffered from, or played a part in, the actions of the company. She read the files of old newspapers to discover additional transactions. She examined the records of government investigations. In short, she was both meticulous and relentless. As historian C. C. Reiger described her approach to her famous work:

> Three years passed before she was ready to begin writing; five years elapsed before her investigations were completed. In that time she had mastered the history of the company, penetrated the technical intricacies of her material, pieced together the evidence, and prepared herself to tell the complicated story in such a way that the average man and woman would understand it.[26]

Several features of Tarbell's work have since become a part of the research phases of investigative reporting: (a) a thorough study of the documents and records related to the investigation, (b) interviews with individuals knowledgeable about the topic, and (c) personal observation of relevant activities.

Ironically, it is possible that some of what Tarbell achieved by studying government records and court documents could not be duplicated today. As the next chapter shows, with the arrival of the Computer Age, governments at all levels have turned to storing their records on magnetic tape or other electronic media. In some cases, the paper records are destroyed after the data have been transferred to electronic form. Thus, it is possible that some of the paper files that Tarbell read would have no contemporary counterparts. However, her extensive perusal of newspaper files might be easier today. She could retrieve at least some of them efficiently through an online database, such as Lexis/Nexis, without the need to travel to the local "morgue" of each of the newspapers.

INVESTIGATIVE REPORTING IN CONTEMPORARY TIMES

Following the flamboyant period of the muckrakers, the press gave less emphasis to investigative reporting. Moreover, the strategies of traditional investigative reporting continued to be refined, but actually did not change greatly between the time of the muckrakers and the beginning of the 1960s. After the extensive disclosures of the muckrakers ended, public interest appeared to decrease.

The Quiet Period

It is difficult to say why the period from the beginning of World War I to the start of the Viet Nam era in the 1960s produced so few great examples of investigative reporting. Perhaps the news-rich events of World War I, prohibition, the depression of the 1930s, World War II, and the start of the Cold War preoccupied journalists. That is not to say that the watchdog was entirely silent. There were some major disclosures during the 1920s; for example, the *New York Times* uncovered some of the details of the Teapot Dome scandal. But there was nothing of the scale of the exposures of Steffens, Tarbell, or Baker. During the 1960s, however, there was a significant resurgence of investigative reporting. At the end of that decade, reporter Seymour Hersh uncovered the story of the My Lai massacre in Viet Nam, and Jack Nelson's investigations during the height of the civil rights movement helped deflate the image of J. Edgar Hoover.[27]

In some ways, the basic mission of the investigative newspaper reporter was pursued during the first half of the 20th century by other kinds of writers. Books became an important medium for exposing significant problems in society.[28] Sinclair Lewis in *The Jungle* described disturbing conditions in the meat packing industry. John Steinbeck's *Grapes of Wrath* revealed in a stark way the terrible conditions of the "Okies" who were forced out of their homes in the dust bowl and into the migrant labor camps of the 1930s. In the 1960s, Michael Harrington's *The Other Americans* provided a factual account of the economic plight of older citizens. In more contemporary times, Bob Woodward's *The Agenda* disclosed the inner workings of a White House struggling with problems confronting the nation.

As their media matured, radio and television broadcasters also produced investigative reports and documentaries designed to expose problems in the society, such as hunger in the U.S., crime and political corruption. An early example was Edward R. Murrow's *See It Now,* which began as a regular series on television in 1951. Murrow made history in 1953 with his critical look at McCarthyism. In 1960, the highly successful program *60 Minutes* went on the air.[29] Today, a number of television programs continue the tradition, but often with a tabloid approach.

The Revival

Two incidents of investigative reporting stood out during the 1970s. One was prompted by the murder of reporter Don Bolles in Phoenix, Arizona. Although few citizens may now recall what it was about, it was remarkable because of the way in which the news industry responded. The case provides a classic example of the methods of traditional investigative reporting. Bolles, of the *Arizona Republic,* was murdered when his car was blown up as a result of his investigations of land development scandals in the area. An organized group, Investigative Reporters and Editors (IRE), formed a year earlier, led a massive inquiry into the crime:

> It was the largest investigative effort in history: months of work by six permanent staffers and 30 other reporters, assisted by 26 news organizations and several foundations; a compilation of 46,000 index cards boiled down from searches of documentary records, interviews, tape recordings; finally, a 100,000-word series [was made public]. . . . In late 1977 three men were convicted of Bolles' murder and others were sought in the conspiracy.[30]

The Bolles murder made journalistic history, but of all efforts at investigative reporting in recent times, none is more familiar to the public than Watergate. It ranks high as a significant episode in the development of investigative reporting because it illustrates the great power of the press and what can happen when it pursues its watchdog role vigorously. Careful investigation by reporters Bob Woodward and Carl Bernstein of the *Washington Post,* supplemented by continuous news coverage by other media over many months, eventually led a U.S. president to resign from office for the first time in the nation's history.

The eventual resignation was a result of a complex series of decisions that were made by the White House team of Richard Nixon.[31] In 1971 he authorized a surveillance team that later was called the "Plumbers." The team's mission was to disrupt its political enemies by using a variety of unethical and often illegal tactics. On June 17, 1972, they illegally entered the Washington headquarters of the Democratic National Committee, located in the Watergate apartment complex. The five-man team was caught as they were planting listening devices in the office of Lawrence O'Brien, the chairman of the Democratic Party.

The next day, the *Washington Post* ran a front-page story linking one of the burglars to the CIA. Bob Woodward and Carl Bernstein, young reporters at the *Post,* were assigned along with others to the developing story. Woodward found a link between the burglars and E. Howard Hunt, a member of the White House staff. At first, the nation's news media gave the events little space. However, after the connection with the White House was revealed, they eagerly published or broadcast further reports.[32]

As the story continued to develop, the *Post* reporters received a great deal of information from an anonymous tipster that they referred to as "Deep

Throat." Over succeeding months, the White House staff and then Nixon himself denounced the revelations and interpretations. They vigorously denied that there was any "cover up." The nation became fascinated with the unfolding events. Finally, Nixon's enemies, seeing his vulnerability, undertook congressional action to initiate impeachment hearings. Tapes of Nixon's conversations in the Oval Office came to light, providing a "smoking gun" implying involvement by the president. Finally, the House Judiciary Committee formally charged Nixon with obstruction of justice, abuse of power, and contempt of Congress. On August 8, 1974, the President announced to an astonished nation that he was resigning, effective the next day. He was promptly pardoned by his successor, Gerald Ford.[33]

Watergate is a classic example of traditional "shoe leather" investigative reporting. If there were any doubts about the importance and effectiveness of investigative reporting, they were surely dispelled by Watergate. The affair has etched itself indelibly into the American consciousness, both as a classic example of investigative reporting in the watchdog tradition of the press, and as an example of political corruption and duplicity. Its very vocabulary is now associated with political misbehavior. The term *gate* has become a suffix to indicate any alleged scandal involving political figures—as in Irangate during the Reagan era and even Nannygate during the Clinton administration. Significant disclosures are now almost always referred to as "smoking guns." Jokes continue about tapes with "18 minutes of silence."[34]

Watergate represents a high point in the development of traditional investigative reporting. It captured the imagination of the public as a glamorous activity. The actions of Richard Nixon and his powerful subordinates were of great importance to the American people. The politicians tried to conceal their misdeeds, but clever reporters protecting the public interest brought them to light. Those revelations of misdeeds brought the investigators prizes and public acclaim. The image of the courageous reporter rooting out corruption among the mighty once again became a significant part of the folklore of the press. After Watergate, enrollments in journalism courses and degree programs in colleges and universities rose sharply.[35]

From a standpoint of methods and strategies, traditional investigative reporting was exclusively a "low-tech" approach. It began with the wits of insightful reporters who then sought confirming evidence for their suspicions. Its investigative strategy was based on leaks of important information by "whistle-blowers" (such as Deep Throat), interviews with people involved in the activities, firsthand observation of situations, uncovering a trail of significant documents (or tapes) that were incriminating. This evidence was corroborated where possible and then interpreted in ways that reflected good news values. Unlike other forms of inquiry, such as social science research, it did not seek broad generalizations that characterized similar classes of events and it did not seek to test explanatory theory concerning independent and dependent variables. It was strictly focused on *news*—timely information of interest and importance to the public.

DEFINING INVESTIGATIVE REPORTING TODAY

Both scholars and practitioners have studied and defined investigative reporting in many ways. One of the most widely quoted definitions appears in a publication prepared by officers of the national professional association, the IRE. They defined investigative reporting in the following terms:

> It is the reporting, through one's own work product and initiative, of matters of importance which some persons or organizations wish to keep secret. The three basic elements are that the investigation be the work of the reporter, not a report of an investigation made by someone else; that the subject of the story involves something of reasonable importance to the reader or viewer; and that others are attempting to hide these matters from the public.[36]

Definitions such as this stress the idea that the goal of investigative reporting is to uncover a situation that someone is *purposely concealing*; that is, they are deliberately attempting to hide it from the public because it is unethical, or even illegal.

This certainly describes investigative reporting as it has been conducted in the past. However, it is too narrow a focus for investigative reporting as it is developing today. The computerization of government records makes it necessary to broaden the definition. As the next section of this chapter shows, investigative reporting is no longer only a matter of clever insights, interviews with whistle-blowers and the discovery of incriminating documents that someone wants to keep secret. Great changes have taken place in the ways in which the records of government transactions are kept. During the last three decades, the use of computers for government record keeping has made the task of the investigative reporter more complex. For example, as noted earlier, Ida Tarbell was able to conduct her inquiry in part by examining paper records of legal actions and government transactions. Contemporary investigative reporters now must cope with magnetic tapes, software, codebooks, strategies for data analysis, and computer hardware if they wish to examine the records of courts and other government agencies. Thus, to fit the new era of computerized government records, the older definition of investigative reporting must be modified.

A definition more appropriate for the years ahead is that of Dennis and Ismach, who wrote that investigative reporting should focus on "all sectors of society that require examination, explanation or airing, but that are hidden from public view."[37] This definition does not require a *deliberate* intent to conceal. Whatever is being examined may be difficult to uncover simply because it is obscured in a large reel of magnetic tape or is otherwise "hidden" by the nature of records rather than improper intent alone. Clearly, however, two features suggested by both the traditional and the more contemporary definitions remain: Investigative reporting concerns those matters that are important to the public and not easily discovered.

In summary, the major lesson of this chapter is that, like all aspects of mass communication, investigative journalism is now and has been in a constant process of change. Its history encompasses that of newspapers themselves—stretching back to Gutenberg and the earliest broadsides, pamphlets, and primitive news sheets by which critics of government spoke out in print. Only as recently as the 19th century, however, did journalists begin systematically gathering facts to support their claims about the issues and events on which they were reporting.

For decades, the process of gathering information for investigative purposes, analyzing it, and preparing disclosures for the public was little influenced by advances in mechanical calculating or electronic computing technology. When governments turned to electronic record keeping, however, a fundamental change came about in the way investigative reporters have to dig out facts about the functioning of agencies of government. Today, if they want to exercise their watchdog function, journalists often have to make use of sophisticated new computer technologies and complex strategies of analysis of digital information that were never a part of the more traditional approach of the past.

As this book explains, computer-assisted investigative reporting began in a small way during the 1960s. It became somewhat more common during the 1970s and came into greater use during the 1980s. By now it has become a part of the routine work practices of many of the nation's newsrooms. In the chapters that follow, various trends that have been a part of this transition are explained and the contemporary nature of CAIR is described and illustrated. In addition, the similarities and differences between the natures and objectives of CAIR, precision journalism, and social science research are made clear. Finally, a formal methodology for CAIR analyses is described.

NOTES AND REFERENCES

1. Elliot Jaspin, "The New Investigative Journalism: Exploring Public Records by Computer," in John V. Pavlik and Everette E. Dennis, *Demystifying Media Technology* (Mountain View, Calif., Mayfield Publishing Company, 1992), pp. 142–144.
2. See: Katherine Gregg and Elliot Jaspin, "1,140 Mortgages Not Listed in RIHMFC Computer File," the *Providence Journal,* City Edition, June 19, 1985, p. 1; "Sons, Daughters of State Leaders Got 8 1/2-Percent RIHMFC Loans," the *Providence Sunday Journal,* June 2, 1985, p. 1.
3. Elliot Jaspin, "The New Investigative Journalism: Exploring Public Records by Computer," *op. cit.,* p. 144.
4. An outstanding and very readable explanation of the origins of these concepts and principles is: Herbert Altschull, *From Milton to McLuhan: The Ideas Behind American Journalism* (White Plains, N.Y.: Longman, 1990).
5. Milton's famous work was first published as: *Areopagitica; A Speech of Mr. John Milton / For the Liberty of Unlicensed Printing / to the Parliament of England.* See: Frederick S. Siebert, *Freedom of the Press in England 1476–1776: The Rise and Decline of Government Control* (Urbana: University of Illinois Press, 1965), p. 195.
6. Michael Oakeshot, ed., *Leviathan: Or the Matter, Forme and Power of a Common-wealth Ecclesiastical and Civil* (Oxford: Basil Blackwell, 1946).
7. John Locke, *Two Treatises on Government* ed., Thomas I. Cook (New York: Hafner, 1947).
8. Charles-Louis de Montesque, *The Spirit of Laws,* translated by Thomas Nugent and reprinted in *Great Books of the Western World,* vol. 38 (Chicago: Encyclopedia Britannica, 1952).
9. Jean Jacques Rousseau, *The Social Contract* translated by G.D.H. Cole and reprinted in (New York: Everyman's Library, 1947).
10. For a discussion of these issues with respect to both revolutions, see: William Ebenstein, *Great Political Thinkers* (New York: Tinehart and Company, 1951), pp. 442–452.
11. For a detailed treatise on how the development of printing helped spread scientific, religious, and political ideas, see: Elizabeth L. Eisenstein, *The Printing Press as an Agent of Change* (London: Cambridge University Press, 1979).
12. The average edition of a particular title during the period of 1456–1499 was between 200 and 1,000 copies. With presses in all the major cities in Europe producing multiple titles during that half century, there are grounds for assuming that millions of copies of books were printed. One estimate places the number at about 8 million. See: Elizabeth L. Eisenstein, *The Printing Press as an Agent of Change* (Cambridge: Cambridge University Press, 1979), pp. 11, 45.
13. Craig R. Smith, *op. cit.,* pp. 1–6.
14. Scandals disclosed by journalists concerning military purchases, atomic waste disposal, and medical experiments on human subjects without their consent illustrate the point. For example, see: "Cold War Guinea Pigs: The Government's Secret Experiments Using

Radiation, Mind Control, Chemicals and Drugs on its Citizens," *U.S. News and World Report,* January 24, 1994, pp. 32–52.

15. Michael Stephens, *A History of the News* (New York: Viking Penguin, Inc., 1988), p. 233.

16. By the mid-1830s, even after steam presses increased the availability of newspapers to the public, almost all editors still received news in the form of packets of information by ship from Europe, by mail from neighboring regions, from observation of court proceedings or from official statements provided by various groups and agencies. As one historian noted, "news was being covered in early nineteenth-century America . . . but with few exceptions, news was not being *uncovered.* American newspapers had yet to discover the power of reporting." Mitchell Stephens, *op. cit.,* p. 225. See also: Richard A. Schwarzlose, *The Nation's Newsbrokers,* Vol. I (Evanston, Ill.: Northwestern University Press, 1989), pp. 11–26.

17. This discussion is based in part on the following sources: Warren T. Franke, *Investigative Exposure in the Nineteenth Century,* Ph.D. Dissertation, University of Minnesota, 1974, pp. 43–47; Oliver Carlson, *The Man Who Made the News* (New York: Duell, Sloan and Pearce, 1942), p. 146; and Mitchell Stephens, *op. cit.,* pp. 242-247.

18. Nils G. Nilsson, "The Origin of the Interview," *Journalism Quarterly,* 48, (Winter, 1971), p. 707.

19. *Ibid.,* p. 248.

20. For a biography of Elizabeth Cochran, describing this and other investigative activities, see: Iris Noble, *Nellie Bly: First Woman Reporter* (New York: Julian Messner, 1956).

21. Timothy W. Gleason, *The Watchdog Concept* (Ames, Iowa: Iowa State University Press, 1990), p. 54.

22. Newspaper readership in the United States reached its peak in 1910, with an average of 1.36 subscriptions to a daily newspaper per household. In 1905, more than 6,000 magazine titles were published in the U.S. See: U.S. Bureau of the Census, *Historical Statistics of the United States: Colonial Times to the Present* (Washington, DC: Government Printing Office, 1960), p. 500.

23. David Mark Chalmers, *The Muckraker Years* (Huntington, N.Y.: Robert K. Krieger Publishing Company, 1980), p. 9.

24. *Ibid.,* p. 45.

25. See: *McClure's Magazine,* Vol. 20, No. 3, January, 1903.

26. C.C. Regier, *The Era of the Muckrakers* (Chapel Hill, N.C.: The University of North Carolina Press, 1932), p. 123.

27. Eileen Keerdoja, "My Lai Massacre," *Newsweek,* April 3, 1978, p. 12; Alexander Cockburn, "Beat the Devil," *The Nation,* Vol. 246, No. 12, March 26, 1988, p. 402.

28. Melvin L. DeFleur and Everette E. Dennis, *Understanding Mass Communication* (Boston: Houghton Mifflin Co., 1994), pp. 526–527.

29. Sidney W. Head and Christopher H. Sterling, *Broadcasting in America,* 5th ed. (Boston: Houghton Mifflin Co., 1987), pp. 73–80; Erik Barnouw, *Tube of Plenty* (London: Oxford University Press, 1975), pp. 171–177.

30. Edwin Emery and Michael Emery, *The Press and America,* 4th ed., (Englewood Cliffs, N.J.: Prentice-Hall, Inc., 1978), p. 372.

31. A 1,000-page record of the Watergate events can be found in: *Watergate: Chronology of a Crisis, Congressional Quarterly* (Washington, DC: U.S. Government Printing Office, 1975).

32. For an account of the Watergate events, see: Carl Bernstein, *All the President's Men* (New York: Simon and Schuster, 1974).
33. The bipartisan House Judiciary Committee voted for impeachment on three counts in late July 1972. By early August, even Nixon's staunch allies were dropping their support. For a summary of these events, see: Edwin Emery and Michael Emery, *op. cit.,* 4th edition (Englewood Cliffs, N.J.: Prentice Hall, 1978), pp. 538–546.
34. The "18 minutes of silence" refers to the deleted portion of a tape recording of a conversation between President Richard Nixon and chief aide H.R. Haldeman on the day after the Watergate break-in. Nixon's secretary, Rose Mary Woods, claimed she accidently caused 18 minutes of the conversation to be erased while she was transcribing the conversation. See: Brian Gorman, "Looking for Scandal? Nixon's Back on Tape," the *Toronto Star,* May 25, 1991, Weekend Section, p. H3.
35. Enrollments in journalism programs in colleges and universities rose steadily from the mid-1970s until 1987, when they began to decline slightly. See: Paul V. Peterson, "Journalism and Mass Comm Enrollment Leveled Off in 1987," *Journalism Educator,* 43, 1, Spring, 1988, pp. 4–10.
36. John Ullman and Jan Colbert, *The Reporter's Handbook: An Investigator's Guide to Documents and Techniques* (New York: St. Martin's Press, 1991), p. vii.
37. Everette E. Dennis and Arnold Ismach, *Reporting Processes and Practices* (Belmont, Calif., Wadsworth Publishing Co., 1981) p. 66.

2

Coming Together: Computers, Government Record Keepers, and Journalists

Computer-assisted investigative reporting emerged, for the most part, as a means by which journalists could examine the performance of government agencies and officials. As later chapters show, there are many other applications of CAIR, such as the development of "in-house" databases for special projects, or assembling factual information for other purposes. However, CAIR is especially important in the analysis of the records of agencies and their policies for oversight and watchdog purposes.

This chapter focuses on two historical developments. One is the accumulation of technology that made possible the electronic digital computer that is now at the heart of storing government records—as well as the basic tool used for analyzing those records. The other is the transition by government agencies from paper to magnetic media for storing information about their transactions.

A decade ago, few journalists would have regarded the history of the electronic computer as relevant to their craft. However, it is now a critical analytical tool. Like it or not, it has become a part of the intellectual heritage of journalism, just as other major technologies, such as the power-driven press, the telegraph, and the linotype did in the past. Furthermore, when federal, and later state and local, agencies made the decision to store the records of their routine transactions in machine-readable form, that transition became a part of the history of journalism. For those reasons, therefore, this chapter traces these two developments for the purpose of showing how they have shaped investigative journalism today.

THE DEVELOPMENT OF MECHANICAL CALCULATORS

The change from storing government records on paper to using computers and electronic media is the end result of an accumulating technology that quite literally began in prehistoric times. It is obviously not necessary to review that accumulation in extensive detail for the purposes of this book. However, a very brief look at its major highlights can serve an important purpose. It can provide a historical perspective on the unfolding of technology that is now making it necessary for investigative reporters to modify the way they do their work. If they are to continue performing their traditional role as watchdogs of government, it is a technology that journalists must now master and use. That perspective leads to the conclusion that it is very unlikely that journalists will ever be able to return to an era of shoe leather reporting where computer technology plays no role. In fact, this brief developmental perspective indicates not only why investigative reporting on government in an electronic age now requires an ability to use computers but also why the need for such proficiency will *increase* in the future.

As a brief review of its development will show, no single individual "invented" the digital, general-purpose, programmable, electronic computers that we use routinely today. They resulted from a step-by-step accumulation of specific solutions to a host of problems by a long list of brilliant human beings over many centuries. Today's computers incorporate such cultural advances as ancient solutions to practical calculating, sophisticated mathematical systems, complex electronic principles, and intricate technological hardware. These various elements were brought together just after World War II to produce the first of the great machines that could be programmed to add, subtract, multiply, and divide at the speed of lightning.

From Stones to Bones: The Earliest Technologies

The earliest steps toward mechanical calculation were taken a very long time ago. The first device was literally a kind of tray (*abex* in Greek, from which we get *abacus*) on which a layer of sand was spread. Then, several parallel rows or furrows were marked in the sand with one's finger. On each row a set of 10 stones (*calculi* in Latin) was arranged along one side. One could then "calculate" by moving the stones from one side of the tray to the other. (The use of 10 stones was probably a consequence of the fact that we have that many fingers.) One line was for single digits, a second for tens, a third for hundreds, and so on. For example, the number 325 could be represented by 5 stones in the single digit row; 2 stones in the tens row and

3 in hundreds row. Even larger numbers were no problem with additional rows. Adding and subtracting could be accomplished by moving stones back and forth, "carrying over" where needed. The system was later refined into a wooden frame with cords and later wires instead of furrows, and beads instead of stones. It was a "user-friendly" device, enabling a person to add and subtract in a remarkably rapid, reliable, and accurate way and providing for "storage" of the answer. It remained in wide use for thousands of years. It is still used by shopkeepers in many third-world countries. It incorporated the basic digital (present/absent) principle of today's computers.

Simple counting, adding, and subtracting served the needs of ordinary people for centuries. However, more complicated requirements arose when human beings began to conceptualize the world around them in terms of forms, shapes, and angles, and to visualize relationships in abstract terms. This led the Greeks to develop geometry. Later, algebra came from the Arab world, along with the concept of zero. These mathematical foundations eventually provided the basis for the modern science of astronomy. Over succeeding centuries, astronomy became increasingly sophisticated in a mathematical sense. The early astronomers used the geometry of the Greeks and the algebra of the Arabs to plot the orbits of the heavenly bodies and to develop forecasts of their positions. As their science progressed, lengthy and precise calculations were increasingly required.

Completing complex calculations by mental manipulation of numbers was dreadfully laborious and punishing. For example, multiplying two 10-digit numbers together (not uncommon in early astronomical calculations) requires 100 separate multiplications of single-digit pairs, plus 20 additions and carry-overs. It was a mind-numbing task that could take the better part of an hour to complete and check thoroughly.[1] Understandably, the "calculators," clerks who were specially trained and hired for the task, made many errors.

A great breakthrough in the ability to calculate, specifically in the laborious task of multiplying large numbers, came through an invention of the English Baron John Napier (1550–1617). He used the newly developed principle of the logarithm (adding the exponents of numbers to obtain the exponent of their product). He did it with an ingenious device that consisted of 14 flat rods, each of which looked rather like a 12-inch ruler of today.[2] The rods were made of ivory because it was a stable substance that did not shrink and expand to any great degree. Because of their appearance, they came to be called Napier's "bones." They worked together as a system. Each was marked with numbers in such a way that, with the right selection of rods, the product of any two numbers could be read with very simple additions. Rather complex calculations could be accomplished far more easily than by using human calculators. Numbers of several places could be multiplied together in this manner.[3]

Calculating "Engines"

Although Napier's bones made certain calculations easier, it was another device—an actual mechanical calculating machine—that was the next major leap forward. A somewhat earlier version of such a machine was said to have been fashioned in wood by the German Wilhelm Schicker (1592–1635) in 1623, but it was apparently destroyed in a fire and only descriptions remain.[4] In any case, the Frenchman Blaise Pascal (1623–1662) independently conceived of, and had built, a device for *mechanical calculation*. His machine (or machines, as there were a number of variations) was an ingenious contraption with metal cylinders, gearwheels and cogs housed in a rectangular container about the size of a modern shoe box.[5] The parts were linked together in such a manner that, by turning a crank, the machine could perform all four arithmetic functions. It was the forerunner of the electrically driven calculators that would become common early in the 20th century.

During the 1600s, the applied science of navigation was assuming more and more importance. England had become a great sea power, and the mathematics that had so benefited astronomy were used to develop practical systems for locating ships on the surface of the globe. At the heart of these systems were elaborate *tables*—such as those showing declinations of the sun and stars during certain periods and at various locations of latitude. When logarithms became available, tables for their use were developed to ease the burdens of navigators calculating the positions of their ships. The need for reliable calculating devices grew sharply to aid in the construction of accurate tables.

A more elaborate and much-improved "calculating engine" was developed by the German Baron Gotfried Leibnitz (1646–1716), codeveloper of calculus (along with Sir Isaac Newton). Leibnitz called his apparatus an Arithmometer.[6] It was based on the principles incorporated in Napier's bones. Like Pascal before him, he improved the device through several models but was constantly handicapped by the limited metal-working technology of his time.[7]

Generally, then, the early stages in the development of mechanical calculation came about as a result of two major factors—scientific advances and the practical needs of government. The inventive genius of Pascal and Leibnitz yielded the first versions of machines that would eventually replace human calculators. In part, they developed them as a answer to the need for increasingly complex and precise arithmetical operations required for developing mathematical theories. Yet, both men understood that such machines would have practical applications. One, of course, was astronomy—which was yielding navigation tables required by politically powerful nations whose ships roamed the world. Those nations gladly funded the development of more advanced machines because they were directly related to such politically important activities. In many ways, as work on mechanical, electric, and then electronic calculation continued, it would be that same conjunction of practical needs of governments, coupled with the inventive genius of scientists, that would lead the way to the development of the computers we use today.

Programming Calculating Machines With Cards

Although the hand-cranked calculating engines undoubtedly made the chores of computation easier, they were not "programmable." That is, an operator had to use them one step at a time. What was badly needed was an "automatic" machine that would complete a series of computations according to a set of prearranged instructions. To use an analogy, the early machines were like playing the piano. Each step had to be completed one at a time by the operator following a planned sequence, just as each key and chord must be struck by the musician as he or she plays along through a musical score. In contrast, a mechanical player piano can perform essentially the same musical composition automatically. Once it is set into motion, it is controlled by the paper roll that provides the necessary instructions. If a system could be devised for instructing a calculating engine to solve a particular problem automatically, far greater precision and efficiency could be achieved.

The idea of programming a machine came from an unlikely source. During the early 18th century, the French silk industry was weaving very complex patterns. By 1725, weavers began to use sequences of cards with holes punched in them that allowed needles to pass through. This permitted threads of varying colors to be introduced into the cloth to form elaborate designs. Over a period of several decades, this technology advanced steadily. It was the master weaver Joseph Marie Jacquard (1752–1834) who perfected the system to a point where a really intricate design, of about 5 by 5 feet, could make use of as many as 24,000 cards. Indeed, the Jacquard principles are still in use today.

The idea of adapting cards to program a calculating machine belongs to Englishman Charles Babbage (1791–1871). With funding from the British government (because of its intense interest in practical navigation), he developed an extraordinarily complex device that truly pushed the frontiers of mechanical calculation to the ultimate limits.[8] It was a time shortly before electrical energy had been harnessed. His *Difference Engine* (named for its arithmetical principle) had to be cranked by hand, but it performed its operations automatically following the instructions provided by a series of cards. Babbage also developed drawings for (but did not actually build) an even more elaborate Analytical Engine that could calculate to 29 places and print out the results.[9] (It was later constructed and it worked well). Perhaps the most significant of Babbage's contributions was not his engines, which would soon be replaced by electrical systems, but the way he designed a *store,* and the manner in which he programmed his machines.

The store of the Difference Engine was an automatic register that included a system for punching cards to record output:

> The store may be considered as the place of deposit in which the numbers and quantities given by the conditions of the question are originally placed, in which all the immediate results are provisionally preserved and in which at the termination all the required results are found.[10]

The card system Babbage used to store results and the use of such cards for programming his machine provided technologies that would be important for later developments. His solution was a direct adaptation of the Jacquard system for controlling weaving looms:

> Those who are acquainted with the cards of a Jacquards loom will readily understand the functions of these cards. [They] consist of pieces of thick paste board, tin plate or sheet zinc pierced with a number of holes; these cards being strung together by wire or tape hinges pass over a square prism.[11]

Although the work of Babbage laid the technological foundation for both card-based programming and the storing of results automatically produced by a machine, with his contributions the age of developing mechanical and hand-cranked "calculating engines" came to an end. His machines were truly marvels of the early 19th-century engineering mind, combined with the great mathematical advances that had been made up to that time. The next major step would be to combine binary computation principles, card-based programming, and the new power source provided by electricity that became available during the final quarter of the 19th century. Once again, government would play a major role.

ELECTRICAL MACHINES FOR STATISTICAL TABULATION

The next phase in the development of the digital computer requires a shift in focus from such fields as mathematics, astronomy, and navigation to problems of governmental *statistics* (in the sense of data concerning the state). As the 19th century drew to a close, the United States was experiencing great difficulty with its decennial census. The U.S. population was increasing at a startling rate, exceeding 20% between 1880 and 1890 alone. It took 8 years to process the 1880 data by hand. Cross-tabulations of combinations of attributes were especially laborious. Thus, it was almost time for a new census before the previous data had been processed, and it was clear that it would get much worse. Furthermore, U.S. agriculture, industry, and other sectors of society were generating large amounts of data that were of great interest to the government. To keep abreast of this sea of information, a mechanical means of swift and accurate counting and cross-tabulation was urgently needed.[12]

The Hollerith Tabulator and the 1890 Census

In 1879, a 19-year-old engineer named Herman Hollerith started working for the U.S. Census as a special agent. During his 3 years with the Census, he gained a deep appreciation of the problem of processing huge amounts of data. He also conceived of the idea of combining the Jacquard binary principle of a needle passing through a hole in a card with the concept of closing an electrical circuit.[13] He worked briefly as a professor at MIT, and then at the U.S. Patent Office. After experimenting with a paper tape approach, Hollerith developed a counting device based on multipunched cards through which needles could pass to close electrical circuits. These would then register accumulated impulses on dials.[14]

The Hollerith tabulator was an immensely practical device, about the size of a small piano. It could very quickly count as many as 40 variables punched in a card as binary entries. Going into business for himself, he decided to compete as an independent contractor for the task of tabulating the 1890 Census. Hollerith was able to try out his system with data from the health department of the City of Baltimore, and it worked well. It was given further trials in New Jersey and New York City, where it was immediately hailed as an important invention:

> [Mr. Hollerith] has introduced a machine which it is claimed will do automatically and by electricity, with correctness and dispatch, the arduous work

of tabulating a vast amount of statistical information . . . it is a most ingenious device, designed . . . with a special view . . . for use in the exhaustive statistics of the 11th Census.[15]

Hollerith won the contract and completed the task in record time.[16] His machines were adopted by census takers in several other countries. The age of electrical data processing had begun. Again, it was the needs of government that provided the necessary stimulus.

Business and Industry Adopt Electric Tabulation

At the turn of the century, U.S. industry had expanded enormously. Businesses of all kinds were faced with the mundane tasks of accounting, payroll calculation, inventory control, and the like that are so familiar today. They quickly discovered that electric counting and tabulating machines could save them great amounts of money as compared to employing a large labor force of clerks. In 1896 Hollerith incorporated his enterprises as the Tabulating Machine Company. He prospered greatly by developing and marketing an entire system of devices that could punch cards, tabulate swiftly, reproduce decks, verify their accuracy, and sort on different variables. He finally sold his company in 1911, and in 1924 its name was changed to International Business Machines (IBM).[17]

FROM CALCULATORS AND TABULATORS TO COMPUTERS

The next step toward the development of a *computer* (as opposed to a calculator and counter) shifted the scene from government records and business-related accounting to the scientific world of academe. The term *computer* as a name for a machine did not come into general use until the 1940s. As was noted earlier, before that time the word referred to a person—a clerk who was skilled in computational procedures. Devices, "engines," and other machines designed to reduce the drudgery of counting, sorting, and calculating were called adding machines, tabulators, or automatic calculators, depending on their use.[18]

Solving Problems of Trajectories

It was the scientific community working with the military to solve problems of artillery trajectories in order to develop practical firing tables that led the way to true computers. Such trajectories involved mathematical curves whose shapes had to be calculated from complex equations.

At first, the computers were electrically driven but based on mechanical principles. The change to electronic systems was a major hurdle. An important step was taken by Vannevar Bush, then a professor at MIT. Using principles developed by James Maxwell and William Thompson (Lord Kelvin), he built an electrically driven machine capable of solving enormously complex differential equations.[19] Bush called his 1927 model a *differential analyzer.* However, it ultimately proved to be like the dinosaur; very impressive at the time, but doomed to extinction. The device worked very well for complex calculations, and was widely used by scientists and engineers for that purpose, including those at the U.S. Army Aberdeen Proving Ground, who calculated trajectories for precise gunnery and aerial bombs. Its major limitation was that it was so narrowly focused that it had few other applications. His final model, built in the late 1930s, set an all-time record for sheer size; weighing over 100 tons![20]

ENIAC: The First Electronic Digital Computer

The final development of the modern stored-program, digital, electronic computer took place just as World War II was ending. It brought together the principles of virtually every advance that has been mentioned, plus the critical principles of *electronics*—the science that deals with the behavior of electrons in various kinds of substances and environments.

During the 1930s, a number of experimenters sought to develop computers based on digital systems that also made use of electronic circuits, rather than purely mechanical shafts, wheels, and cogs driven by electrical energy. In 1937, Howard W. Aiken, then a graduate student at Harvard, began to design a computer that would use the punched card approach. It was not actually an electronic system, but it worked well. Aiken went to work for IBM and in 1943 completed the Automatic Sequence Controlled Calculator (ASCC), which was taken over by the Navy and finally moved to Harvard as the Mark 1.

The first true electronic digital computer was one built in 1937 and 1938 by Professor John V. Atanasoff and his assistant Clifford Berry at Iowa State College. Although it was relatively small, slow, and designed for the narrow purpose of solving simultaneous linear equations, for the first time it incorporated (over 300) vacuum tubes.[21] This was a major step forward, for the first time making use of the principles on which today's electronic computers are based. Atanasoff had to wait until 1990 to gain recognition for his work when he was awarded the National Medal of Technology by

President Bush. After his death in 1995, his wife explained how he had developed the idea of an electronic computer:

> In 1937 he was working on ways to help graduate students complete lengthy calculations when he decided to clear his mind with a long drive. After 189 miles, he stopped at a roadside bar in Illinois, where, over several bourbons, he developed the concepts behind modern computing.[22]

Another pioneer, John W. Mauchley of the University of Pennsylvania, working with J. Presper Eckert, took Atanasoff's electronic approach much further. Mauchley and Eckert envisioned a purely electronic computer that promised much greater speeds and more general applications than any earlier model. The Pennsylvania team worked in cooperation with the U.S. Army's Ordinance Department at Aberdeen Proving Ground, and substantial government funds were obtained to construct one of the most famous of all the machines of the 1940s.[23] It was the Electronic Numerical Integrator and Computer (ENIAC). Construction was commenced in 1943 and it became operational in 1945, just after World War II ended. It was immediately dubbed the "electronic brain" by the press and was the wonder of its time.

ENIAC was a huge device, about 100 feet long and 8 feet high. Built in a U-shape, it used more than 18,000 vacuum tubes, 70,000 resistors, 10,000 capacitors and miles of wires and cables. It was programmed by wiring boards and setting panels of 6,000 switches by hand. Its immediate goal was to calculate firing tables, but it was a true general-purpose computer. It was incredibly slow and inefficient by today's standards (a small notebook computer has vastly more computing power and speed), but it was the scientific wonder of its time.

The new giant solved problems never before possible, including critical calculations for the H-bomb. In comparison with later solid-state machines, it was a maintenance nightmare. Insects often shorted some of its circuits, causing errors that had to be "debugged." Every time it was turned on several vacuum tubes failed, so it had to be left running and constantly monitored. Nevertheless, ENIAC was the first card-based, digital, general-purpose, electronic computer.[24]

The Contemporary Computer Revolution Begins

In many ways, the modern Computer Age, in terms of widespread use for routine problems, began during the 1950s. It was the adoption of the computer by U.S. business and industry during the period that deeply established the machines as a common part of our contemporary culture.

The tabulator, sorter, and its related machines had been in wide use for several decades, but electronic computing had not been a part of daily operations of large groups in the public and private sector. By the beginning of the 1950s, however, all of the technology had been developed and major manufacturers began to see a vast market for machines that could be used by trained lay operators, rather than only by mathematicians and research scientists.

It was the vision of great profits to be made from computers that led IBM, Remington Rand, Northrup, Raytheon, and a number of other corporations, to design, manufacture, and market a selection of machines designed for various purposes and applications. Very quickly, standardized languages were developed—FORTRAN (FORmula TRANslating system) for statisticians and COBOL (COmmon Business Oriented Language). The Cold War also played an important part in the progress of the new Computer Age. Both applied science and the military used and influenced the designs of computers extensively. For example, the structure of data files by such agencies as the Atomic Energy Commission still shapes the way in which information is stored in major online databases.[25] All of this expanded the market and led to rapid development of mainframe machines of increasing speed and capacity.

The first federal agency to use a large mainframe computer, outside of the military, was the U.S. Census. It purchased the very first UNIVAC manufactured by Remington Rand (in 1951) for use with the 1950 census data. However, computers did not immediately spread to other agencies of government because they did not need vast tabulating and calculating power. Routine record keeping on electronic media would wait for additional developments that would make it possible for routine clerks to prepare computerized "documents." Meanwhile, government agencies continued to generate paper records. Their volume increased substantially after Congress passed the Administrative Procedure Act of 1946. For the first time it became mandatory for all federal agencies to keep and maintain records that were to be open to inspection by the public (with some exceptions).

A critical technological transition during the decade of the 1950s was the change to *solid state* systems. This came about after the transistor was developed in 1947.[26] This small electronic device contained essentially the same circuits as the vacuum tube for influencing the flow of a stronger electric current between grids powered by fluctuating weaker currents. However, in the transistor, the circuits were embedded in a small piece of "solid state" silicon (rather than a hollow glass bulb). The transistor was cheaper to produce, created very little heat, was far more efficient, and served the same functions as the vacuum tube it replaced. Early in the 1950s, the manufacture of computers using vacuum tubes came to an end and production of reliable solid state computers began. Later, this led to the development of miniaturized integrated circuits on silicon chips, which are at the heart of computers today.

As their use increased, the social effects of powerful computers were widely feared by critics, who maintained that privacy and other important qualities of life were being threatened. Their concern was that "Big Brother" (meaning the Orwellian concept of intrusive central government) would be able to use the new technology invasively to keep track of everyone and dehumanize them to the status of a number.[27] The now-venerable 80-column IBM card, with its stern warning "Do not fold, spindle, or mutilate," began to appear in everyone's mailbox as companies turned to computerized billing. In many ways, anticomputer feelings generated during this period are still a part of our shared attitudes and beliefs.

THE GOVERNMENT BEGINS USING COMPUTERS FOR ROUTINE RECORD KEEPING

There were various reasons for the delay in the use of computers by government for routine record keeping. One was that the venerable IBM cards of the early period, with only 80 columns and 10 rows, provided only limited storage. Furthermore, they were relatively fragile by comparison with today's storage media. They deteriorated with repeated handling and swelled under conditions of high humidity.[28] A second reason was that government records had to be kept by routine clerks, not by scientists with advanced technical skills. Thus, the technology in use had to be reasonably user friendly so that people with limited training could prepare and manage the records. Such a technology was not available until the development of the interactive computer screen and software that made it possible for users to follow simple directions and procedures.

Magnetic Tape and the Interactive Keyboard

The most common medium for storing records today is magnetic tape.[29] It is durable, reliable, and capable of storing vast amounts of information in relatively small space. Various other document and record-storing media were used prior to the adoption of tape—16 mm film, microfiche, discs, and so forth. Magnetic tape was first used by the Germans in World War II. Its use as a storage medium for electronic records began in the late 1950s. During the next two decades, after a number of tape formats were tried and abandoned, it was standardized. Although CD-ROM is coming into wide use, tape became so widely established for large-scale data storage that it is likely to remain an important medium for the foreseeable future.

A major advance that made computers much easier to use came in 1960. It was the interactive computer, where the operator can type numbers and letters on a keyboard and they will appear on a screen. This permits them to be checked and edited before being entered into a computer's memory. The hardware was developed by the Digital Equipment Company, and Dan Murphy of MIT prepared the necessary software. It was the forerunner of today's word-processing programs.[30] This made it possible for people who could use a typewriter to make entries into a computer. It made it much easier for clerks with limited computer skills to generate, store, and recover records.

The number of computers in use by federal agencies rose sharply after 1960. For example, in 1955, when Congress first began hearings on the Freedom of Information Act (FOIA), federal agencies were using only 45 mainframe computers.[31] About a decade later, in 1966, when FOIA was finally passed, estimates indicate that 3,000 were in use.[32] By 1986 that number had soared to approximately 25,000 mainframes and more than 125,000 of the (then) new microcomputers.[33] By 1990, the number of mainframes had nearly doubled to 48,000.[34] The use of microcomputers more than doubled in a single year, from 490,000 in 1987 to more than a million by 1988.[35]

The widespread adoption of computers by the federal government was paralleled at the state and local level. A survey completed in 1985 revealed that 97% of U.S. cities used computers to store and retrieve at least some information. That represented an increase of 90% from the previous decade.[36] Another survey completed in 1988 indicated that virtually all state and municipal governments use computers in some way.[37]

A Tidal Wave of Electronic Records

The acquisition of huge numbers of computers has not reduced the number of government records kept by agencies of governments. If anything, it has increased them. In other words, machine-readable records have increased to astronomical proportions.

One way of viewing the explosion in computer use by the federal government is to note the increase in spending on information technology that took place during the 1980s. According to an Office of Technology Assessment report, the government spent about $9.2 billion on information technology in 1982. In 1988, the figure was $15 billion.[38] Only 3 years later, by 1991, it had grown to $17 billion.[39]

Still another index of progress in the transition to computerized records is provided by the growth in the number of accessible databases produced and maintained by the federal government. This is a difficult matter to pin down in terms of numbers because no one keeps a careful count of how many are actually available. However, various estimates have been made by different sources. For example, in 1987 a major commercial indexer, Information USA, tallied 4,200 files in its *Federal Database Finder,* a published guide to accessible federal data sources. In that same year, the Government Accounting Office tallied 7,782—triple the number available in 1983. The GAO survey concluded that, "Federal agencies maintain hundreds of thousands of electronic records and databases. No one really knows how many. A far smaller number, about 7,800, mostly databases, are available for sale on magnetic tape or diskette."[40] In 1990, the *Federal Database Finder* listed more than 8,000 databases and electronic bulletin boards.[41] By 1995 the number was growing so fast that keeping count was almost impossible.

Whatever the actual number today, it is clear that it is very large and that it is growing at an accelerating pace. There are a variety of reasons why this is the case. One is that government itself has grown sharply in recent decades. The U.S. federal government is the largest producer and publisher of information in the world.[42] For example, the Patent and Trademark Office alone has an archive of 28,000,000 documents, which led Congress as early as 1980 to urge it to computerize.[43]

As more agencies provide services for more citizens, the flood of records will increase on an annual basis. For example, such agencies as the Social Security Administration, Veteran's Administration, the Justice Department, and the Department of Defense each engage in millions and millions of transactions annually for which, *by law,* records must be kept. The number and size of agencies continues to grow, in spite of politicians' periodic promises to reduce the size of government. To provide a perspective, every 4 months the government generates "a stack of records equal to all those produced in the 124 years between George Washington and Woodrow Wilson."[44] In an another illustration, the National Oceanic and Atmospheric Administration, a relatively small agency by comparison, has so much data stored on tapes that if the effort could "start now and go real fast, it would take 1,100 years to publish it all."[45]

Although all of these electronic records may seem massive, their size, weight, and bulk pales by comparison with the paper they are replacing. To illustrate the problem, the Navy cruiser the *U.S.S. Vincennes,* a vessel of only intermediate size, carries 26.6 tons of paper in filing cabinets that weigh 9.3 tons, for a total of 35.9 tons of dead weight that must be carried wherever the ship goes.[46] In another illustration, at the small Federal Maritime Commission, a few clerks keep track of shipping tariffs, manually updating data in three-ringed binders by replacing over 750,000 pages annually.[47]

As the transition from paper to computer records continues, however, it is not without its problems. One source of difficulty has been changing technology. Earlier machine-readable records can be difficult to recover when technology changes. For example, the most extensive record of Americans who served in World War II now exists only on 1,600 reels of microfilm pictures of computer punch cards.[48] Even if these millions of cards were reconstructed, there are few machines around today that could read them. Similarly, many early tape formats are now obsolete and the machines that were able to handle them have long since been junked. In addition, human shortcomings are always a problem. Code books are often lost. This results in a well-preserved record that no one can decipher—just a tape full of numbers.

Another way in which government records are lost, or become unavailable to many, is through private vendors who charge for online access to government records. In order to recover costs, agencies sometimes sell their records to private businesses who then place them into databases that are offered as online services. Users can gain access to these for a fee. This discriminates on the basis of affluence. Furthermore, the private vendors often discard records that they deem unprofitable and data that may be historically significant are lost forever.

THE ADOPTION OF COMPUTERS IN NEWSROOMS

After computers became widely available, it was inevitable that they would find their way into the news business. This happened in several ways and it set the stage for the eventual development of computer-assisted reporting.

The first entry by a computer into a newsroom took place in the early days of television. As explained in the following, it was under circumstances that would forever change the way that broadcasters provide reports on election night. The second entry was the widespread adoption of computers by newspapers and other news organizations for routine business purposes. For example, newspapers began to use large computers not only to process payrolls and related information, but also to automate the mechanics of virtually every task related to preparing copy and getting it printed. The third entry took place during the 1980s as commercial firms developed online database services providing abstracts or full text of publications of many kinds. These proved to be a rich resource for journalists. At first they were used mainly by newspaper librarians, but they are now used by reporters themselves. This occurred during the same decade as the small personal computer joined its mainframe counterpart in the news industry. This was slow at first, and it took place mainly as a part of the general adoption of microcomputers by American society at large.

   When all of these elements came together, reporters began to have access to resources that would change the nature of news reporting considerably. With microcomputers and modems they could access electronically stored information in full-text online services, electronic bulletin boards, and federal data services. These extended greatly the sources and amount of information available to develop stories. Then, with microcomputers available, they were able to make increasing use of software for spreadsheet analysis, database construction, and statistical manipulation to examine government records in electronic form. In the final section of this chapter, therefore, the movement of computers from science labs and business settings onto the desks of reporters is briefly traced.

Reporting a Presidential Election

During the evening of November 4, 1952, the age of electronic computing came together with the age of mass communication. It was an event of which historians took little note, but it would forever change the way that journalists reported elections to the public. In one of the earliest television coverages of a presidential election, CBS made use of the Remington Rand UNIVAC, which had been programmed to predict the outcome of the election on the basis of early returns.[49] It was the contest between Dwight D. Eisenhower, the great hero of World War II, and Adlai E. Stevenson, the champion of the Democratic Party.

   All of the pollsters and pundits predicted a very close contest. Political wisdom had it that Stevenson might be the winner, because the Democrats had controlled the White House through three elections with Franklin D. Roosevelt and then through the two terms of Harry S. Truman. Others predicted that Eisenhower would win because of his popularity as an effective leader during the war. Both Eisenhower and Stevenson were impressive candidates, and absolutely no one was predicting a strong win by either.

It had taken weeks for the computer experts to work out the formulas for predicting the outcome as a statistical projection from partial returns. It had never been done before. To develop the formulas, they had to go back to previous elections and feed in partial data to see if the results could have been predicted at the same points in time. It seemed to work, but everyone was nervous because the computer had to perform in the glare of national television. If it flopped, it would be a highly visible disaster for both fledgling industries.

Finally, by election evening, all was ready. Two news broadcasters would present the returns and provide analyses on the air as the evening progressed. One was Walter Cronkite, then chief Washington correspondent for CBS, and the other was Charles Collingwood, a newscaster for CBS.

Actually, three separate UNIVACs were used because no one was sure that the machines were up to the task. The computer operators anticipated glitches, bugs, and problems. The three machines were located in Philadelphia at the Remington Rand factory. Direct wires went to the TV studio. One computer performed the main calculations. A second duplicated the projections to make certain to catch any errors. A third remained on standby as a backup in case of equipment failure. (They all worked perfectly.)

As the team went on the air, things got very tense very quickly. By 9:00 p.m., with only 7% of the vote counted, UNIVAC predicted a landslide for Eisenhower. It was a startling forecast of 438 electoral votes for the Republican candidate and only 93 for the Democrat. UNIVAC said that the prediction was statistically significant at a level of 100 to 1. That was so wild and unexpected a prediction that no one believed it. After all, it was supposed to be a close race. In a state of near panic, both the computer experts and the broadcasters discounted the machine's results. The statisticians and programmers quickly tinkered with their formulas to try to get results that would be more realistic. The TV newscasters covered and stalled by saying that the machine was taking more time than had been anticipated.

But, no matter what assumptions were fed into the formulas, UNIVAC steadfastly predicted an Eisenhower landslide. Finally, after waffling, stalling, and reporting far more conservative estimates (that they had literally made up), the newscasters finally conceded to the machine. By midnight they reported that UNIVAC had been right all along.

The final count was unbelievably close to the early UNIVAC predictions made on the basis of only 7% of the returns. Eisenhower received 442 electoral votes (UNIVAC had predicted 438). Stevenson received 89 (UNI-VAC had predicted 93).

In the days that followed, newspapers were caustic in their criticism of the TV newscasters who had refused to believe the computer.[50] One editorial headline gloated that "Machine Makes Monkey Out of Man."[51] CBS commentator Edward R. Murrow summed up the situation concisely in his conclusion that: "The trouble with machines is people."[52]

In spite of the debacle, a major step had been taken. Computers had entered the newsroom. Since 1952, computer projections of the outcomes of elections on the basis of partial returns have been a standard part of television broadcasts on election nights.

In the decades that followed, computers came into wider use in the U.S. business community, and they quickly found their way into the world of the newspaper. Various mainframe systems were adopted to process payrolls, keep track of subscriptions, manage various kinds of advertising information, and automate presses. Typewriters began to disappear from the newsroom. They were replaced by "dumb" terminals linked to the mainframe. Such video display terminals (VDTs) were dumb in that they permitted reporters to prepare their stories on screen (and others to modify and process them for final printing) but they could not be used to process data or for other interactive functions. That would not be possible until the arrival of the now ubiquitous microcomputer.

Americans (and Reporters) Adopt the Microcomputer

Beginning in the early 1980s, the small desktop computers that are so common today began to appear on the market. Apple was the pioneer, followed quickly by Radio Shack, Compaq, and KayPro, and finally in 1983 by IBM. From the beginning, IBM made a historic decision to make its designs and architecture public. No licensing agreement was needed to duplicate them. This permitted numerous other manufacturers to make "clones" that were IBM compatible. Dozens of brands came on the market and prices came down quickly. The technology advanced rapidly, and a vigorous software industry sprang up to supply user-friendly programs for word processing, spreadsheet analysis, and many other kinds of tasks. The small computers were adapted for hundreds of uses.

The adoption of the microcomputer within American society is still continuing, but between 1983 and the end of the decade, millions were eagerly purchased by businesses, the government, colleges, public schools, and organizations. In addition, millions of families purchased them for home use. The acquisition of microcomputers by U.S. families followed a typical S-shaped accumulative curve of adoption over time. In 1990, the number of adopters reached nearly a quarter of U.S. households.[53] By 1995, 33% of U.S. households had a computer at home.[54]

Adoption curves have been widely studied by social scientists who specialize in research on the adoption of new technology of all kinds.[55] In contemporary urban–industrial societies, there is a constant flow of new technical products and other kinds of innovations. The process by which they spread through the society is well described by the theory of the *adoption of innovation.* The theory is widely applicable to many fields, and it describes the stages by which a device like a microcomputer is adopted by users. It is applicable to the process by which the microcomputer came into wide use in American society and in newsrooms.

Briefly described, the adoption process begins with an *awareness* stage in which those who will ultimately adopt an innovation learn of its existence but lack detailed information about it. Awareness is followed by an *interest* stage, during which those who contemplate adoption will devote increasing attention to the innovation and seek additional information about it. In an *assessment* stage, individuals use the information obtained to evaluate the applicability of the innovation to their lives. In a *trial* stage, a small number of individuals acquire and test the innovation to determine its utility. Finally, in an *adoption* stage, the new adopters use the innovation on a full scale. After this, others adopt it and the accumulation of users follows a characteristic S-shaped curve.

Not all adopters make their decisions at the same time. The overall rate of adoption can be plotted as a proportion of those in the relevant population who have done so at a particular point in time. Rogers maintained that, when plotted in this way, several rather general *categories* of adopters can be identified on the basis of their "innovativeness."[56] These categories are the *innovators, early adopters, early majority adopters, late majority adopters,* and the *laggards,* who hold out until a very late stage. Rogers also identified a different set of stages by the kinds of actions that are taken within an organization that adopts an innovation. These five stages are called *agenda-setting* (administrators see the innovation as a potential solution to a problem), *matching* (an innovation with a particular problem), *redefining/restructuring* (changing conditions in the organization so that the innovation can be acquired), *clarifying* (how it is to be used), and *routinizing* (its day-to-day use once it has been adopted).[57]

Both processes have relevance for the adoption of computers in the newsroom. At first, it was an individual adaptation as reporters acquired their own computers. Later, it was done via organizational decisions.

Looked at newspaper by newspaper, during the earliest period, the curve starts at zero level and begins to rise very slowly because only a few innovators acquired the item. Then, in a second stage, it begins to accumulate a bit faster as early adopters take up the item. This is followed by a period in which the accumulation curve rises at its greatest rate as the early majority adopters make their acquisition decisions. It then starts to slow as late majority adopters take up the item and become part of the curve. Finally, as the curve levels out, only a few laggards are added. The overall pattern that results is the so-called S-shaped curve.

Along with other Americans, reporters acquired and began to use their own personal microcomputers. At first, reporters used their personal computers for word processing, as replacements for the typewriter. Many brought them to the office to use because management was reluctant to supply them. Eventually, newspapers began to provide them, and as modems and communication software became available, they began to be used in more sophisticated ways. One of the most important was to connect their computers via telephone lines to *online databases* that could provide rich sources of information to aid in the development of stories. At first, this was done mostly by librarians, but it soon spread to reporters themselves.

As the next section shows, the adoption of such commercially vended databases by newspapers followed its own S-shaped curve and it further encouraged the widespread use of microcomputers in the newsroom. Once they were there, however, reporters began to experiment with using them for the analysis of records of government.

Newsrooms Adopt Online Databases

As early as 1980, Anthony Smith predicted that the rapidly expanding use of computers, along with the growth of various kinds of electronic databases (which had just started to be available), would forever change how reporters gather and formulate the news.[58] Today, his insightful prediction has become a reality. Online databases have been widely adopted by American journalists as a routine tool for gathering, transmitting, enhancing, disseminating, storing, and even making the news.

Databases are now used in several ways by most U.S. dailies. For most, the old paper "morgue" of clipped stories has been replaced by a computerized library in which the paper's own stories are stored. Second, commercial databases are routinely searched by reporters seeking various kinds of background information. Third, some newspapers construct their own databases on specialized topics. These can be valuable in developing particular categories of stories. Finally, the analysis of the computerized records of government agencies has become increasingly common. The present section of this chapter discusses the way in which the adoption of online databases took place during the last decade.

By the beginning of the 1980s, commercial vendors such as Mead Data Central's Lexis/Nexis, Knight Ridder's VU/TEXT, the Dow Jones News-Retrieval service, and others were online with full-text coverage of many newspapers and other periodicals. During the decade they became increasingly valuable tools for journalists. A reporter using a personal computer with a modem could call up stories on a given topic that appeared in newspapers, magazines, and newsletters in various parts of the country. Today, such services have greatly expanded and vendors also provide detailed information on corporations, litigation, legislation, campaign financing, and a host of other topics. Other kinds of databases are available as well. For example, science-oriented CDP Online allows access to more than 150 databases of technical journals in fields ranging from astronomy to zoology.[59] Thus, rapid and relatively easy access to enormous amounts of information is revolutionizing newswriting.

As the 1980s began, most papers were not subscribing to online services, and only a few innovators were using them. By 1983, however, these numbers increased and the curve appeared to be entering the early adopter phase.[60] By 1984, their advantages were becoming clear to newsroom managers, but the high cost was an inhibiting factor. At the time, Nexis contained full text of 25 newspapers and wire services, 100 full-text magazines and newsletters, and 60 abstracted periodicals of the *New York Times* Information Bank.[61]

By the middle of the decade, the acquisition of such database services for journalism continued to follow the classic S-shaped adoption curve.[62] It is not possible to plot that curve in an exact manner because no one systematically kept track of the data. Jacobson and Ullman pointed out that "trade press articles have followed the trend, but their data are largely anecdotal in nature."[63] However, the curve can be roughly reconstructed from a limited number of studies that have examined the use of online databases by journalists in one part of the country or another. For example, in 1983, Ullman surveyed 97 U.S. dailies with circulations of 100,000 or more.[64] Of the 57 who replied, 20 (i.e., 35%) were subscribing to one or more databases. These tended to be the larger newspapers. Many respondents indicated that costs were a limiting factor. This was confirmed in 1986 when Soffin and his associates surveyed newspapers in Michigan. They found that only a few of these smaller newspapers were subscribing to databases. Indeed, half said that they saw no real need for them.[65] In a study of editorial writers at 27 newspapers that was reported in the same year (1986), Kerr and Niebauer found that the majority did not use online databases.[66]

In another study focusing on the first half of the 1980s, Miller examined the use of online databases by newspapers and concluded that their use was not extensive. However, he noted that it had quadrupled between 1982 and 1986.[67] Thus, it seems clear that during the first half of the 1980s, many newspaper managers became aware of databases. A few innovators began to use them as the decade began, and then, by the middle of the 1980s, the rate of adoption appears to have advanced to the early adopter stage.

By mid-decade, the rate of adoption continued to increase. A study of newspapers listed in the 1986 *Editor and Publisher Yearbook* by Jacobson and Ullman yielded a figure of 29% who used at least one database.[68] In 1988, Miller reported a survey indicating that more than half of the 155 newspaper respondents (and many broadcasters) were using databases.[69] From there, the curve appears to have moved into the early majority stage. By the end of the 1980s, a study of 105 newspapers showed that about 90% subscribed to commercial databases.[70] In addition, De Riemer indicated in 1991 that over 80% of the 131 reporters studied in a survey of four regional newspapers used databases regularly.[71]

Larger studies, done later, show lower rates of adoption. For example, in 1996 Steven S. Ross and Don Middleberg published the results of a survey sent to more than 6,000 writers and editors from almost all of the nation's dailies, large weeklies, and business magazines. The researchers reported that almost one fourth (23%) of the 751 respondents said that they went online to use the Internet and commercial information services once a day or more. A similar proportion (24%) said they went online to obtain information at least once a week. Overall, 68% said they or their staffs used such online services at least once a month. In addition, the results indicated that America Online was the most popular commercial service used by the respondents.[72]Another survey, completed in 1995 by American Opinion Research, reported that 57% of 854 newspaper editors and publishers said that their papers were using online services. In addition, many of the others indicated that they planned to begin using databases soon.[73]

Although precise data remain elusive, with a large proportion of newspapers now making use of computers for online searching, it does appear overall that the industry has entered into the early majority stage of adoption. This leaves only the late majority and the laggards to begin using online services during the remainder of the 1990s. In a rough way, then, the adoption of online database services in the newsroom appears to be following the typical pattern of five stages—from innovators to laggards—out-lined by Rogers.

Reviewed from a somewhat different perspective, the studies noted also indicate that a *qualitative* pattern of change took place during the 1980s in the way in which such databases are used in the newsroom. The change was in who did the searching. When they were first adopted, online services were controlled largely by librarians. A considerable controversy developed as to whether reporters themselves should be allowed direct access. It was librarians who managed the newspaper's own computerized records, and when online databases became available, they did all of the searching because they had the necessary skills. At first, reporters were required to get management authorization, story by story, to request such searches. Even if they had the skills, few were allowed to do their own searching.

These controls made sense at the time. Management was rightly concerned with costs, and online services were very expensive. However, late in the 1980s, things changed: First, more reporters learned how to search efficiently. Second, the cost of subscriptions and use of online databases leveled off with increased competition among database vendors. And third, as hardware costs decreased, more reporters were provided with desktop computers to use. Although some managers still keep a very tight rein on who can go online, others have come to believe that the benefits outweigh the costs in the use of online databases. The information they provide can improve the quality of stories and it can increase the amount of news coverage one reporter can manage in a given period of time. Thus, the use of online resources can actually be less costly than having additional personnel—an important consideration during a time of declining per capita circulation curves.

In summary, the use of computers by working journalists is not something that appeared out of nowhere during the last decade or so. It is the latest development in a process that extends back to the time when people drew lines on a tray of sand and used stones instead of fingers to keep track of simple calculations. Those beginnings provided the basis for great scientific advances as the technology of tabulation and calculation developed over several centuries. It was not until the 20th century was well under way that computing advanced into the electronic age. The result was a great technological revolution that by the present time has touched nearly every aspect of society, including journalism. With access to vast amounts of information available from online databases on almost any topic, many reporters now routinely use desktop computers to assemble information in minutes that would have taken hours or even days to gather in a paper-based library. The result is a capacity to provide the public with news stories with greater accuracy and richness than was possible before.

In many ways, it was the adoption of computers in the newsroom that paved the way for an important change in the nature of American journalism. The rate of adoption accelerated with the declining cost of hardware and the creation of easy-to-use software. The presence of desktop computers, used first for word processing and then for database searching made them a familiar device for reporters. This factor, in turn, caused innovative individuals to experiment with new uses for the computers. This led to the development of computer-assisted investigative reporting.

The changes discussed in this chapter provided the foundation of a significant development in the field of journalism. The next chapter shows in greater detail how the combination of computers and the change to electronic records led to a new form of investigative reporting. Journalists with the required computer hardware, software, and skills can now assemble and analyze databases for specific investigations, or review the entire record of a public agency, or even the performance of a specific official, over a span of years in ways that were never possible during the era of paper records.

NOTES AND REFERENCES

1. This example and details concerning John Napier's invention were adapted from F. Gareth Ashurst, *Pioneers of Computing* (London: Frederick Muller, Ltd., 1983), pp. 1–17.
2. For a detailed description of Napier's accomplishments, see: Herman H. Goldstine, *History of Numerical Analysis from the 16th through the 19th Century* (New York: Springer-Verlag, 1977).
3. The device was soon developed into the slide rule by William Oughtred, another mathematician. See: A. J. Sly, *A Short History of Computing,* 2nd ed. (Hatfield, Australia: The Advisory Unit for Computer Based Education, 1976), p. 7.
4. F. Gareth Ashurst, *Pioneers of Computing* (London: Frederick Muller, Ltd., 1983), p. 19.
5. For a more detailed account and a readable biography of Pascal, see: Mortimer Ernest, *Blaise Pascal* (London: Methuen, 1959).
6. Ashurst, *op. cit.,* p. 45.
7. Ashurst, *op. cit.,* p. 44.
8. Phillip Morrison and Emily Morrison, *Charles Babbage and His Calculating Engines* (New York: Dover Publications, Inc., 1961).
9. For general descriptions of the Difference Machine and Babbage's Analytical Machine, see: Dionysius Lardner, "Babbages's Calculating Engine," *Edinburgh Review,* July, 1834, No. CXX, and L. F. Menabrea, "Sketch of the Analytical Engine Invented by Charles Babbage," *Bibliotheque Universelle de Geneve,* October, 1842, No. 82, trans. Ada Augusta, Countess of Lovelace.

10. Charles Babbage, "On the Mathematical Powers of the Calculating Engine," unpublished manuscript dated December, 1837, reprinted in: Brian Randell, *The Origins of Digital Computers: Selected Papers* (New York: Springer-Verlag, 1975), pp. 17–52.

11. *Ibid.,* p. 20.

12. Keith S. Reid-Green, "The History of Census Tabulation," *Scientific American,* Vol. 260, No. 2, February, 1989, pp. 98–104.

13. There is some dispute as to whether he first conceived of this idea or whether it originally came from some other fellow worker. In either case, it was Hollerith who transformed the concept into a reality. See: F. Gareth Ashurst, *op. cit.,* pp. 80–81.

14. The new machine was immediately patented by Hollerith (U.S. Patent 395,781, June 8th, 1887). He had worked in the U.S. Patent Office and understood the process very well.

15. The quotation is from the *New York Post.* See: Geoffrey D. Austrian, *Herman Hollerith: Forgotten Giant of Information Processing* (New York: Columbia University Press, 1982), p. 41.

16. He also competed successfully for the Census of 1900.

17. Charles Bashe, Lyle R. Johnson, John H. Palmer, and Emerson W. Pugh, *IBM's Early Computers* (Cambridge, Mass.: The MIT Press, 1986), p. 6.

18. By the early 1950s, the term *computer* came to mean a stored-program, electronic digital computer. See: A. W. Burks, "Electronic Computing Circuits of the ENIAC," *Proceedings of the Institute of Radio Engineers,* 1947, pp. 756–757.

19. Bush was a renowned scientist in his time. He designed the machine that broke the Japanese codes before World War II and was chief scientific advisor and administrator under Franklin D. Roosevelt, being administratively responsible for the Manhattan Project among others. See: J. Crank, *The Differential Analyzer* (New York: Longmans, Green and Company, 1947).

20. Ashurst, *op. cit.,* p. 104.

21. Clark R. Mollenhoff, *Atanasoff: Forgotten Father of the Computer* (Ames, Iowa: Iowa State University Press, 1988).

22. "John V. Atanasoff, at 91; Credited with Developing First Computer," *The Boston Globe,* June 17, 1995, p. 14.

23. Other electronic calculators were developed during the period, such as the Selective Sequence Electronic Calculator (SSEC) of IBM, which became operational in 1948. See: Charles J. Bashe, *et. al., op. cit.,* pp. 47–59.

24. For full details of its construction and use, see: Arthur W. Burks, "From ENIAC to the Stored Program Computer: Two Revolutions in Computers," Paper presented at the International Research Conference on the History of Computing, Los Alamos, New Mexico, 1976; Reprinted in N. Metropolis, J. Howlett, and Gian-Carlo Rota, eds., *A History of Computing in the Twentieth Century* (Orlando, Fl.: Academic Press, 1980), pp. 311–344.

25. Diane H. Smith and Kent A. Smith, "Online Government Databases: Into the Maelstrom," *Database,* 11, 3, June, 1988, p. 56.

26. J. Bardeen and W. H. Brattain, "The Transistor, A Semi-Conductor Triode," *Physics Review,* 74, July, 1948, pp. 230–231; See also: W. H. Brattain, "Genesis of the Transistor," *The Physics Teacher,* March, 1968, pp. 109–114.

27. For example, see: Wilson P. Dizard, Jr., *The Coming Information Age: An Overview of Technology, Economics, and Politics,* 3rd. ed. (White Plains, N.Y.: Longman, 1989), pp. 3–4.

28. Charles J. Bashe, Lyle R. Johnson, John H. Palmer, and Emerson W. Pugh, *op. cit.,* pp. 1–33, 193.

29. Although newer storage systems are being used, such as robotic stackers, jukeboxes, and other systems, magnetic tape remains a major medium. See: Peter J. Interland, "Sea of Change Underway for Storage Solutions," *LAN Times,* 8, 17, September 2, 1991, p. 52.

30. J. Markoff, "Digital Fetes the 'Germ' That Began a Revolution," *New York Times,* December 16, 1990, Business Section, p. 11.

31. David Morrissey, "Update: FOIA and Computer-Assisted Journalism," address at the 1991 conference on computer-assisted reporting at Indiana University's National Institute for Advanced Reporting, March, 1991.

32. Martha Mulford Gray, "Computers in the Federal Government: A Compilation of Statistics," Special Publication 500-46, National Bureau of Standards, Institute for Computer Sciences and Technology, April, 1979.

33. *Managing End User Computing in the Federal Government,* U.S. General Services Administration, Information Resources Management Service, No. 2, September, 1986.

34. *Automatic Data Processing Equipment in the Federal Government,* General Services Administration, Federal Equipment Data Center, April, 1990.

35. *Microcomputer Survey Report,* General Services Administration, Office of Federal Information Resources Management, September, 1988.

36. Sig Splichal and Bill F. Chamberlin, "The Battle for Access to Government Records Round Two: Enter the Computer," unpublished paper, University of Florida, August, 1991, p. 2.

37. D. Brundy, "Computers and Smaller Local Governments," *Public Productivity Review,* 12, 1988, p. 184.

38. W. John Moore, "Access Denied," *National Journal,* January 20, 1990, p. 121.

39. Morrissey, *op. cit.,* 1991.

40. These various figures are from the Bureau of National Affairs, Inc.'s "Daily Report for Executives," DER No. 154, August 11, 1989.

41. Matthew Lesko, *Federal Database Finder,* 3rd ed. (Kensington, MD.: Information USA, 1990).

42. Julius J. Marke, "Public Access to Computerized Government Information," *New York Law Journal,* January 28, 1992, p. 4.

43. "Daily Report to Executives," *op. cit.,* p. 17.

44. Donald A. Ritchie, "Oral Histories May Help Scholars Plow Through the Rapidly Accumulating Mass of Federal Paper," *Chronicle of Higher Education,* 35, November 2, 1988, p. A44.

45. Quote from Carl C. Abston, Chief of NOAA's Systems Integration and Planning Office in Boulder Colorado, in Rick Vizachero, "Feds Have Big Plans for CD-ROM; Compact Disk Read-Only Memory," *Government Computer News,* 10, 7, April 1, 1991, p. 1.

46. Eben Shapiro, "CD's Store the Data But Sifting's a Chore," the *New York Times,* Sunday, August, 4, 1991, p. F9.

47. "Daily Report to Executives," *op. cit.,* p. 7.

48. "History Lost in Computers," Associated Press release published in *The Syracuse Post Standard,* April 2, 1991, p. A-1.

49. This account is based on the following source: Harry Wulforst, *Breakthrough to the Computer Age* (New York: Charles Scribner's Sons, 1982), pp. 161–171.

50. See, for example, an editorial in the *Washington Post,* November 8th, 1952.

51. From an editorial in the *Journal* of Jacksonville, Florida, November 11th, 1952.

52. Joel Shurkin, *Engines of the Mind* (New York: W.W. Norton and Company, 1984), p. 253.

53. John Carey, "Looking Back at the Future: How Communication Technologies Enter American Households," in John V. Pavlik and Everette E. Dennis, *Demystifying Media Technology* (Mountain View, Cal.: Mayfield Publishing Company, 1993), pp. 32–39.

54. John Carey of Greystone Communications, Dobbs Ferry, NY, tracks the penetration of various media into U.S. households. He bases the 33% figure on data received from the Electronic Industry Association and A. C. Nielsen (personal correspondence).

55. A classic work on the adoption of innovation is: Everett M. Rogers and F. Floyd Shoemaker, *Communication of Innovations: A Cross-Cultural Approach* (New York: The Free Press, 1971). See especially, pp. 52–70. See also: Everett Rogers, *Diffusion of Innovations,* 3rd ed. (New York: The Free Press, 1983).

56. Everett M. Rogers, *Diffusion of Innovations,* 3rd. ed. (New York: The Free Press, 1983), pp. 245–251.

57. Everett M. Rogers, *Communication Technology: The New media in Society* (New York: The Free Press, 1986). For a discussion of the diffusion of microcomputers in the organizational setting of a high school system, see: "The Innovation Process in Organizations," pp. 137–147.

58. Anthony Smith, *Goodbye Gutenberg: The Newspaper Revolution of the 1980's* (New York: Oxford University Press, 1980), p. 206.

59. For example, Lexis/Nexis provides coverage of hundreds of business and news sources, industry and trade publications and federal publications that contain information on corporations, new bills before Congress, legal records, and tax information. Knight-Ridder's VU/TEXT provides full-text retrieval service for more than 50 newspapers and over 1,500 business publications. Several others, such as Dialog, provide a similar range of information services.

60. Tim Miller, "Information, Please, and Fast; Reporting's Revolution: Data Bases," *Washington Journalism Review,* September, 1983, pp. 51–53.

61. Tim Miller, "The Database as a Reportorial Resource," *Editor and Publisher,* April 28, 1984, pp. 70–71, 104.

62. For a specific analyses of the diffusion of online databases, see: Everett M. Rogers, *Communication Technology: The New Media in Society* (New York: The Free Press, 1990), pp. 117–149.

63. Thomas L. Jacobson and John Ullman, "Commercial Databases and Reporting: Opinions of Newspaper Journalists and Librarians," *Newspaper Research Journal,* 10, Winter, 1989, p. 16. For early discussions of database use and search strategies for journalists, see: Kathleen A. Hansen and Jean Ward, "Journalism and Library Research: Combining Methodologies in a New Search Model," *Research Strategies,* 1, 4, 1983, pp. 167–175.

64. Frederic F. Endres, "Daily Newspaper Utilization of Computer Data Bases," *Newspaper Research Journal,* 7, 1, Fall, 1985, pp. 29–35.

65. Stan Soffin, *et al.,* "Online Databases and Newspapers: An Assessment of Utilization and Attitudes," Paper presented at the annual meeting of the Association for Education in Journalism and Mass Communication, San Antonio, 1987.

66. John Kerr and Walter E. Niebauer, Jr., "A Base-Line Study on the Use of Outside Databases, Full Text Retrieval Systems By Newspaper Editorial Page Writers," Paper

presented at the annual meetings of the Association for Education in Journalism and Mass Communication, Norman, Oklahoma, 1986.

67. Tim Miller, "The Data-Base Revolution," *Columbia Journalism Review,* September/October, 1988, pp. 35–38.

68. Jacobson and Ullman, *op. cit.,* p. 18.

69. Tim Miller, *op. cit.,* p. 36.

70. From data presented by D. Ashenfelder, speaker at the Conference on Advanced Investigative Methods for Journalists, Indiana University, Indianapolis, March 1990.

71. Cynthia De Riemer, "Commercial Database Use in the Newsroom," Paper presented at the annual meetings of the Association for Education in Journalism and Mass Communication, Boston, 1991.

72. Steven S. Ross and Don Middleberg, "The Media in Cyberspace II: A National Survey," Columbia University Graduate School of Journalism and Middleberg and Associates, 1996. Results can also be found on the internet (http://www.mediasource.com).

73. *Communications Daily,* Vol. 15, No. 122, June 12, 1995, p. 7.

3

Freedom of Information Laws: The Legal Status of Electronic Records

As the age of computerized records began, one of the first obstacles journalists encountered in exercising their oversight function was gaining access to the files of government agencies. Under the old rules, getting a document was usually not all that difficult. One went or wrote to the agency, specified the document requested, and a copy was more or less promptly produced. As the same agencies developed ways of recording their transactions on magnetic media, however, some also developed a considerable reluctance to make those records available to the public. A number of years passed, during which federal and state courts had to refine the status of electronic records as opposed to those filed on paper.

Even today, there are a number of reasons why agencies may drag their feet or openly resist requests for files of computerized records, and such resistance does not necessarily mean that they are trying to conceal mismanagement or wrongdoing. That had been the situation in the case of the Rhode Island mortgage records cited in chapter 1, in which files were eventually obtained by Elliot Jaspin and his colleagues only by going to court and calling in the State Police. It may also have been the case with at least some federal agencies that resisted disclosure when reporters first started to ask for computer tapes. However, the legal status of electronic information remains unclear in many ways. In addition, there were other grounds on which agencies resisted requests for records of their transactions. For example, providing file after file to reporters and others could easily place a considerable work load on already busy personnel. It must also be recognized that Congress has failed to provide sufficient resources to agencies to enable them to comply with large numbers of FOIA requests.[1] In addition, an agency's work load is compounded if it must *restructure* its files in some way—that is, do special computer searches or perform some other data manipulation in order to provide a requesting citizen with particular kinds of information that has been requested. There is also the issue of *privacy*. After all, federal files contain sensitive information about all of us—tax returns, records of our earnings, passport applications, information about military service, and many other kinds of information.

For many reasons, therefore, some federal agencies, as well as others at the state and local level, have been reluctant to hand out their records, whether on paper or in machine-readable form. In fact, for nearly a century and a half, federal agencies were not even required to keep records! However, the entire area of federal record keeping began to change following World War II. The first major step took place when Congress passed the 1946 Administrative Procedure Act. It was the foundation statute that required all federal agencies to maintain records of their transactions. A second and critical step took place in the mid-1960s, when a "Freedom of Information" law was passed and signed. All of the states have since enacted similar legislation in one form or another and access to the records of public agencies is now provided on a far more open basis. However, as this chapter explains, it was not always an easy transition, and it should not be assumed that all went well after these laws were passed. There were many legal barriers to breach and even today gaining access to public records in a form that an investigator needs may be a complex task.

ENSURING CITIZEN ACCESS TO THE RECORDS OF PUBLIC AGENCIES

The Freedom of Information Act was written with the noble intention of providing an "open society in which the people's right to know is cherished and guarded."[2] When the act was signed by President Lyndon B. Johnson in 1966, it not only created a right of public access to government information but also made that right enforceable.[3] A major question concerns how free that access is even today. It is toward that issue that this section is addressed.

The 1966 law was drafted at a time when most agencies of the federal government kept their records in the form of paper documents (or miniature pictures of paper documents on microfiche or film). Shortly after this, however, the medium of record keeping changed. No longer were transactions recorded only on paper and stored in filing cabinets. Records of agency transactions became electronic entries on magnetic computer tape. This transition caused a number of problems because the law, written in the language of paper, was inadequate for addressing the problems of a computer age. Although the law was amended in 1974 and 1986, it failed to resolve many controversies that arose when citizens first tried to get access to the computerized records of government. The law remains, essentially, a law of paper access.

In order to understand how computerized records are interpreted under the Freedom of Information Act, it is necessary to look at the history of that law and a number of precedent-setting legal cases that resulted from controversies concerning the right to obtain computerized information. Clearly, many of these issues remain unresolved. These unresolved issues along with the accumulated court rulings have had a direct impact on the development of CAIR. It is also helpful to compare freedom of information laws at the state level, and to discuss the elements of an "ideal" freedom of information law.

The Administrative Procedure Act of 1946

There is no provision in the Constitution of the United States that requires federal agencies to give citizens access to their records. Indeed, as already noted, federal agencies were not even required by law to *keep* records until the Administrative Procedure Act was signed in 1946. For the first time, the act required the following: "PUBLIC RECORDS.—Save as otherwise required by statute, matters of official record shall in accordance with published rule be made available to persons properly and directly concerned except information held confidential for good cause found."[4] Furthermore, the law required that each agency publish in the *Federal Register* descriptions of its organization and the places, methods, and procedures whereby the public could make requests or secure information. (The *Federal Register* is an official newsletter in which the announcements of the government are disseminated.)

This foundation legislation also carefully defined the term *agency*, and specified the nature of a "person or party" (who would be entitled to request information or records from an agency). It even defined the terms *rule* and *agency action*. More important for this discussion, however, is the fact that the law did not define what constitutes a *record*. Furthermore, the (precomputer-era) law used such terms as *papers, forms,* and *reports* that were "published." Even today, the amended law retains this paper-oriented language and provides no definition for the term *record*.

The Freedom of Information Act of 1966

During the decade of the 1960s, many Americans grew increasingly dissatisfied with their government. Pressures mounted from a growing number of concerned citizens for full disclosure of the activities of all federal agencies and bureaucracies. In 1966, Congress passed a lengthy amendment to the Administrative Procedure Act, and called it the Freedom of Information Act.[5] This amendment, commonly referred to with the acronym FOIA, placed the burden of compliance squarely on the agencies and required that they prove that they were justified when denying access to records. It also clarified the conditions under which agencies could legally withhold records by specifying nine exemptions to the Act. In order to protect against unwarranted invasions of personal privacy, the law permitted agencies to delete identifying details, but required that the agencies justify any such deletions in writing.

The FOIA amendment was written with some very real "teeth" to enforce its provisions. If records were not released, citizens could register a complaint in federal court about the agency. The court could then enjoin the agency and order the production of any records improperly withheld. More forcefully, the statute stated that "in the event of noncompliance with the court's order, the district court may punish the responsible officers for contempt."[6] Finally, a provision was included requiring that such court cases "take precedence on the docket over all other causes and shall be assigned for hearing and trial at the earliest practicable date and expedited in every way."[7] These were strong measures indeed.

In 1974, an additional amendment set time limits for responding to FOIA requests and allowed uniform fees to be established for the direct costs involved in locating and duplicating records.[8] These fees could be waived or reduced if the information could be considered "as primarily benefiting the general public."[9] It also allowed courts to assess reasonable attorney fees and other litigation costs when records were withheld improperly. The 1974 amendment required that agencies determine within 10 business days of the receipt of a request for records whether or not the agency would comply with the request. In "unusual circumstances," however, these time limits could be extended with written notice. Decisions not to comply with appeals were to be made within 20 business days.

The Freedom of Information Act was amended most recently in 1986.[10] The FOI Reform Act of 1986 established categories of requesters and granted preferred status to the press, educational, and noncommercial scientific users. Commercial users could be charged for document search, duplication, and review costs. Those with preferred status could receive records without charge, or reduced charge if disclosure was "in the public interest and contributes significantly to public understanding of the operations or activities of government."[11] The 1986 amendment also narrowed the exemption from disclosure for records compiled for law enforcement.

Thus, what we usually refer to as the Freedom of Information Act is not a single statute, but an expanding body of legislation with interpretations modified by amendments and a long list of court cases. Throughout all of the amendments, however, much of the wording of the original 1946 law—the paper language—remains intact. The word *record* is never defined; the word *computer* never appears. Issues concerning the changing technology of record storage, retrieval, and access are not addressed.

LEGAL TANGLES RESULTING FROM THE TRANSITION TO COMPUTERS

The Scottish poet Robert Burns is perhaps remembered best for his caution that "the best-laid plans of mice and men" [often go astray]. The same generalization can readily be applied to the FOIA or to its counterparts at the state level. Clearly, the detailed plan of Congress almost foundered on the rocks of bureaucratic intransigence and confusion. The result was a tangle of legal challenges and court cases that complicated the "right to know," at least as far as computerized records are concerned. This section focuses on the evolving legal process that is clarifying the nature of FOIA and how it is used by citizens who request access to records of public agencies.

Concern with federal records in computer form was not a problem when the 1966 law was first designed. When Congress first held hearings on the FOIA in 1955, the federal government used only a small number of computers, and all agencies kept paper records in filing cabinets. At present, as explained earlier, all agencies of the federal government store records in computerized form. A similar trend has taken place at the state and local levels.[12] Thus, it is not surprising that as the technology changed after the law was passed, new questions and problems of interpreting FOIA arose.

Since FOIA was enacted, the number of requests for federal records has soared. That number is still growing sharply. For example, in 1988, FOIA requests totaled 394,914 from all federal agencies.[13] Only a year later, a Congressional committee estimated that approximately 500,000 requests were being filed each year under the FOIA statutes.[14] By 1991, federal agencies received a total of 589,391 requests.[15] These requests currently cost the federal government more than $67 million each year to process.[16] One agency alone, the Federal Bureau of Investigation, reported in 1996 that $21,082,010 was spent during the previous calendar year on processing requests for information under FOIA and the Privacy Act.

Soon after the transition to electronic media began, people started to request information in machine-readable form. The law, however, implied that the government need not provide them in this form. Problems stemming from this source continue to plague journalists and others who want to examine the computerized records of government agencies. In fact, the confusion has allowed some agencies to use the law as written to block attempts by reporters and others from gaining access to their records. To show the dimensions of these legal tangles, six major issues are examined. Each has been addressed by the courts as they have attempted to adjudicate disputes between those who want information and agencies that are asked to provide it. These six issues center on the following questions:

1. What is a "record?"
2. In which "formats" can information be obtained?
3. What constitutes a "new" (newly created) record?
4. What is the nature of a "search?"
5. What defines a "reasonable effort" to comply with a request?
6. What is the legal status of software and codebooks used to decipher computerized records?

What Is a Record?

One of the first problems concerning the application of FOIA to electronic records was whether or not the FOIA provisions applied only to paper records and documents or to computer records as well. Susan Long, an academic researcher, asked for computer tapes containing information that the Internal Revenue Service (IRS) had compiled for the Taxpayer Compliance Measurement Program in order to study the application of IRS policies throughout the country. The IRS refused, claiming that computer tapes were not "records" as intended by FOIA. This was the landmark case of *Long v. Internal Revenue Service* (1979).[17] The Court concluded that FOIA applied to computer tapes as well as paper documents. Speaking for the majority, Judge Kennedy concluded:

> In view of the common, widespread use of computers by government agencies for information storage and processing, any interpretation of the FOIA which limits its application to conventional written documents contra-

dicts the "general philosophy of full agency disclosure" which Congress intended to establish.[18] We conclude that the FOIA applies to computer tapes to the same extent it applies to any other document."[19]

The U.S. Supreme Court addressed this same issue in 1980.[20] In *Forsham v. Harris,* the Court cited the Records Disposal Act, a statute that included machine-readable materials in its definition of agency records, and concluded that this definition also applied to FOIA.[21] Finally, in *Yeager v. Drug Enforcement Administration,* the U.S. Court of Appeals for the District of Columbia reaffirmed the applicability of FOIA to computerized records.[22] This court concluded that "it is thus clear that computer-stored records, whether stored in the central processing unit, on magnetic tape or in some other form, are still 'records'" for the purposes of FOIA.[23]

These decisions represented a major victory for journalists and other users: Because records in computer form were now defined legally to be the same as paper records, citizens had a legal right to request them from agencies. However, as the questions that follow indicate, other barriers to access remained.

In What "Formats" Can Records Be Obtained?

Although it is now clear that the information stored in computers is subject to FOIA, requesters are not guaranteed access to the information in formats other than paper. In other words, the courts have also ruled that agencies do not have to supply their records in the form of machine-readable media. This decision rests with the custodian of the agency's records.

A landmark case testing this issue was *Dismukes v. Department of the Interior.*[24] The plaintiff had asked for a nine-track computer tape that listed the participants in the Bureau of Land Management's California oil and gas leasing lotteries. The Department of the Interior denied the request, saying that the information was available only on microfiche. The court ruled that an agency has no obligation to accommodate the requester's preference for the format of the information; only to provide the information in a "reasonably accessible form." The court held that the agency could determine the form in which to make its records available.

The format issue also arose in *National Security Archives v. CIA.*[25] Here, the plaintiff, a public interest research group, requested a computerized index of all FOIA requests filed with the CIA. The intelligence agency, however, provided the index on 5,000 pages of paper. The National Security Archives argued that the size of the printout made analysis impossible and demanded the actual computer tapes instead. The judge, citing the *Dismukes* ruling, dismissed the case. In another case in 1991, the court also reaffirmed the reasoning behind *Dismukes.* In *Coalition for Alternatives in Nutrition and Health Care, Inc. v. Food and Drug Administration,* the court said that the agency could determine the form in which records are made available.[26]

In still another format case, *International Computaprint Corporation v. U.S. Department of Commerce,* a private database vendor requested magnetic tapes containing all trademarks registered since 1980, all active registrations, and all pending applications from the Patent Office.[27] Although the Patent Office had the information in a computerized database, it provided the information in 289 reels of microfilm and said the information could also be obtained online in the Office's public reading room. The agency further claimed that these formats were equivalent to the computerized database. Computaprint personnel tried to use the terminals in the public reading room to download the information, but were asked to leave the machines at 1-hour intervals so that others could use the system. Computaprint personnel estimated that it would take about 8 years to get all of the information they wanted by using the reading room in this manner. Computaprint therefore argued that the formats were not equivalent. Nevertheless, the judgment of the court favored the agency.

Whereas federal courts have ruled that agencies may determine the format in which records will be released under the FOIA, a few state courts have shown more flexibility. For example, in *Brownstone Publishers, Inc. v. New York City Department of Buildings,* the court said that an agency that maintains electronic records must provide them in that form when requested.[28] The publishing company wanted a tape rather than a printout that would have exceeded 1 million pages. The court noted that requiring the publishing company to search manually through more than 1 million pages of paper printouts undermined the principle of maximum access.

It is clear from the cases described here that agencies can, in effect, deny access to information by burying that information in unusable mounds of paper or other nonelectronic formats. This represents a barrier for journalists and other users of large databases of government records. A million-page printout and a computer tape containing the same data are not equivalent formats. One cannot calculate even simple totals or averages, or extract specific cases, by manually sorting through a million pages of numbers.

What Constitutes a "New" Record?

FOIA does not require agencies to create "new" records for requesters. Agencies are required only to provide access to what are called records in being—information that the agency has already prepared in the form in which the agency uses it. Some agencies, such as the Department of Defense, have interpreted this in the past to mean that they need not provide information for which there is no existing printout.[29] In other words, as an extreme example based on that position, if it is necessary even to hit the return key on a computer to produce a printout, then a "new" document would be created.

This issue has been repeatedly challenged. For example, in *National Labor Relations Board v. Sears Roebuck,* the Board declined a request for additional explanatory materials that would describe the circumstances of certain litigation.[30] The U.S. Supreme Court, agreeing with the petitioner, stated the following: "The Act does not compel agencies to write opinions in cases in which they would not otherwise be required to do so. It only requires disclosure of certain documents which the law requires the agency to prepare or which the agency has decided for its own reasons to create."[31] For another example of the issue of records in being versus new records, consider an agency such as the Interstate Commerce Commission that routinely makes safety inspections of large trucks that haul freight across state lines. A report is filed for each inspection and this information makes its way into a computer database. These records may be filed by date, by region, or by whatever is convenient for the agency. Under FOIA, those specific records must be available to the public. However, the agency is not required to assemble those records for a requester by, say, size of truck (unless it has already done so), because that would be a "new" record or document, rather than one that is already "in being."

A related example is *Kele v. U.S. Parole Commission.*[32] In this case, a prison inmate requested information on certain kinds of crimes. The parole commission refused to provide the information because its computer files were organized by inmate name, not by the type of crime. Thus, organizing and extracting the information by crime would result in the creation of a new document.

What Constitutes a "Search?"

Under FOIA provisions, a citizen may ask an agency to search through its "files" for a specific record, such as the results of a particular civil suit. Such requests are common, and it was relatively easy for an agency to comply when paper records were kept in filing cabinets. However, in the age of electronic records, the term *search* usually means that someone must write a program that tells the computer to go through a data tape and locate, extract, and print that specific record. The issue here is whether these two types of searches (manual vs. computer programmed) are the same. This controversy remains unresolved.

A considerable debate has developed around this issue. Citizen groups insist that writing a program to extract specific information from a computer database is comparable to the manual process for paper records. Agencies opposed to this point of view maintain that developing a computer program to extract information results in the creation of a new document, which is not required.

This comparison of computer programming to record creation was challenged in *Public Citizen v. Occupational Safety and Health Administration* (OSHA).[33] The public interest group asked for information concerning specific companies that was contained in a computerized database of OSHA's enforcements of workplace safety. The agency responded that although the information on those companies was in its database, new computer programming would be required to retrieve the records. Public Citizen claimed that the retrieval of the records by programming was merely a form of searching rather than record creation. The suit was settled when OSHA later agreed to provide the information.

In another case, *Clarke v. U.S. Department of Treasury,* a federal district court ruled that the creation of a special computer program to extract the names and addresses of registered institutional owners of certain bonds exceeded the Treasury Department's obligations under the FOIA.[34]

Although courts have ruled that agencies are not required to program their computers for requesters, some agencies have been willing to do so. Furthermore, future debate on this issue may be helped by the decision of at least one agency, the Department of Energy. The Office of Hearings and Appeals within the agency determined that programming might be considered a part of the search process rather than the creation of a new record when merely retrieving information already existing in a database.[35] However, it is unlikely that agencies will be required to do more extensive programming in response to FOIA requests. Again, the lesson here is that journalists themselves will need to know how to extract specific cases from complex files of raw electronic data.

What Constitutes a "Reasonable Effort?"

The question here concerns the amount of effort to which an agency must go, and how much of its resources it must devote, to providing information in response to a FOIA request. Several court cases have addressed different aspects of this issue.

When problems have arisen involving paper records, the courts have based their interpretations as to what is "reasonable" on the amount of effort required by the agency to fill the request. In cases involving computer records, as already discussed, some courts have concluded that any new programming or modification, no matter how easy, would result in unreasonable effort. Indeed, in many cases, writing programs to retrieve computer records may require significantly less effort and take considerably less time than lengthy manual searches for large numbers of paper records. Furthermore, the question of what is reasonable extends to the segregation of exempted portions of records, compiling summaries of records, and statistical manipulations of data.

An example of a controversy over the issue of extent and effort is provided by the previously mentioned *Long v. IRS*.[36] Susan Long wanted the IRS to delete personal identifiers from tax compliance data so that the data would no longer fall under an FOIA exempted category and could be released to her. The IRS refused, saying that would involve the creation of a new document. On appeal, the court said that deleting the names, addresses, and social security numbers from the data would not result in the creation of a new document because the identifiers were "reasonably segregable" and would not place an unreasonable burden on the agency.

However, in a related case, the court reached a different conclusion concerning the limits of reasonableness when asked to segregate data. In *Yeager v. Drug Enforcement Agency,* the court applied a test of reasonableness based on whether the request was "functionally analogous" to what would have been done in a manual search.[37] Furthermore, the court concluded that the capabilities of computers should not result in additional duties for the agencies. Although a task may be possible to do, the court said, "we are not persuaded that Congress intended any *manipulation* or *restructuring* of the substantive content of a record" (italics added).[38]

The manipulation of records or data was also addressed in the previously mentioned case of *Kele v. U.S. Parole Commission*.[39] The plaintiff, a prison inmate, requested statistical information on convicted murderers. The court ruled in favor of the Parole Commission, saying that performing statistical analyses for requesters "would transform the government into a giant computer research firm captive to the whims of individual requesters at great public expense."[40]

Thus, it is clear that although existing data can be requested under FOIA, further analysis of those same data cannot be demanded. Moreover, considering the tone of the court's ruling, it is unlikely that this will change. This is another critical issue for journalists and other users of government data.

It means that it is up to requesters to do any sorting, statistical analyses, or other manipulations of information contained in databases acquired under FOIA. An agency may agree to provide a tape containing the records as the agency prepared them, but unless journalists and other users have the skills needed to process and analyze these records in being, they will remain locked out from the information they wish to obtain.

What Is the Status of Software and Codebooks?

Without appropriate software, raw data on agency tapes or other electronic media cannot even be accessed, let alone analyzed. However, the FOIA status of software used by agencies to create and manipulate their databases of records is uncertain at this time. Most agency regulations make no mention of software and agency practice in this area is inconsistent.

Some requesters claim that the software used to create a record cannot be separated from the record itself and should be considered an integral part of the information it contains. They point out that they cannot use the data if they do not have the agency software and programs that go with the data. They conclude, therefore, that agencies should be required to provide these essential keys to using their records.

Most agencies, however, claim that software is a tool used to manipulate the data rather than part of the record itself. It would seem that the agencies have a strong case here. One reason is that agencies often do not create their own software. They buy it from a commercial vendor or service. Commercial software licensing agreements contractually define the uses to which it can be put and they set limits on the degree to which it can be passed on to others. Also, such software may fall under the "trade secrets" exemption of FOIA. At present, this means that journalists and others who obtain an agency's tapes must provide their own software and programming to use the data.

The legal status of codebooks that describe the information on a computer tape is a little clearer. Computer tapes can be prepared in different formats for particular hardware systems (IBM, VAX, etc.) and with different layout designs. The ways in which information is recorded on a tape may be incomprehensible without an explanation. For example, a number 1 in column 14 may indicate the subject has a prior criminal record, and the number 5 in column 15 may indicate that the subject served a 5-month jail sentence. However, there is no way to tell this without a some kind of coding key to decipher the meaning of the numbers—usually a printed document that accompanies the computer tape. In *Seigle v. Barry,* the court ruled that when a public record is maintained in such a way that it can only be interpreted by the use of a code, then the codebook must be provided.[41]

The issues discussed in the six preceeding questions illustrate some of the difficulties courts and agencies have when trying to apply FOIA intentions to computer records. Thus far, agencies and the courts have based many of their decisions on analogies to paper records. The unique characteristics of computerized information, however, often make this inappropriate. In several cases, the courts have expressed a need for Congress to clarify the many gray areas resulting from the application of FOIA laws to electronic information.

Variations Among State Freedom of Information Laws

In addition to the federal statutes, every state has its own freedom of information law or laws. Although these are patterned after the federal statute and share many of the same problems, many state laws have incorporated some improvements. To illustrate, at least 34 states specifically address computer records in their laws. They define public records as including all information kept by government agencies "regardless of physical form or characteristics" (or some variation of this phrase). The New York state law, for example, defines a record as "any information . . . in any physical form whatsoever including, but not limited to . . . computer tapes or discs."[42] An additional 14 state laws provide definitions that are broad enough that an interpretation clearly can be made that computer records are included.[43]

The recognition that computer records are public information, however, does not answer all of the legal questions. Only in a few exceptional states can a requester demand a computer tape. Four states (Rhode Island, New Hampshire, Kansas, and Montana) say or infer that agencies may release only printouts or printed copy of the information. Only three states (Texas, Washington, and Wisconsin) specifically permit access by anyone, regardless of the purpose for which the information is sought. Seventeen states set definite time limits for the production of records. At least 16 state public records laws clearly allow for the deletion of exempt information, but few address the issues of software, programming, and data manipulation.

Researcher Sandra Davidson Scott has identified a minimum of 12 elements for a good state law concerning the access of computerized records.[44] These include a definition of public records that is broad enough to include those that are computerized, a requirement that exemptions be explicitly stated and narrowly construed, and access be assured for all citizens regardless of purpose. Furthermore, the deletion of restricted information must be allowed so that the remaining information may be released rather than restricting the entire record. The requester's form of the information must be met when records are maintained in that format, and access must include all of the information on computer tapes, including record layout, density blocking, codebooks, and so on. Instructions must be provided for the proper maintenance and storage of records as well as their destruction. Finally, time limits must be set for the production of records and sanctions must be stated for failure to comply with the statute.

THE CONTINUING EVOLUTION OF FOIA

In an effort to settle some of the controversies and difficulties surrounding FOIA and electronic information, Senator Patrick Leahy (D-VT) introduced a bill in the U.S. Senate in 1991 to amend Title 5 of the U.S. Code. This bill, called the Electronic Freedom of Information Act of 1991, was to ensure public access to information in an electronic format.[45] In introducing the legislation, Leahy noted that new technologies should mean more and easier access to government information, but he complained that this was not always happening. He said that "some agencies use computers to frustrate rather than to help requesters."[46] Although this bill was not passed, it is important to note that it finally defined the term *record*:

(1) the term "record" includes all books, papers, maps, photographs, data, computer programs, machine readable materials, and computerized, digitized, and electronic information, regardless of the medium by which it is stored, or other documentary materials, regardless of physical form or characteristics.[47]

The bill also defined a *search* as including either a manual or automated location of records. It required agencies to provide records in the format in which they were requested by any person, as long as the agency maintained their records in that format. However, even if the agency did not usually keep its records in an electronic form, the amendment stated that the agency must make "reasonable efforts" to provide information in electronic form when requested. The bill also directed agencies to publish electronically by computer telecommunications all information that is required to be in the Federal Register as well as an index of all information stored in electronic form by the agency and a description of any new database. It also provided an incentive for agencies to respond to FOIA requests by allowing agencies to keep a percentage of the fees collected from requests. Certainly, this bill would have been an improvement if passed. However, even this proposed legislation would have left many issues unsettled, such as the extent to which agencies must go when responding to requests or the nature of software and programming.

In 1995, Senator Leahy introduced another bill to amend the FOIA. The "Electronic Freedom of Information Improvement Act" defines the term *record* to mean "all books, papers, maps, photographs, machine-readable materials, or other information or documentary materials, regardless of physical form or characteristics." A *search* is defined as "a manual or automated review of agency records that is conducted for the purpose of locating those records." In addition, the bill instructs agencies to provide records in any form or format that is requested, when the records are available in that format. It also extends the period in which agencies must determine whether or not they will comply with a request from 10 to 20 working days. Finally, the bill requires agencies to process requests on a first-in, first-out basis and allows agencies to keep one half of the fees collected from FOIA requests in order to offset the costs of compliance. The proposed legislation was still under debate during the summer of 1996.[48]

AGENCY STRATEGIES FOR NONCOMPLIANCE

Although various FOIA definitions and issues have been addressed by the courts, many problems of access by journalists and others remain unresolved. Most agencies respond promptly to most requests for records within the framework of FOIA. However, there are some that do not, and strategies for avoiding disclosure may be used by agencies that are not eager to comply. The FOIA statutes and rulings themselves continue to offer fertile ground for delaying or avoiding release of information that is requested. And, as they grow in complexity, with additional amendments and precedents set by the courts, still other grounds for resistance or denial will develop. Because of that complexity, two important questions about access to computerized records remain: First, what are a citizen's actual chances of receiving requested information under the FOIA provisions, and second, what are some of the tactics and strategies of resistance bureaucrats have used in their efforts to avoid compliance with such requests?

It would be incorrect to say that most agencies resist disclosure of their records. Indeed, many try very hard to provide information that is requested. A request that is likely to be acted on favorably must spell out in a letter exactly what records are requested by whom on what issue or topic for what period. The greater the specificity, the greater the chances for success.

Requests that are properly made avoid presenting an agency with grounds for delays or reasons for denying a request.

Unfortunately, however, there appear to be a number of procedures that agencies have used to keep journalists or other citizens from gaining access to the records they request. Considerable insight into the tactics and strategies of avoidance used by agencies can be gained from a 1989 nationwide survey conducted by the Freedom of Information Committee of the Society of Professional Journalists (SPJ). They contacted reporters and editors all over the country to determine what problems they had encountered in dealing with agencies under FOIA. The results of the survey indicated that agencies frequently resist providing their records to journalists.[49] What strategies do agencies use in blocking legitimate requests? Just how do they deny access to their records? In the sections that follow, six specific techniques that were identified in the SPJ survey are discussed.

Delay

The results of the SPJ survey of journalists showed that it was common for agencies to delay compliance with FOIA requests. In spite of the fact that the federal law mandates that agencies determine whether or not to respond to requests within 10 working days, excessive delay was the most common complaint of the journalists surveyed.

This is a difficult problem with which to deal. When journalists who were requesting information from their government asked agencies to explain why such lengthy delays were occurring, the reply was often that there were "unmanageable backlogs" of requests that they had to deal with. For example, as of May 1996, the FBI had a backlog of 15,259 requests and a 4-year wait for some of those requests to be processed.[50] Certainly, backlogs are a problem for the agencies. The number of FOIA requests continue to increase, whereas the resources with which to process the requests often do not. However, some of the delays encountered by respondents to the SPJ survey were so excessive that they seemed truly unreasonable. One journalist reported that he had filed an application in July 1988. Several months later he asked agency officials why they had not complied. The reply by the individual in charge was, "You think you have it bad? One person has been waiting since 1983."[51]

Differential Treatment

Although there are exceptions, agency guidelines provide for a first-come, first-served system. That is, the first to apply should be the first to receive the information requested and no one in a given category of users—such as journalists—should arbitrarily be given priority. What actually happens, some critics claim, is that agency officials respond more promptly to some requests than others. For example, large news organizations with bureaus in Washington, DC tend to be served promptly and have little difficulty in getting the records that they want. Television networks receive the same treatment. In contrast, individuals from news organizations in locations remote from Washington, and small newspapers generally say that they receive requested information much more slowly.

Selective Deletion

Journalists also complain that agency officials often "edit" the records—that is, selectively delete information. As a result, it can be impossible to examine the functioning of officials whose records are protected from scrutiny. This strategy of selective deletion occurred with the tapes containing the records of the U. S. Courts that are described in this book. The records contained 5.5 million court cases for the entire United States for an 18-year period. They included all criminal, civil, and appellate transactions appearing before the federal courts during that period. After the records arrived, it was discovered that the agency had removed the names of all federal judges who had been involved in these cases. No reason was given for these deletions. This, of course, made it impossible to examine their records. That is, it was impossible to compare the performance of judges in different districts to reveal how they had handled various categories of lawsuits, criminal trials, and other actions.

Hiking Fees

According to the SPJ survey, this is a commonly used tactic for heading off requests for records. In spite of the fact that the federal government provides guidelines governing fees for various categories of users, some agencies have imposed prohibitive fees.

In addition, many states have worked out separate systems for assessing fees, and there is great variation. In fact, some have no standard formula that applies to all agencies. Moreover, in many states, the freedom of information statutes are worded quite vaguely. In specifying what it may cost to obtain records, the statutes use such phrases as "reasonable fees may be charged." Other difficulties arise where some kind of searching is involved. The state may provide no clear rules as to what charges citizens must pay when this kind of operation must be performed. Leaving such matters to the discretion of the agencies has resulted, in some cases, in prohibitive charges imposed on the requester. An example is provided by a group in Minnesota that requested a computer-generated list of physicians who performed abortions. The list was relatively small, a few hundred names at most. The Minnesota group was told that the price would be between $2,500 and $4,000.

Switching Formats

The exact format in which an agency must provide records when they are requested is not specifically mandated by the FOIA. Thus, the requester may ask for a particular format (such as magnetic tape) but the agency is free to supply the records in whatever format it chooses. This can provide a convenient way for the agency to make it difficult or even impossible for an investigator to conduct the analysis for which the records were sought. A classic case is one that was mentioned earlier—that of *Dismukes v. Department of Interior.* A lawsuit was filed to obtain the records on computer tape. The Department of the Interior maintained that it was willing to supply the information, but only on microfiche. The Court held that the agency had the right to specify the format.

As mentioned earlier, agencies are not always trying to block requests when they respond to a request for information in one format by indicating that it can only be provided in another. Records are not always available in the format requested. Each agency designs its record system around its own needs, and not for the convenience of journalists or other users. Thus, some records are kept in formats that would be difficult to use in an analysis, and the agency may have had no reason to prepare them in another. Still, if an agency claims that it has no computerized records of relatively recent transactions, and that they exist only on paper, there are clear grounds for suspicion.

Denying Data Exist

On more than one occasion, an agency has simply denied that it has records of the type requested. Such a denial occurred in connection with an analysis of the records of the federal courts discussed in chapters 6 and 7. One part of the analysis focused on the performance of federal prosecutors in 11 "big city" judicial districts. A request was made to the U.S. Justice Department for a database on the handling of cases by the U.S. Attorneys in charge of those districts. The agency claimed that it had no such records but this was later shown to be false.

A truly determined agency can frustrate a request for records in many other ways. Certainly, all of the tactics and strategies discussed in this chapter are open to determined officials. They can protest on the grounds of "unreasonable effort," fail to provide codes for deciphering records, refuse on the grounds that new records have to be prepared, selectively delete material with claims of protecting privacy, refuse to grant fee waivers, charge exorbitant fees, switch to difficult formats, enforce the paper-only rule, and so on. If all else fails, agencies can always stall with the assumption that the person making the request will ultimately get tired and go away.

In overview, although the intent of Congress, and of legislators in the respective states, generally has been to provide for open government, the end result has not always achieved that goal. According to Paul McMasters, deputy editorial director of *USA Today,* and a Chairman of the Freedom of Information Committee of the SPJ, the nationwide survey of journalists conducted by his group revealed "a graphic montage of agencies routinely violating the FOIA, robbing the public of needed information and jeopardizing good government."[52] The SPJ maintained that federal and state agencies routinely block the efforts of citizens who request information within the freedom of information provisions.

In spite of the survey data and the conclusions of SPJ, conflicts of this kind are seldom simply confrontations between the good guys and the bad guys. Federal and state agencies often lack funding for the specialists needed to comply with FOIA requests. Government workers may already have their hands full just keeping up with the routine work of their agency. Few resources may be left to provide information rapidly to everyone who requests it.

Another important point is that the federal government is not a research agency that can perform all kinds of computer analyses for citizens. Many ask the agency to group and sort information in ways that meet their objectives. Such requests are frequently vague and a considerable effort would be required to comply even if an agency had the best of intentions. It is far easier for an agency to provide basic records in being, and let the user go from there. Such records may require sophisticated data manipulation of a type that can go beyond the skills and hardware of many who request the records. Sometimes, when that happens, the agency response is seen as noncooperative. An important conclusion, then, is that although agencies often make life difficult for those who request government records, the user can also be part of the problem. Often, misunderstandings or limitations on skills pose barriers that can be as insurmountable as those used by agencies that resist disclosure. Perhaps the most significant lesson is that if freedom of information is to remain a reality, rather than just an ideal, improvements will have to be made by users as well as government.

NOTES AND REFERENCES

1. Eric A. Sinrod, "Freedom of Information Act Response Deadlines: Bridging the Gap Between Legislative Intent and Economic Reality," *The American University Law Review,* 43, Am. U.L. Rev. 327, Winter, 1994.
2. U.S. Senate, the FOIA Source Book, Committee on the Judiciary, Subcommittee on Administrative Practice and Procedure, 93rd Congress, 2nd Session, 1974. President Johnson's comments upon signing the bill into law.
3. Clearly, not everyone cherishes or guards the public's right to know. For example, NASA has been accused of teaching employees how to avoid disclosing information. Congressional investigators recently found a set of instructions for handling FOIA requests. This NASA document instructs employees to mix up documents and camouflage handwriting so that the document's significance would be less meaningful, and tells employees to rewrite and even destroy documents "to minimize adverse impact." See: "Congressman Says NASA Taught Workers How to Hide Data," in the (Syracuse) *Post Standard,* Feb. 28, 1992, p. A-3.
4. Sec. 3 (c) of the Administrative Procedure Act (Public Law 404); 60 Stat. 238 (1946).
5. 5 U.S.C. sec. 552 (Public Law 89-487), 1966.
6. Sec. 3(c)(b) of the Freedom of Information Act (Public Law 89-487), 1966.
7. *Ibid.,* sec. 3(c)(b).
8. Public Law 94-409; 90 Stat. 1247 (1976).
9. *Ibid.,* sec. (4)(A).
10. Public Law 99-570 (100 Stat. 3207-44), 1986.
11. *Ibid.,* sec. (4)(A)(iii).
12. Martha Mulford Gray, "Computers in the Federal Government: A Compilation of Statistics—1978," National Bureau of Standards Special Publication 500-46, April 1979.
13. W. John Moore, "Access Denied," *National Journal,* Vol. 22, No. 3, January 20, 1990, p. 121 (start of article).
14. John Markoff, "Computers Challenge Freedom of Information Act," *New York Times,* June 18, 1989, section 1, p. 25.
15. See 1992 *Annual Reports, Access Rep.* March 31, 1993.
16. Katherine J. Brophy, "Sharing Secrets on How to Keep Them," *Inform,* March 1991, p. 42.
17. 596 F.2d 362 (9th Cir. 1979).
18. S. Rep. No. 813, 89th Cong. 1st Sess. 3 (1965).
19. 596 F.2d 362, 365 (9th Cir. 1979); see also Senate Report No.13, 89th Congress, 1st Sess. 3 (1965) for the intentions of Congress concerning FOIA. For an excellent account of legal controversies surrounding FOIA and electronic records, see Jamie A. Grodsky, "The Freedom of Information Act in an Electronic Age," in *Informing the Nation: Federal Information Dissemination in an Electronic Age,* U.S. Congress, Office of Technology Assessment (Washington, D.C.: U.S. Government Printing Office, October, 1988).
20. 445 U.S. 169, 186 (1980).
21. 44 U.S.C. sec. 3301.

22. 678 F.2d. 315 (D.C. Dir. 1982).

23. *Ibid.,* 678 F.2d 315.

24. 603 F. Supp. 760 (D.D.C. 1984).

25. Civil Action No. 89-0142 (D.C. District Court), 1989.

26. Civ. No. 90-1029 (D.D.C.), 1991.

27. Civil Action Nos. 87-1848, 88-0839 (D.C. District Court), 1988.

28. 550 N.Y.S. 2d 564 (N.Y. Sup. Ct.), 1990.

29. 32 C.F.R. Part 286, 1987 (Fed. Reg. vol 52, No. 132, July 10, 1987).

30. 421 U.S. 132 (1975).

31. 421 U.S. at 161-62 (1975).

32. Civ. No. 85-4058 (D.D.C.), 1986.

33. Civil Action No. 86-0705 (D.C. District Court), 1986.

34. WL 1234 (E.D. Pa.), 1986.

35. Decision and Order of the Department of Energy, Office of Hearings and Appeals, KFA-0158 (May 26, 1988).

36. *Op. cit.,* 596 F.2d 362, 1979.

37. *Op. cit.,* 678 F.2d 315 (D.C. Cir.), 1982.

38. *Ibid.*

39. *Ibid.,* Civil Action No. 85-4058 (D.C. District Court), 1986.

40. Memorandum of Points and Authorities in support of defendant's motion to dismiss, p. 19.

41. 422 So.2d 63 (Fla. 4 D.C.A.), 1982.

42. N.Y. Pub. Off. Law Sec. 86(4).

43. For information and summaries of state public records laws, see: Jane E. Kirtley, ed., "Access to Electronic Records," (Washington, D.C.: The Reporters Committee for Freedom of the Press), 1990; Sandra Davidson Scott, "Computer Technology v. Laws on Access," paper presented at the annual convention of AEJMC in Boston, August, 1991.

44. Sandra Davidson Scott, "Computer Technology v. Laws on Access," paper presented at the annual meeting of AEJMC in Boston, August, 1991.

45. Senate Bill 1940, 102nd Congress, Sess. 1, 1991.

46. Julius J. Marke, "Public Access to Computerized Government Information," *New York Law Journal,* January 28, 1992, p. 4.

47. 5 U.S.C. sec. 552(f); as proposed in the "Electronic Freedom of Information Improvement Act of 1991" (Senate Bill 1940).

48. Senate Bill 1090, 104th Congress, Sess. 2, 1995; See also: Testimony of Robert Gellman, Privacy and Information Policy Consultant, before the Subcommittee on Government Management, Information and Technology as reported by the Federal Document Clearing House, Inc., June 14, 1996.

49. For a summary of the Committee's findings, see "Life on the FOIA Front: Delays, Misrepresentation, Over-editing, Favoritism," *The Quill,* December 1989/January 1990, pp. 18–19.

50. Richard A. Ryan, "Access to Public Information Still a Fight," *Detroit News,* July 4, 1996, p. A1; Larry Bivens, "Freedom of Information: Ask And You Shall Wait," *Detroit News,* July 5, 1996, p. A1.

51. *Ibid,* p. 18.

52. *Quill, op. cit.,* p. 18.

4

Computer-Assisted Investigative Reporting: Its Development, Definition, and Current Status

Public records have always been an important resource for investigative reporting. That is as true now as it was when Ida Tarbell and her colleagues tracked down documents for their investigations at the turn of the century. Today, as the previous chapter showed, technological advances have made the older approach inadequate, or in many cases obsolete. As governments began storing their records on computers, many of the facts and details that journalists were accustomed to finding on sheets of paper were located in bits and bytes on magnetic computer tapes.

At first, when journalists began conducting computer-assisted projects, it was a cumbersome and difficult task. To examine the records of a government agency with a computer, they first had to create their own database from paper documents. Moreover, they had to use a mainframe computer with neither ready-made software nor an interactive screen on which to type their instructions. More recently, as personal computers became commonplace in newsrooms, some reporters began to see the potential of employing the machines that they had been using only for word processing for counting, sorting, and comparing various kinds of information that they could obtain on magnetic tape.

This computer-assisted approach opened investigative possibilities that had not been possible in the paper-only era. It was not simply a matter of gaining access more quickly to the same information that they used to find on paper documents—it was much more. If reporters obtained the computer tapes of a government agency's records, not only could they zero in on specific information about particular cases, but they also had access to the thousands or even millions of transactions in an agency's entire file. Furthermore, they could *manipulate* and *rearrange* the data in various ways to make comparisons and discover patterns that otherwise might remain hidden. With the power of the computer, in other words, reporters could identify trends, relationships, and other patterns that would never have been apparent when paper records were stored in file folders within long rows of cabinets.

It was this ability, to use the electronic records of a government agency as a resource for investigating its performance, going beyond the barriers posed by paper, that gave rise to computer-assisted investigative reporting. CAIR made it possible to examine and statistically manipulate the full range of an agency's past activities. There was little that could remain undetected, as had been the case with a sea of paper. Thus, CAIR greatly extended the ability of journalists to exercise their oversight functions. The new strategy did not replace the objectives and techniques of more traditional investigative reporting; but, it did greatly enhance them.

CAIR DEFINED

Like almost any complex aspect of journalism, complete consensus does not exist as to just what CAIR is or how it should be performed. Some even feel that a term such as *computer-assisted journalism* has no more meaning than *pencil-assisted journalism*. The fact that a computer is used as a tool to help generate an investigative report, such critics argue, is incidental. The essence of such journalism, they maintain, is in the insights of the reporter and his or her skill in following leads, reaching conclusions that can be verified, and writing the story.

The critics have a point. No amount of computer expertise can replace the creativity, motivation, and communication skills required for effective reporting. CAIR is not a substitute for those features of the traditional approach. To be effective it must be, above all, good journalism in the commonsense meaning of that term. Therefore, to develop an adequate definition of CAIR, one must begin with the clear recognition that it is an *extension*, rather than a *replacement* of the wisdom, doggedness, insights, suspicions, and effective writing of the old-fashioned investigative reporter.

The nature of investigative reporting (with or without computers) was defined in a previous chapter, in which the views of various practitioners and journalism scholars were compared. Essentially, the definition that was set forth was based on two principles: (a) investigative reporting concerns matters that are important to the public, and (b) they are not easily discovered. The chapter concluded that investigative reporting need not be defined strictly in terms of secrecy or wrongdoing as has often been the case.

Finally, in defining CAIR as an extension of traditional investigative reporting, one must deal with a rather confusing set of concepts and their terminology that has developed as computers became commonly used tools by reporters. Many of these terms seem to be used interchangeably to describe any or all aspects of the new area. One such term is *computer-assisted journalism* (CAJ)—also called *computer-assisted reporting* (CAR) or even *database journalism.*

Computer-assisted journalism (CAJ) is an umbrella concept. It includes at least three major ways in which reporters are now using computers to develop news stories: The first was discussed in chapter 2. It is based on searching publicly available or commercially vended online databases (such as Lexis/Nexis or Dow Jones), electronic bulletin boards, or even the Internet. As explained earlier, the main objective here is to locate sources or to assemble background information on a person, topic, or issue in order to flesh out a news story.

CAJ also includes the creation or construction of "inhouse" databases for specialized uses in newsrooms. These unique databases often incorporate a variety of information collected or gathered by reporters from several different sources for use in a special investigation. Two examples are described later in this chapter—The *Seattle Times* investigation of the Green River murders and *Newsday*'s series on "The Confession Takers."

Another form of CAJ is computer-assisted investigative reporting (CAIR), which is the central focus of this book. Broadly speaking, it is the application of computers to the practice of investigative reporting. For example, computers and related software are used to analyze electronic records—especially those related to, or generated by government—in order to conduct oversight investigations and to disclose newsworthy situations revealed by the findings.

In addition, journalism scholar Philip Meyer believes that other sources of information created or analyzed with the use of a computer could be included in the definition of CAJ or CAIR. These could include findings from survey research, public opinion polls, field experiments, or content analyses. Clearly, then, the definition of CAJ can include a number of applications and concepts. Undoubtedly, the definition may change as more practitioners add their voices to the discussion.

With these explanations in mind, the focus of this book is on the *historical development* and the *methodology* of computer-assisted investigative reporting (CAIR) as it focuses on the analysis of electronic public records.

This is perhaps the most complex area of computer-assisted journalism and, therefore, the area most in need of explanation and discussion.

THE PIONEERS

The use of computers by journalists to analyze the records of government actually began during the 1960s. Little notice was taken of the strategy at the time. A short time later, during the 1970s, the number of newspapers performing and reporting on CAIR analyses began to grow. By the end of the 1980s, the practice became more common.

The Earliest CAIR Analyses

Although it is difficult to pinpoint with certainty when the first "true" example of CAIR occurred, Clarence Jones of the *Miami Herald* may have been the first journalist to use a computer to analyze public records. In 1968, Jones hired law students from the University of Miami to enter data into a computer from the paper records of 682 people booked into the Dade County jail on vice charges during a 1-year period. Jones then persuaded Clark Lambert, the newspaper's systems manager, to write COBOL programs to sort the data and to do some cross-tabs. This simple analysis, "A Scientific Look at Dade Justice," revealed evidence of bias in the Dade County criminal justice system.[1]

In 1967, following the civil rights riots in Detroit, Philip Meyer used a computer to analyze survey data from African Americans who lived in the riot area. The data were used to test popular theories concerning the causes of the riots. For example, some people thought that those who participated in the riots did so because they were at the bottom of the economic ladder and had no opportunity for advancement or expression. Furthermore they also believed these rioters were poorly educated, frustrated, and hopeless. However, Meyer's analysis showed that people who had attended college were just as likely to participate in the riots as those who had failed to finish high school. In addition many believed that the root cause of the riots was the difficulty that African Americans who were raised in the South had in assimilating into the culture of the North. In fact, more of the rioters were raised in the northern United States. Meyer's analysis resulted in a series in the *Detroit Free Press* titled, "The People Beyond 12th Street."[2]

An important pioneer in government database analysis was David Burnham, then of the *New York Times*. In a large-scale 1972 project, he used a computer to analyze records from the New York City police department. He prepared a two-part series showing unexpected and large differences in the numbers and rates of crimes reported throughout the city and in the ability of each precinct to make arrests.[3] Burnham obtained population figures, crime reports, and arrest statistics from each of the city's precincts and this information was entered into the newspaper's computer. Next, simple rates of reported crime and rates of arrest for each precinct were calculated. This information provided the basis for his first lengthy story.

The story indicated that the homicide rate in Harlem—the number of murders per 1,000 residents—was 328 times higher than the same rate in Kew Gardens, Queens. Furthermore, the robbery rate on the west side of Manhattan was twice as high as that on the east side. Although it had been widely documented by social scientists that poor people in urban areas are more likely to be victims of crime than middle-class and upper class residents, this was not generally understood by the New York public in the early 1970s.

The second story examined the number of arrests in each precinct in relation to the number of reported crimes. It also investigated the number of officers assigned to each precinct in relation to the residents living in each precinct. These data demonstrated that, for example, the police in Hunts Point made twice as many robbery arrests in relation to reported robberies as the police in East Harlem. It also showed large differences in the number of policemen assigned to each precinct. The upper east side had 3.2 officers per 1,000 residents, whereas the west side had only 2.4 officers.[4]

A year and a half later, on August 5, 1973, the *Times* published another computer-based story prepared by Burnham.[5] In this case he was concerned that a great deal of the public's fear of crime was related to the unstated concern of White middle-class and upper class residents that they were most likely to be the targets of violent crime by Blacks. Burnham wanted to separate these fears from the facts.

To achieve his objective, Burnham obtained a random sample of 100 handwritten reports completed by police officers immediately after they were present at the scene of a murder. The sample of 100 cases was drawn from a group of homicides that had occurred 12 months before the research began. This ensured that the cases would have had time to work their way through the court system. Burnham then searched the court files for the related records that contained information on the person or persons who had been arrested for each murder. The data extracted from the police and court (paper) records were transferred to punch cards and read by the computer operated by the *Times'* business department.

The computer calculated percentages of victims and their murderers for different racial categories from the sample. The story reported that 48% of all murders involved Blacks killing Blacks; only 9% involved Blacks killing Whites. Projecting the sample percentages to the entire city, the story reported that a Black resident of New York City was found to be eight times more likely to be murdered than a White resident.

Still another story by Burnham was published by the *Times* on July 30, 1973.[6] This story ranked each of the city's 71 precincts in both the numbers and the rates of homicides, burglaries, and robberies according to 1970 census characteristics (such as race, income, age, and employment) using the computer of the Rand Institute in New York City.

This analysis showed that in the 10 precincts with the highest homicide rates, the populations were, on average, 54% Black, 28% Hispanic, and 18% White. The median income in these precincts ranged from $4,950 to $10,966. In the 10 precincts with the lowest homicide rates, the populations were, on average, 2% Black, 6% Hispanic, and 92% White. Median income in these areas ranged from $10,003 to $20,865. Burnham consulted social scientists about these figures. Their explanation was that the disparity in income led to frustration and aggression and was compounded by patterns of discrimination, poor schools, and lack of opportunities in poor neighborhoods. Some of the information presented in the story had never before been available, even to the police.[7]

These were truly pioneering efforts that helped to establish the new CAIR movement in journalism. These investigations focused on problems that were of deep concern to the entire community. Burnham continued to develop computer-assisted projects. In 1989, he and Professor Susan B. Long established one of the first research organizations devoted to CAIR analyses at Syracuse University. Called Transactional Records Access Clearinghouse (TRAC), it is associated with the S.I. Newhouse School of Public Communications. The purpose of TRAC is to acquire the electronic records of major federal agencies, to analyze the records, and to provide the information to the press, academicians, Congress, and public interest groups.

The CAIR Movement Begins

The early experiences of both Jones and Burnham show that as CAIR was getting its start, reporters had to enter information obtained from paper documents into a computer by hand. At the time, the records they used were not conveniently available on magnetic tape. Like many of the pioneers, they had to design and develop their own databases around the special needs of the issues they were investigating. Today, as explained in chapter 2, thousands of databases are available on tape from a host of agencies. Nevertheless, many investigative reporters must still develop their own databases of specialized information related to their news objectives.

Also in the early 1970s, other reporters began similar projects. Donald Barlett and James Steele of the *Philadelphia Inquirer* conducted a comprehensive computer analysis of a court system, perhaps the first such investigation by a newspaper. They followed the progress of 1,034 defendants through the court system.[8] They gathered information from more than 10,000 court documents and 20,000 pages of transcripts. Next, they laboriously coded the information and then punched it into IBM cards for use in an IBM 7090 mainframe computer. The analysis was completed with the help of Philip Meyer, who at that time was a reporter in the Knight-Ridder Washington Bureau, and the story on unequal justice ran on February 18, 1973.

In 1978, Rich Morin and Fred Tasker of the *Miami Herald* may have been the first reporters to directly access and analyze public records that a government agency itself compiled and maintained in computerized form.[9] They acquired the tape of tax assessment records for Dade County, Florida. Using a mainframe computer and SPSS software, along with help from Louise McReynolds, they compared the sale prices of property to the assessed valuations in Dade County. Their results showed that expensive property was assessed at a lower effective rate than low-priced property.

These same investigative reporters conducted still another study using public records. In this case it was crime records from Monroe County, Florida (which includes Key West). These records were maintained by the county in a computerized format. After analyzing these data, Morin and Tasker concluded that individuals convicted of felonies that were drug related were treated more leniently and were less likely to get jail time than individuals charged with other crimes.

CAIR ANALYSES BECOME INCREASINGLY COMMON

By the mid-1980s, CAIR projects were taking many forms. For example, as described earlier, Elliot Jaspin obtained a computer tape from the Rhode Island Housing and Mortgage Finance Corporation. The tape contained the records of 35,000 mortgages that were supposed to provide low-interest, subsidized home financing for low-income and middle-income buyers. He used a computer to sort the records by interest rate and discovered that large loans at the lowest rates had been awarded to the sons and daughters of high-ranking state officials.[10] Furthermore, mortgages totaling $44 million were either deleted or never entered into the agency's computer file. Some of the missing records were from a loan program that was kept open, long after the public was told it had closed, to provide mortgages for "special people" such as bank officials and RIHMFC employees.[11] The investigation into this scandal in the Rhode Island agency later resulted in 25 indictments.

In another dramatic example, after a series of tragic deaths of schoolchildren in school bus accidents in 1985, reporters Jaspin and Maria Johnson set out to investigate the causes. They knew that all of the school bus drivers had been certified by local police chiefs as having safe driving records. Wondering if this were really true, Jaspin and Johnson obtained the state's computer tapes of all traffic offenses for the prior 3 years. They used a computer to match the names of the state's 1,367 bus drivers with the same names on the tapes and found that more than 25% had at least one traffic violation. They also discovered that some of the drivers had large numbers of serious violations. Some had been charged with driving under the influence of drugs or alcohol; others had invalid licenses or had been involved in serious accidents.

These findings prompted Jaspin and Johnson to check the computer records of criminal offenses for the state and to match the names of the bus drivers with the court records. They found that some of the drivers had been convicted of felonies, including drug dealing.[12] As a result of their investigation, the entire licensing procedure was changed and 65 bus drivers had their licenses revoked.

All of the computer-assisted projects up to this time, or at least the overwhelming majority, had been performed on mainframe computers. This often was awkward because newspapers that had their own mainframe needed it for billing, payroll, and other administrative purposes. Furthermore, a knowledge of specialized computer languages, programming, and software was required. Alternatives, such as renting space on a university computer, were expensive. By the mid-1980s, however, personal computers were finding their way into newsrooms. This led Jaspin to seek a way to replace mainframe computing with personal computers where possible. If this were achieved, it would bring down the cost of computer-assisted reporting and make it accessible to virtually every newspaper in the United States.

The Development of Specialized Software

While Jaspin was a fellow at the Gannett Center for Media Studies at Columbia University in 1989, he developed a PC-based system for accessing nine-track computer tapes. He purchased a nine-track tape drive and hooked it into the back of an IBM-compatible PC. Then, with the assistance of Dan Woods, he developed a special software program that he called "nine-track express." The system mimics the functions of a mainframe computer. The entire system—tape drive, PC, and software—can be purchased for $9,000 to $12,000.[13]

Jaspin stresses that his system does not replace the need for a mainframe computer in all cases. A desktop computer may contain vastly less storage and working space. A very large dataset may still require a mainframe computer. However, in many cases, not all of the data need to be examined for a particular story. This is where Jaspin's system helps: The software extracts only the data that are needed. For example, a magnetic tape containing all hospital admissions for a state may have millions of records and go back several years. But perhaps the reporter is investigating whether women who give birth and have medical insurance are more likely to have a caesarean section than women with no insurance. Thus, only those records of women who entered a hospital for a birth need to be extracted from the database and examined. This "divide and conquer" approach makes large databases accessible to newsrooms with ordinary desktop computers for analyses that otherwise might not be possible.

Several newspapers are now using Jaspin's system. Some, such as the *Dayton Daily News,* have a special room set aside (that they call the "nerd room") with PCs, attached tape drives, and a collection of computer tapes. Jaspin's system is simple to use and was designed for reporters who have little or no programming knowledge. The program converts the format in which the data are stored on the computer tape into a format that can be read by a PC. It then allows the user to select the fields or variables to be imported to the PC. After the data have been downloaded into the PC, they can be transferred to a database or spreadsheet program such as DBase, Paradox, or Lotus, for analysis. Jaspin's software also provides procedures for checking whether the tapes may have been tampered with in an attempt to make them unreadable.

In 1989, Jaspin founded the Missouri Institute for Computer-Assisted Reporting at the University of Missouri. It was later renamed the National Institute for Computer-Assisted Reporting (NICAR). Although Jaspin no longer heads the institute, it continues to train journalists in the use of his system and provides experts and the use of the university's mainframe computer when necessary.[14]

As described, early CAIR projects used information gathered from paper records that was manually keyed into a computer. At first these records usually came from one source, such as criminal court records or arrest records. The resulting computer file mirrored the paper records and contained the same, or a portion of the same, information. But in time, reporters began to build computer files with information gathered from diverse and multiple sources. This resulted in the creation of unique databases. Many newspapers now routinely build their own inhouse databases.

Constructing Unique Databases

Although the majority of CAIR projects focus on analyses of existing public records, another approach has been developed. For some investigations, no database exists, yet the reporters may have or can develop a host of facts that could be analyzed effectively in various ways with the use of a computer. Thus, some investigative reporters have obtained interviews, public documents, arrest records, crime scene reports, and other kinds of information and designed their own computer files in order to search the data for patterns and relationships. Two specific examples illustrate the procedure.

The Confession-Takers of Suffolk County.   Among the first reporters to create their own complex databases of records were Thomas Maier and Rex Smith of *Newsday*. Their efforts had a dramatic outcome. In 1985, a series of highly publicized jury verdicts in Suffolk County (in Long Island, NY) caused great concern. Citizens were shocked when juries failed to convict individuals accused in three homicides. One was an alleged mob hitman accused of killing a prominent lawyer; another was a drifter accused of stabbing a nurse to death; still another was a teenager accused of kicking a dying friend and dragging the body into the woods. The District Attorney's office protested that the cases had been handled properly and the system had not broken down. Maier and Smith wanted to take a deeper look.[15]

The reporters decided, however, that they wanted to go beyond an examination of those few cases currently in the public eye. They wanted to examine how all criminal cases were handled and to look at the overall effectiveness of a system that affected the lives of so many people in the county.

It took Maier and Smith the next 6 months just to gather all of the information that would be needed. They carefully reviewed the cases of 361 people charged with homicide in Suffolk County during an 11-year period. A six-page data sheet was designed and completed for each case. It included as many as 78 facts for each case, such as age, race, sex, prior criminal background, and details of the murder and the victim. This information was drawn from the records of indictments, statements from suspects, arrest records, and court transcripts. In addition, more than 300 interviews were completed with prosecutors, defense lawyers, defendants, judges, and jurors. All of the information compiled about each case was entered into a computer to develop a unique database about the Suffolk County cases. For comparison, similar data were gathered on more than 700 homicide cases in six other suburban counties in five states.

The computer analysis revealed striking differences between Suffolk County and the other jurisdictions. One of the most glaring differences was that the Suffolk police achieved a much higher rate of confessions from their suspects than the other counties. In fact, confessions were obtained in 94% of the murder cases—a rate that experts claimed was far above the average for the nation.

Some of the Suffolk County confessions had curious features. For example, one included statements that had been handwritten entirely in English but signed by a suspect who spoke and read only Spanish. Another was signed by a suspect who was illiterate. Still another confession had been signed by a mentally retarded defendant, saying he fully understood his Miranda rights.[16] There was also a confession that had been taken and signed by a woman as she was led from the emergency room, sedated with valium and still dressed in only a hospital gown. Furthermore, a substantial number of confessions were oral statements, for which there was no proof other than the word of a police detective.

Maier and Smith's five-part series, "The Confession Takers" (published in the Suffolk edition of *Newsday*), showed that the high confession rate actually led to fewer convictions than in the other jurisdictions studied because of serious questions about how those confessions were obtained.[17] Soon after the series appeared, the Suffolk County legislature began its own investigation into the police department. The police commissioner and most of the homicide squad later resigned.

The Green River Murders.   In another dramatic case, a unique database developed by investigative reporters also yielded important information. In 1986, reporters Carlton Smith and Thomas Guillen of the *Seattle Times* decided to investigate the role of the police in handling the Green River murders, a series of homicides in which 48 young women were killed, with their bodies dumped in or near the Green River, south of Seattle. It was the nation's worst case of serial murders. The reporters wanted to know how one person could continue to murder so many women while virtually surrounded by police.[18]

Smith and Guillen tried to get the information they needed from the police, but their requests were met with foot-dragging and refusals. The police claimed they needed to maintain tight security. The reporters decided they would have to find another way to learn what the police knew and how the investigation was being carried out.

Using the state Public Records Act, the reporters requested and received a long list of documents. These included arrest logs, police expense vouchers, budget requests, internal memos, mileage logs, and case reports. They also obtained almost 5,000 arrest reports, traffic citations, and various court records. The information in these documents made up the first part of their database.

As a next step, the reporters gathered information on all of the known victims. This included the address, the names of all relatives, friends, and associates of the victims. It also included such details as the type of vehicle most often linked with a victim, missing clothing or jewelry (items often kept as souvenirs by serial killers), who was closest to the victim when she disappeared, and so on. These records made up the second part of the database.

Smith and Guillen wanted to know what the police were doing at the time each of the women were killed. They also wanted to know what clues were being overlooked and what was preventing the police from catching the killer. The reporters compiled lists of all the people who were arrested for any reason and released, especially on the dates that the women were killed or first reported missing. They also went through the mileage logs, work schedules, and vacation schedules of all the vice squad. The reporters thought that if they could put all of these pieces together, they would have a sort of time-and-motion study of the victims, the police, and the people who were in the area at the same time.

Under the direction of Steven Wainwright, the paper's systems manager, the information they had gathered from all of their sources was entered into the Atex editing system. The data were then transmitted by modem to an IBM PC XT and imported into R:Base for analyses. The data required 17 megabytes of disk space for storage. The database was periodically updated when new information came in.

As a result of developing this unique database, the reporters were able to trace, almost minute by minute, the movements of the police during the investigation. They were able to show, for example, that one night, while the police were focusing on a "penny-ante" gambling raid, the killer murdered two women—one at 8:00 p.m. and another at 9:00 p.m. Perhaps if more police had been working the "strip" (an area of hotels near the airport from where most of the women had disappeared), this could have been prevented. The reporters concluded that the King County Police simply were not prepared to handle a large, complex investigation. The police failed to see the connection between many of the murders.

The reporting team also assembled a profile of the killer from the data. In addition, they showed that the killer had knowledge of the activities of the police. It was clear that the killer was active only when the police were not. This led the reporters to suspect that the murderer, if not a policeman, at least had inside information on police activities.

As the killings continued, the database provided a rich source of information and was "mined" for stories for months. The reporters followed the police investigation closely and continued to gather information for the database for more than 2 years. The stories published included a six-part series that appeared in the *Seattle Times* between September 13 and 18, 1987.[19] In time, the police became interested in the database the reporters were developing and began providing information to the reporting team. When the police changed tactics and began arresting the customers of prostitutes, the homicides stopped. Unfortunately, the Green River killer has never been caught.

CAIR in the National Interest

Although unique databases can yield dramatic news stories, the source used in many newspapers' computer-assisted projects has been the records of national, state, or municipal government agencies that reveal information about local issues, operations, or officials. This is consistent with the local orientation of most newspapers. Some of the larger papers, however, have made extensive use of federal records to develop stories of national interest.

One paper in particular has made extensive use of national databases. *USA Today* began doing computer-assisted projects in 1989. The goal was to produce stories unobtainable by traditional reporting methods and to specialize in the investigation and analysis of both federal agency records and those of every state. These often are enormous databases that have required the use of mainframe computers.

USA Today's first computer-assisted project investigated the health of the nation's savings and loan institutions (S&Ls). It was a large and complex undertaking. The 3-month effort analyzed all of the 1988 computerized quarterly financial reports submitted to the Federal Home Loan Bank Board. These included records from all 3,046 S&Ls throughout the nation. The total assets, liabilities, net worth (and net worth as a percentage of assets) were calculated for each.

The study showed that the nation's solvent S&Ls held troubled loans totaling $19.3 billion, or about 42% of the total capital held by such institutions. Furthermore, 391 S&Ls in 38 states were insolvent, meaning that their liabilities exceeded their assets. Another 393 were "troubled" and faced serious financial problems. The study showed that Texas led the nation with the largest number of insolvent S&Ls, followed by Illinois, Louisiana, California, and Florida. In other words, the crisis was national, not just regional. The paper published several stories on the health of the S&Ls, including a state-by-state ranking of every institution.[20] These stories captured the attention of the nation and demonstrated the severity of the problem.

As their next CAIR project, *USA Today* conducted an analysis of the Environmental Protection Agency's (EPA) Toxic Release Inventory. The EPA completed its first inventory in 1987, but the data were not available on computer tape until 1989. This annual inventory lists detailed information on 328 toxic chemicals released by industries throughout the nation into the environment.

The analysis showed that, in 1987, 7 billion pounds of toxic chemicals were pumped into the air, land, and water by 19,278 factories. Calhoun County, Texas, led the nation in total toxic emissions. Amax Magnesium in Rowley, Utah, was the biggest air polluter; Aluminum Co. of America (ALCOA) in Point Comfort, Texas, dumped the most on land; and Agrico Chemical in Uncle Sam, Louisiana, was the major water polluter.[21] Several stories were published.

USA Today also completed projects using other national databases, resulting in stories on such issues as diversity in the U.S., drug arrests and minorities, big cities and rape, and campus crime. A three-part series on the country's deadliest roads analyzed all of the fatal accident records of the National Highway Traffic Safety Administration and the Federal Highway Administration.[22] The newspaper's "Banks on the Brink" series analyzed financial data on 12,296 banks obtained from the Federal Deposit Insurance Corporation.[23] The newspaper now employs several full-time specialists for this type of reporting.

As this review has shown, CAIR projects are characterized by great diversity and flexibility. Clearly, they depend on the creativity and imagination of the reporters who design them. They can range from a straightforward analysis of census data to the development of a highly specialized database around the activities of a serial killer. Moreover, they are often a part of a broad strategy that includes interviewing, the use of paper records, and other features of more traditional investigative reporting. However, computer analyses of existing or created databases can provide insights and conclusions that can lead a community to take corrective action that might not have been possible without the disclosures provided by such an effort. And that, after all, is the major purpose of the watchdog function of the press. Thus,

CAIR is more than a fad. Because of its successes, this mode of investigative reporting is becoming an important part of American journalism.

THE CONTEMPORARY STATUS OF CAIR IN THE NATION'S NEWSROOMS

Since the mid-1980s, the number of CAIR stories that have appeared in the nation's newspapers has grown considerably. Their number continues to increase, and a remarkable range of topics and issues have been investigated. Moreover, CAIR was by no means confined to large dailies serving major metropolitan areas. Even smaller papers were producing such stories for their readers.

CAIR as Everyday Journalism

By the early 1990s, too many CAIR projects had been produced to include a complete inventory here. However, to illustrate the great variety of stories that have been uncovered through CAIR analyses, the following summaries provide an overview of the kinds of topics, issues, and projects that have been and can be pursued:

• Reporters from the *Charlotte Observer* gathered information on candidates running for elected offices and their contributors from publicly available financial reports and created an inhouse database. Their analysis resulted in several stories that were printed between June 16 and 20, 1985, detailing the status of campaign financing and legislative voting patterns in North Carolina.[24]

• In 1985, *Detroit Free Press* reporters examined the computer records of the Michigan State Department of Corrections and discovered widespread problems in the state prison system. As a result of the series that was published between September 22 and 28, the state's record-keeping system was overhauled.[25]

• Members of the *Boston Globe*'s Spotlight Team produced a seven-part series on money laundering in 1985. Using data obtained from the Federal Reserve Board and the U.S. Treasury, the project attempted to measure the extent of laundering both in New England and the nation. The project explained how launderers used offshore banks in Latin America, the Bahamas, and elsewhere to hide drug profits, and traced the cocaine and cash flow between Colombia and a major drug distribution operation in Rhode

Island. It detailed the banking industry's failure to comply with cash reporting laws and the failure of regulators to enforce the laws. The series was credited with helping pass the 1986 amendments to the Bank Secrecy Act, which expanded cash reporting requirements for banks and other institutions. The series won the 1986 George Polk Award for investigative reporting.[26]

• A 1986 computer analysis of the biographical records of 1,542 professional athletes on the rosters of the National Football League's 28 teams by reporters for the *Dallas Times Herald* showed that 6 of every 10 players failed to earn their college degrees, even though most of these former collegiate stars attended U.S. universities as full-time students for 4 or 5 years.[27]

• Reporter Judy Holmes of the *Asbury Park Press* undertook an investigation of caesarean surgery and related issues in the nine hospitals located in the newspaper's coverage area in 1988. She acquired the computer tapes of hospital admissions from the Department of Health and, with the help of Elliot Jaspin, extracted and analyzed the data from women admitted for live births. Two stories were published. The first story showed that local hospitals were continuing the practice of routinely performing caesareans for women who had previously had one such delivery. The second story demonstrated that there was a higher rate of caesarean deliveries among women with private insurance as compared with women covered by Medicaid.[28]

• Reporter Cheryl Imelda Smith and Projects Editor Barry Katz of the Syracuse *Herald-Journal* conducted a year-long investigation in 1988 of the distribution of health problems and health care in Onondaga County in central New York State. They obtained nine computer tapes containing 8.5 million records covering hospital admissions in six counties, and then extracted the data for Onondaga County. The analysis identified unexpected patterns and problems of health care that were related to income. A series of articles probed the ways in which the county's health professionals related to the poor, who had higher rates of illness and disease than those with greater affluence.[29]

• A computerized study by the *Los Angeles Times* of 18,315 adults who underwent heart bypass surgery in California in 1986 revealed that the hospitals with the highest death rates did relatively fewer bypass operations than those institutions with lower rates. The study also showed great variations in typical costs for bypass patients—from a high of $59,000 to a low of $16,000. The statewide median charge was $27,700.[30]

• A computer analysis by the *Washington Post* of the state's $16.8-million scholarship program indicated that students at Maryland's private colleges received a disproportionate share of scholarship money compared with those at public institutions. The records of 25,932 students who applied for state scholarships for the 1988–89 school year were examined.[31]

• Sara Fritz and Dwight Morris of the *Los Angeles Times* analyzed 220,000 separate expenditures reported to the Federal Election Commission by 798 candidates who were seeking seats in the U.S. House of Representatives in 1990. The analysis showed that 65% of the campaign funds of incumbent congressmen were spent on items that had little or nothing to do with winning the support of ordinary voters. Many used the campaign funds as giant slush funds, and spent the money on expensive cars, real estate, tuxedos, club memberships, Broadway show tickets, lavish entertainment, personal travel, or portraits of relatives.[32]

• A *Newsday* examination of the records of 10,000 Long Island ambulance calls found that response times in Nassau and Suffolk were worse than the counties claimed and well below national standards, which indicate that 90% of all calls should be answered within 10 minutes. Only 51% of Suffolk ambulance calls were answered in that time; in Nassau, the figure was 56%.[33]

• In 1990, *Newsday* reviewed the safety and crash records for more than 140 of the world's airlines over a 20-year period. A computer analysis of more than 700 accidents worldwide showed that the odds of dying on many foreign carriers were significantly higher than on any U.S. carrier.[34]

• A *Washington Post* computer study revealed that congressional candidates were getting more of their campaign funds from outside their home states. In the 1988 election cycle, out-of-state contributions made up 25% of all individual donations, up from 16% in 1984. In the 15 months ending March 31, 1990, 50 Senators and 107 House members received a majority of their large individual donations from out of state.[35]

• Using the computer tapes of billing information and building specifications from the Water Bureau and the Finance Department, New York *Newsday* found that tens of thousands of property owners had been forced to pay more than they owed for water and sewer use due to widespread errors in the billing and metering systems. Furthermore, at least 15% of the houses in Brooklyn and Queens had incorrect size information that could make their water bills too large. More than $2 million was billed to vacant lots between June 1990 and August 1991.[36]

• The *Dayton Daily News* analyzed almost 2 million computer records and reviewed thousands of documents from the Occupational Safety and Health Administration, and found that employers with unsafe workplaces had little to fear from criminal prosecution. In 20 years, only one employer was sent to jail for violating federal safety standards. Employers pay small fines when found at fault for accidents, even when workers are killed or crippled. The median fine for such accidents from 1972 through 1990 was $500.[37]

• A computer analysis by the *New York Times* compared the sale prices of more than 25,000 houses in the five boroughs of New York City with assessors' estimates of values. The study found significant errors in the estimated value of almost half of the houses. The study also found that owners of houses that sold for $75,000 to $150,000 paid an average of 13% more in property taxes, proportionately, than the owners of houses that sold for $250,000 to $400,000.[38]

• A *Washington Post* computer study revealed that carjackers in the Washington area seized at least 245 vehicles from motorists and fatally shot four drivers during an 8-month period in 1992. The study showed that carjackers most often strike late at night and almost always use guns. The crimes are most likely to occur in neighborhoods plagued by other types of crime or in shopping centers near suburban highways. Nissans and luxury cars were most frequently targeted.[39]

• A computer analysis by the *Seattle Times* of 93 unsolved arsons that occurred during a 2-month period indicated that a majority of the fires were likely the work of one individual or a group of people working together. The investigating team analyzed approximately 3,500 "pieces" of information about the fires, and found a number of patterns and similarities. Most of the fires were set in rapid succession over a short period of time in garages and carports. The analysis also showed that in most of the fires set in residences, someone was home at the time, often asleep.[40]

• Reporters from the *Washington Post* studied patterns of sickness and health and their causes and consequences in a 1994 study of the metropolitan area's neighborhoods. Their computer analyses revealed that residents of low-income neighborhoods in Washington, DC were hospitalized three times as often as people in high-income areas for asthma, diabetes, high blood pressure, and other health conditions that are usually controlled by regular and routine medical care. In addition, the neighborhoods where residents were hospitalized most often tended to be those where doctors were scarce. The reporters analyzed the records of 230,000 patients discharged from local hospitals, along with population data from the 1990 U.S. Census. They also reviewed the fields of medicine practiced by the 14,000 physicians in the area.[41]

• The *St. Petersburg Times* published in 1995 the results of an 18-month study of 3,151 petitions for the involuntary psychiatric treatment of the elderly filed by hospitals in Pinellas County. Reporters were granted access to sealed court records. They entered the information from the petitions into a database along with results from interviews with psychiatrists, hospital administrators, mental health advocates, judges, lawyers, and patients. The results revealed that the county led the state in petitions for involuntary treatment, even though other counties in Florida had as many or more elderly residents. In many cases, the forced stays in psychiatric wards were too great a strain on the elderly patients, whose physical health rapidly deteriorated.[42]

Clearly, then, investigative reporters using computers to analyze various kinds of records have produced a remarkable variety of stories. Although the given examples, for the most part, appeared in larger papers, later sections of this chapter indicate that even small papers in local communities are a part of this movement.

Prize-Winning CAIR Stories

Although CAIR analyses can be complex and time consuming, many have paid off, both in terms of important information disclosed to the public and in formal recognition of the reporters who completed the projects. In fact, a large number of CAIR stories have won prizes. For example, Bill Kovach, curator of the Nieman Foundation for Journalism, said that approximately half of the nominees in one recent contest were made up of reports based entirely or mostly on computer-assisted reporting. Each one, he said, had either revealed or illuminated an important activity or issue of public interest.[43]

Several computer-assisted projects have received Pulitzer Prizes. In 1986, Mary Pat Flaherty and Andrew Schneider of the *Pittsburgh Press* won the Pulitzer for specialized reporting with a series revealing corruption in the organ transplant business. They disclosed that a world market had developed for transplanted organs obtained from Third World countries.[44] The following year, Andrew Schneider and Mathew Brelis won a Pulitzer for a series of 14 articles in which they documented dangerous health problems and drug and alcohol addictions among airline pilots and flight crews of major airlines that were undetected during medical exams.[45]

The 1989 Pulitzer for investigative reporting was awarded to Bill Dedman of the *Atlanta Journal and Constitution* for a series titled "The Color of Money." His analyses demonstrated the existence of racial discrimination in the approval of mortgages by the Atlanta banking industry. The computer study compared census data with federally mandated bank reports on 109,000 home purchase and home improvement loans made over a 6-year period in the metro area. The results showed that Whites received five times as many home loans from Atlanta's banks and savings and loan institutions as Blacks of the same income. As a result of the series, the nine largest banks in Atlanta announced that they would make $65 million in loans available in the city's Black neighborhoods.[46]

The 1989 Pulitzer award for Public Service was won by the *Anchorage Daily News* for a 10-day series called "A People in Peril." It detailed the high rate of suicide, alcoholism, and despair among Eskimos, Indians, and Aleuts in Alaska. A total of 22 reporters contributed to the series. The database that they developed tracked Native American deaths and alcohol-related incidents in every borough and village in Alaska.[47]

Reporters Lou Kilzer and Chris Ison of the Minneapolis *Star Tribune* won the 1990 Pulitzer for investigative reporting for a series of stories titled "A Culture of Arson." The series exposed "shoddy" investigations by St. Paul's longtime fire chief and linked the chief to individuals who profited from arson. The reporters analyzed computerized property and fire records and focused on 200 fires that had occurred in St. Paul during a 25-year period.[48]

Marjie Lundstrom and Rochelle Sharpe of the *Gannett News Service* were awarded the 1991 Pulitzer for national reporting for a four-part series that revealed that hundreds of deaths related to child abuse go undetected each year because of errors and problems in death investigations nation-wide. The reporters conducted a computer study of all 49,569 death certificates of children under the age of 9 who died in the United States during a 1-year period. The results showed that in many of the most suspicious child deaths nationwide, no autopsy was performed, even though an autopsy is crucial in detecting child abuse.[49]

Pulitzer Prizes also were awarded in 1992 and 1993 for computer-assisted stories. In 1992, Jeff Taylor and Mike McGraw of the *Kansas City Star* uncovered fraud and waste in the U.S. Department of Agriculture, as well as favoritism toward powerful food lobbies. In 1993, reporters for the *Miami Herald* covered Hurricane Andrew and discovered that, among other factors, lax building codes contributed to the devastation. Also in 1993, all three Pulitzer finalists in investigative reporting relied on government databases for their projects.[50]

In 1996, the Raleigh *News and Observer* was awarded the Pulitzer Prize for Public Service for its groundbreaking coverage of the state's powerful hog industry. The 5-part series, "Boss Hog: North Carolina's Pork Revolution," described how giant agricultural corporations had replaced small, family hog farms in eastern North Carolina, a region where pigs outnumbered people. Reporters Pat Stith and Joby Warrick showed that enormous lagoons of animal waste were threatening water supplies and fouling the air with noxious odors. The series also demonstrated the strong influence the hog industry wielded over state regulators and legislators. The series depended heavily on computerized records searches.

A few months after the series was published, eight hog waste lagoons burst and millions of gallons of feces were spilled into waterways, causing massive fish kills. As a result of the series and the spills, new laws regulating the industry were adopted.[51]

Computer Analyses of Records in More Routine Reporting

Although Pulitzers and other prizes have gone to a number of CAIR projects, many journalists emphasize that computer-assisted reporting is not just for big award-winning or long-term projects. It is also an everyday tool that can be used for routine and quick-hit stories. Reporters at the *St. Petersburg Times,* for example, used computerized census data to develop a kind of "man-bites-dog" story that there were 431 Eskimos living in Florida. They also used census data to help single readers find romance by sorting out those counties where single members of one gender outnumber the other.[52]

For routine reporting, the *Kansas City Star* stores driver's license records, voter registrations, and county assessor records on the paper's mainframe computer. The data are analyzed not only for long-term projects, but also for quick stories such as landlords who unknowingly rent to crack dealers, or fire fighters with suspended licenses who still drive fire trucks on emergency calls.[53]

Computer-assisted techniques are also being used in less noticeable but more fundamental ways. For example, Associated Press reporters were able to track down a suspect in the 1995 Oklahoma City bombing of the Alfred P. Murrah Federal Building. They used a post office box number to get a street address from a database of motor vehicle registrations.[54]

Many newspapers are acquiring their own magnetic tape and CD-ROM libraries. At the *Dayton Daily News,* for example, stored databases include the 1980 census data, 1990 census data, Ohio teacher revocations, Ohio teacher certifications, charities in Ohio, Federal Procurement Data Center tapes on defense spending in Ohio, Dayton city payroll, state medical database of hospital admissions, driver's licenses, bank mortgage data, and campaign contributions. In addition to these, many reporters on the paper build their own databases for routine analyses as information is acquired. The data are used not only for long-term projects, but also for routine stories such as a local department store that owed back taxes of $700,000.[55]

A number of newspapers have established programs of computer-assisted reporting and perform computer analyses on a relatively regular basis.

These include the *Akron Beacon Journal, Asbury Park Press, Atlanta Constitution, Boston Globe, Boston Herald, Dayton Daily News, Hartford Courant, Kansas City Star, Los Angeles Times, Minneapolis Star Tribune, New York Times, Newsday, Philadelphia Inquirer, Raleigh News and Observer, St. Louis Post Dispatch,* and the *Wall Street Journal.*[56] As noted earlier, *USA Today* started its program in 1989 and now employs five specialists for CAIR.[57] At the *Raleigh News and Observer,* 28 reporters completed more than 100 computer-assisted stories in a 4-year period.[58] It is clear, then, that computer-assisted reporting has developed into a routine part of many newsroom operations.

Additional evidence supports the adoption of this type of journalism. According to a recent survey of 192 daily newspaper editors, more than half of newspaper readers in the United States now subscribe to papers that have undertaken at least one computer-assisted project.[59] Approximately 52% of the editors responding said that their newspapers had begun to analyze the computerized records of government agencies. These newspapers had completed an average of seven (and median of four) such computer analyses. One third of these editors, however, claimed that their papers had completed 11 or more computer analyses in one year alone. These analyses were of local and state government records as well as large federal databases. Several created their own databases from paper records. All of this suggests that many of the nation's newspapers are doing computer analyses of government records on a fairly regular basis. Finally, 75% of all of the editors who responded believed that the ability to analyze the computerized records of government will be very important in the years ahead.

NOTES AND REFERENCES

1. Clarence Jones, "A Scientific Look at Dade Crime," the *Miami Herald,* December 15, 1968. The project resulted in several stories. For additional information about the project, see: John McMullan, "A New Concept Is Born," the *Miami Herald,* December 15, 1968.
2. Philip Meyer, "The People Beyond 12th Street: A Survey of Attitudes of Detroit Negroes After the Riot of 1967," *Detroit Free Press,* reprint, 1967. See also: Philip Meyer, *The New Precision Journalism* (Bloomington: Indiana University Press, 1991), pp. 17–18.
3. David Burnham, "A Wide Disparity Is Found in Crime Throughout City," the *New York Times,* February 14, 1972, p. 1; "Police Efficiency Constant All Over City, Study Finds," the *New York Times,* February 15, 1972, p. 1.
4. Additional details of these stories were provided by David Burnham in an unpublished paper, "Trying to Cover the New York City Crime Scene," presented at the Symposium on Computer-Assisted Investigative Reporting at the Newhouse School of Public Communications, Syracuse University, May, 1989.

5. David Burnham, "Murder Rate for Blacks in City 8 Times That for White Victims," the *New York Times,* Sunday, August 5, 1973, p. 1.
6. David Burnham, "Crime Rates in Precincts and Census Data Studied," the *New York Times,* July 30, 1973, p. 1.
7. David Burnham, *op. cit.,* 1989.
8. For a description of several examples of CAIR, see: "Computers and Investigative Reporting: A Selected Chronology," a display prepared by the Freedom Forum Center for Media Studies, 1990.
9. This example of Tasker and Morin's project was cited by Philip Meyer during a presentation, "Reporting in the 21st Century," at the annual meetings of AEJMC in Montreal in August, 1992.
10. Elliot Jaspin, "Sons, Daughters of State Leaders Got 8 1/2 Percent RIHMFC Loans," *Providence Journal,* June 2, 1985, p. 2.
11. Katherine Gregg and Elliot G. Jaspin, "1,140 Mortgages Not Listed in RIHMFC Computer File," the *Providence Journal,* June 19, 1985, p. 1.
12. Maria Miro Johnson and Elliot G. Jaspin, "R.I. System Fails to Fully Check Driving Records of Bus Applicants," the *Providence Sunday Journal,* May 11, 1986, p. 1.
13. Elliot Jaspin, "Introducing Nine-Track Tape Analysis," presentation at the conference on computer-assisted reporting sponsored by Indiana University's National Institute for Advanced Reporting, Indianapolis, Indiana, 1991.
14. Jaspin is now the Systems Editor for Cox Newspapers in Washington, DC.
15. Details about the investigation by *Newsday* into homicide confessions in Suffolk County were provided by Thomas Maier during the Symposium on Computer-Assisted Investigative Reporting at the S. I. Newhouse School of Public Communications, Syracuse University, May, 1989.
16. The "Miranda rights" refer to the Miranda warning rules that every police officer must state to a suspect prior to any questioning. These include the right to remain silent, notification that anything the suspect says can and will be used against him or her in a court of law, the right to consult with a lawyer and to have the lawyer present during any questioning, and if the suspect cannot afford a lawyer then the court will obtain one if desired by the suspect. See: James A. Inciardi, *Criminal Justice* (Orlando, Fla.: Academic Press, Inc., 1984), pp. 286–288.
17. Thomas Maier and Rex Smith, "The Confession Takers," *Newsday,* Suffolk edition, a five-part series printed on Dec. 7–19, 1986.
18. Details about the investigation by the *Seattle Times* into the Green River murders and the creation of the database were provided by Steven Wainwright, the systems manager for the paper, during the Symposium on Computer-Assisted Investigative Reporting at the S. I. Newhouse School of Public Communications, Syracuse University, May, 1989.
19. Carlton Smith and Thomas Guillen, "Green River: What Went Wrong?" a six-part series appearing in the *Seattle Times* on Sept. 13–18, 1987.
20. Wendell Cochran, "Behind the S&L Crisis," *USA Today,* February 13, 1989, p. 3B; Wendell Cochran, "The S&L Mess," *USA Today,* August 14, 1989, p. 1A.
21. Rae Tyson and Julie Morris, "The Chemicals Next Door," *USA Today,* July 31, 1989, p. 1A.
22. Carolyn Pesce, "USA's Deadliest Roads," *USA Today,* September 4, 1990, p. 1A; Larry Sanders, "The 500 Counties Where Risk of Road Fatalities is Highest," *USA Today,* September 5, 1990, p. 8A.
23. Larry Sanders, "The USA's Most Troubled Banks," *USA Today,* May 26, 1992, p. 3B.

24. This example is described in "Computers and Investigative Reporting: A Selected Chronology," an exhibit prepared by the Freedom Forum Center for Media Studies, 1990.

25. *Ibid.*

26. The seven-part series on money laundering in the *Boston Globe* ran during the week of Sept. 29, 1985. The Spotlight Team consisted of Stephen Kurkjian, Daniel Golden, Peter Gosselin, and M. Malone.

27. Christopher Bogan, *Dallas Times Herald*, "41% in NFL Graduate from College," reported in the *Los Angeles Times*, January 27, 1986, Sports, p. 32.

28. Judy Holmes, "Caesarean Sections," *Asbury Park Press*, Dec. 11, 1988, p. F1.

29. Cheryl Imelda Smith, "Health and Wealth," a three-part series in the Syracuse *Herald-Journal/Herald American*, Feb. 26–28, 1989.

30. Robert Steinbrook, "Heart Surgery Death Rates Found High in 1 in 6 Hospitals," the *Los Angeles Times*, July 24, 1988, Part 1, p. 3.

31. Amy Goldstein and Richard Morin, "Md. Scholarships Leave the Needy Behind," the *Washington Post*, August 13, 1989, p. A1.

32. Sara Fritz and Dwight Morris, "Campaign Cash Takes a Detour," the *Los Angeles Times*, October 28, 1990, Part A, p. 1.

33. Adam Z. Horvath, "Emergency! Long Island's Ambulance Crisis," *Newsday*, Nassau and Suffolk Edition, December 18, 1988, News Section, p. 4.

34. Glenn Kessler and Ford Fessenden, "Where Safety Takes a Backseat," *Newsday*, December 16, 1990, News Section, p. 4.

35. Richard Morin and Charles R. Babcock, "Out-of-State Donations to Candidates Are on the Rise," the *Washington Post*, July 31, 1990, p. A1.

36. Penny Loeb, "Leaks in Water Bureau," *Newsday*, City Edition, December 23, 1991, News Section, p. 7.

37. Mike Casey and Russell Carollo, *Dayton Daily News*, "Employees Paying With Their Lives in Hazardous Workplaces," reported in the *Atlanta Journal and Constitution*, June 9, 1991, Section B, p. 1.

38. Alan Finder and Richard Levine, "Unequal Burden: New York's Property Tax," the *New York Times*, July 6, 1991, Section 1, p. 1.

39. Debbi Wilgoren, "Carjackers Put Drivers on Defensive," the *Washington Post*, August 16, 1992, p. A1.

40. Tomas Guillen, Kate Shatzkin, Dee Norton, Duff Wilson, Dave Birkland, Kay Kusumoto, and Peter Lewis, "More Than 60 Arsons Linked—Computer-Aided Study Finds Many Similarities," the *Seattle Times*, October 25, 1992, p. A1.

41. Amy Goldstein, "Worlds Apart: Health Care in Washington," a three-part series in the *Washington Post*, July 31–August 2, 1994.

42. Carol A. Marbin and Stephen Nohlgren, "A Dangerous Age: A Times Investigation," a five-part series in the *St. Petersburg Times*, May 21–27, 1995.

43. Bill Kovach addressed the participants of a conference on computer-assisted journalism at Indiana University's National Institute for Advanced Reporting, Indianapolis, Indiana, March, 1992.

44. See, for example, "SPJ/SDX Meeting to Focus on Pittsburgh Press' Consecutive Pulitzers," PR Newswire, November 10, 1987. Mary Pat Flaherty and Andrew Schneider's series on organ transplants ran in the *Pittsburgh Press* on November 3–10, 1985.

45. Eleanor Randolph, "Medical Reporter Wins 2nd Consecutive Pulitzer," the *Washington Post,* April 17, 1987, p. A3; "Winners of Pulitzer Prizes in Journalism, Letters and the Arts," the *New York Times,* April 17, 1987, Section B, p. 4.
46. Bill Dedman, "The Color of Money," the *Atlanta Journal and Constitution,* May 1–4, 1988. The project was completed with the assistance of Dwight Morris.
47. Elinor Craig, "Mac Database Helps Daily Win Pulitzer," *MacWeek,* Vol. 3, No. 16, p. 14. The series was titled "A People in Peril" and ran in the *Anchorage Daily News* during January, 1988.
48. See: "Reporters from Star Tribune Win Pulitzer," United Press International, Regional News, April 12, 1990. The series was published in the Minneapolis *Star Tribune* on October 29–30, 1989.
49. Marjie Lundstrom and Rochelle Sharpe, "Getting Away with Murder: Sloppy Investigations Leave Child Murders Undetected," Gannett News Service, December 12, 1990; Marjie Lundstrom and Rochelle Sharpe, "Getting Away with Murder: It's Easy to Kill a Child—And Bury the Secret," Gannett News Service, December 12, 1990.
50. "And the (Pulitzer) Winner Is . . . Computer-Assisted Reporting," *The Freedom Forum,* September, 1993, p. 7.
51. Craig Whitlock, "N&O Hog Series Takes Top Pulitzer," *Raleigh News & Observer,* April 10, 1996, p. A1; See also: Pat Stith and Joby Warrick, "Big Pork Helps Its Friends," *News & Observer,* February 26, 1995, P. A9.
52. Bill Adair, The *St. Petersburg Times* Census Project," presentation at the 1992 conference on computer-assisted reporting, at Indiana University's National Institute for Advanced Reporting, Indianapolis, Indiana, March, 1992.
53. Katherine Corcoran, "Power Journalists," *Washington Journalism Review,* November, 1991, p. 31.
54. See: *Editor & Publisher* Magazine, Interactive Communications Section, May 20, 1995, p. 20.
55. Max Jennings, "What Small Newspapers Can Do Without Big Resources," 1992 conference on computer-assisted reporting at the National Institute for Advanced Reporting at Indiana University, March 20, 1992.
56. A partial list of newspapers with programs of computer-assisted reporting was prepared by John V. Pavlik, The Freedom Forum Center for Media Studies at Columbia University, 1990.
57. Karen Jorgensen, "Reporting in the 21st Century," a presentation at AEJMC convention in Montreal, August, 1992.
58. Pat Stith, "Management of Computer Resources: In-House Training of Reporters and Editors," presentation at the 4th annual conference on computer-assisted journalism at Indiana University's National Institute for Advanced Reporting, Indianapolis, Indiana, March 12, 1993.
59. Cecilia Friend, "Computerized Records and Newspapers," *Editor and Publisher,* December 26, 1992, pp. 9–10. The survey, the first comprehensive look at U.S. newspapers and computer-assisted reporting, randomly sampled all U.S. dailies but made the probability of selection proportionate to circulation size. Thus, papers with larger circulations were weighted more heavily than smaller papers. The survey achieved a response rate of 82%.

5

Basic CAIR Techniques:
As Used in Contemporary
Newsrooms

The previous chapters of this book have provided *background* information essential to understanding the origins and nature of CAIR. The opening chapter explained how it is related to, and an extension of, traditional approaches to investigative reporting. Additional chapters described the development of computers, the evolution of the legal statutes governing computerized records of government, and the kinds of stories that have been generated through CAIR analyses since the 1960s. The remaining chapters in the book focus on *methods*—the techniques and procedures of data examination as well as the criteria for accepting or rejecting conclusions that are appropriate for CAIR analyses and reporting. This chapter lays a foundation for those that follow by explaining what methods have been used in the past and in recent times by journalists who have analyzed electronic records to develop stories. The remaining chapters build on this foundation and present a systematic *methodology*—a logic of analysis suitable for CAIR. That methodology will include some of the techniques and strategies that are discussed here, but it will also incorporate additional features derived from other sources. Illustrations of CAIR methodology in use will be provided within the context of a large-scale case study.

A formal methodology for CAIR that is explicitly stated is important. Just as social scientists make use of methods suitable for assembling and analyzing data obtained in their experiments, surveys, and other research efforts, journalists whose goal is to analyze computerized records for investigative purposes must also do so. To achieve this goal, a methodology must first be developed and stated formally. The initial formulation of that methodology in the remaining chapters of this book provides a beginning point around which consensus can be achieved concerning which tech-niques, procedures, and strategies provide trustworthy results and how best to report the findings of CAIR analyses to the public.

BASIC CAIR TECHNIQUES

As a first step in developing a formal methodology for CAIR, this chapter systematically reviews procedures that have been discussed and advocated by its pioneers. It also summarizes ways in which contemporary working journalists have actually conducted a large number of such investigative projects and prepared news stories about them for their readers. We begin, therefore, with a summary of the analytical procedures and strategies used by the CAIR pioneers whose work was discussed in previous chapters.

Burnham's General Formula

Pioneering reporter David Burnham developed a broad conceptual framework to use when investigating a government or public agency. When Burnham joined the *New York Times,* he became concerned about how to figure out what stories to cover in his new beat—a very large one that then included 30,000 police officers, five district attorneys, several court systems and hundreds of thousands of crimes. Burnham was not sure where to begin looking for information and stories. The possibilities seemed endless. He began interview-ing others and asking whether anyone had some kind of formula that would help to identify important topics for investigation. He received an interesting answer from Alfred Blumstein, who at that time was the head of the science and technology task force of President Lyndon Johnson's Commission on Law Enforcement and Administration of Justice. He told Burnham that he should focus his energies on stories that show whether the police, district attorneys, or judges achieve their stated goals, and if not, to look for what prevents these agencies from working the way they should.[1]

This turned out to be an excellent strategy. For example, in virtually all communities, the purpose of the police is to ensure the safety of the public. Quite clearly, however, they do not always do so. In such cases, what problems or procedures stop the police from achieving this goal? Or, in another example, the purpose of the federal Occupational Safety and Health Administration (OSHA) is to guarantee workers' safety on the job. How-ever, it often happens that workplaces are unsafe. What problems or procedures prevent OSHA from achieving its goal? In this sense, says

Burnham, the formal goals of an agency serve as a standard of measurement. He recognizes that all institutions are flawed to some extent, and it may be unrealistic to expect an institution to achieve its stated goals completely. Thus, the difficulty of achieving the assigned goals must be considered. Nevertheless, some agencies fall far short of achieving the purposes for which they were designed, and it is these on which an analysis can focus.

Burnham found this "formula" to be helpful and used it repeatedly when investigating various government agencies. It also provides a starting point when confronting the internal electronic records of an agency. In other words, says Burnham, two key questions must be asked: (a) What is the stated purpose or mission of the agency? (b) What problems or procedures prevent the agency from achieving its stated purpose or goal? These two general questions can help to guide the data analysis.[2]

Jaspin's Advocated Procedures

Elliot Jaspin carried this conceptualization process on to a second step. With a general starting point or question in mind, what must be done with the data to get answers? For example, how can the problems that prevent an agency from accomplishing its mission be found in the computerized records? That is, what specific techniques can be used to pull out the information needed from the tape or database? Jaspin discussed four techniques that journalists can use when searching for answers in a sea of electronic information.[3] Specifically, these are searching, counting, sorting, and cross-indexing.

1. *Searching.* By this technique, Jaspin refers to looking for one occurrence of something, such as an individual's address from a database of drivers' license records. If, as Jaspin relates, a person one day gets into his or her car and suddenly runs down a group of people crossing the street, the only fact a reporter may be given at the scene of the accident is the person's name. The reporter will want to interview family and neighbors, and probably would check the telephone directory for an address. However, the individual may not be listed in the directory, or there may be several people with the same name. It may be more efficient to use a computer and search through all the drivers' licenses that have been issued in the state. Virtually all adults will have applied for a license, and additional information such as age, address, height, and weight will be recorded in those records.

2. *Counting.* Jaspin refers here to finding the number of times something occurs, such as the number of convictions obtained in murder cases. A public official running for reelection, for example, may announce that he or she

was responsible for the aggressive prosecution of drug offenses or violent crimes while in office, and that this resulted in a specific (high) number of convictions. A reporter on deadline may not have the time to verify these claims. With the state's criminal court records loaded in a computer, however, the reporter could quickly find those records where convictions in the candidate's jurisdiction were obtained and count how many there were.

3. *Sorting.* By this Jaspin means ranking facts in ascending or descending order, or finding the largest or smallest of something, such as the amount of overtime pay received by city workers. Jaspin discusses an incident where a source told reporters that large amounts of overtime were being paid to members of the police department. The paper purchased a computer tape containing the city's payroll records and computed the total paid to every city worker during a 1-year period. Next, the totals were sorted from highest to lowest. This showed that a patrolman who worked double shifts for several months earned more than the governor did that year.

4. *Cross-indexing.* Jaspin explains this in terms of matching information in one file or database with information in another. In his project involving the deaths of three children in Rhode Island who were killed by school buses, he and his colleagues obtained a list of all school bus drivers in the state. They entered the names from that list into a database that contained the names of those in Rhode Island who had received traffic tickets during a 3-year period. By this means the reporters found school bus drivers with traffic violations. The same procedure was used in entering the names of the bus drivers into another database of criminal court records. Here they found that some of the drivers also had felony convictions.

Others have advocated similar procedures. The "searching" approach described by Jaspin has been referred to as "finding the needle in a haystack." Others have added that trends occurring over a period of time can be charted and verified by sorting and ranking data.[4]

Meyer's Suggested Strategies

Philip Meyer has also described many procedures that are suitable for CAIR analyses. In his book *The New Precision Journalism,* he advocated the use of the entire body of social science strategies and methods. As a simple first step, however, he wrote that many stories derived from databases can be developed by comparing groups or subgroups as a simple first step.[5] This can be accomplished most easily by the following techniques:

1. *Cross-tabulation.* This is a display, usually in the form of a table, that divides a group of individuals or things into two or more categories and shows the frequency of occurrence. For example, in examining customer satisfaction, the owners of various kinds of cars could be further divided into the percentage of vehicle owners who were satisfied or dissatisfied with their purchase. In another example, individuals convicted of murder could be categorized by race and then the percentage who received a sentence longer than, say, 10 years could be calculated for each racial group. Such comparisons may indicate whether or not an association exists between the categories or variables.

2. *Comparisons of means.* In this procedure, the average value of two or more groups or categories are calculated and compared. For example, the average annual income of female-headed households could be compared with that of male-headed households and two-parent households within a particular geographical area. Or, the average cost of a stay at one hospital resulting from a surgical procedure such as heart bypass surgery could be compared with similar stays in other hospitals in the state where the surgery is performed.

Meyer expressed concern that limited levels of computer use among journalists may be impeding the development of CAIR. He explained that many of the reporters currently using databases of public records for stories fail to tap into the full power of the computer. Instead, they use the computer simply to do the same tasks that they have always done. Meyer referred to these journalists as "computer cowboys."[6]

Meyer believes that, for the most part, many reporters are restricting their analyses to the counting, sorting, ranking, and matching procedures that Jaspin described. A typical story, for example, might list the 10 drunkest drivers in the state (those with the highest blood alcohol level at the time of their arrest). Or, the story may name the county employee who received the most overtime pay during the year. Although this makes a good story, there are only a limited number of this type of "worst (or least) offender" stories that can be obtained from any one database. This leaves the majority of the information in the database untouched. Furthermore, although the computer is used to go though vast numbers of records (technically qualifying it as an example of computer-assisted reporting), the strategies used (sorting, matching, or ranking) do not extend beyond those reporters have used in the past with pencil and paper. Computers, of course, can do more. Thus, Meyer believes that journalists must learn and incorporate a broader array of analytical procedures and basic statistical methods into computer-as-sisted analyses. Journalists who fail to consider statistical methods can make serious errors. They may, for example, reach the conclusion that the averages of two groups differ, or claim that an association between two factors is present, when the findings could have been the result of chance alone. From this point of view, the use of simple strategies can provide a good starting point, but they may not be enough. Additional strategies and methods that extend the capacities of computer analyses must be considered so that CAIR can continue to evolve as a powerful tool of oversight.

TECHNIQUES AND PROCEDURES USED IN 130 CAIR STORIES

Having looked briefly at the strategies of analysis used and advocated by the CAIR pioneers, the next step in establishing a foundation for the development of a methodology for CAIR is to look closely at the methods contemporary journalists are actually using to conduct their analyses of electronic records. To achieve this goal, an examination of 130 contemporary CAIR stories was completed for this chapter. The results not only reveal what procedures and techniques are currently in use, but they also indicate whether there is any factual basis for the "cowboy" hypotheses expressed by Meyer.

The first step in conducting the review was to obtain as many examples of recent CAIR news stories as possible so that their methods and strategies of analysis could be examined. Ideally, such an examination would be based on reviewing a representative sample from the entire population of all computer-assisted investigative news stories published in any of the 1,600 or so dailies, plus all other U.S. newspapers, during the last several years. However, no one knows how many of these projects have been completed; there is no list of every story published. Furthermore, not all newspapers are part of online databases such as Lexis/Nexis, and many computer-assisted stories are difficult to identify. This means that even a diligent search of existing databases would not produce a sampling frame, or complete list, of every story. Therefore, as an alternative approach, what is essentially a convenience sample was used.

To assemble a sizable number of recent CAIR stories, the first step involved a search of all newspaper files in the Lexis/Nexis system. The search terms were designed to uncover any stories in the files that were based on computer analyses of electronic records. This included such terms as *computer-assisted reporting, computer-assisted journalism, computer-assisted investigative reporting, computer-assisted investigative journalism, computer-assisted analysis, computer analysis,* and *computer study.*

This strategy turned up more than 250 stories published during the previous 8 years. Each of these was read carefully to determine whether it was indeed an example of computer-assisted reporting conducted by the newspaper. Just under 100 survived this test. Those eliminated were found to contain the search terms, but did not actually discuss a specific CAIR project, or the analysis was conducted by outsiders rather than reporters themselves. To this set of stories were added over 30 others that had been collected at various conferences, workshops, and symposia devoted to computer-assisted journalism.

The result of these efforts was an assembly of 130 CAIR stories that had appeared in a variety of U.S. newspapers and met the criterion of being based primarily or in significant part on a computer analysis of electronic records. That is, in each, the data and conclusions developed by the analysis were central to the topic of the story. These stories had appeared in newspapers of many kinds. They ranged from the *New York Times,* the *Washington Post,* and *USA Today* to small papers such as the *Waterbury Republican American,* the *Lansing State Journal* (Michigan), and the *State Journal Register* (Springfield, Illinois). Papers of all sizes and circulations were included from all regions of the country.

The next step was to develop a system for classifying and counting the various procedures and techniques that had been employed in these analyses. These ranged from simple frequency counts through a variety of basic statistical indices on up to multifactor associations. Each had to be explained in the newspaper story in such a way that the ordinary reader, not skilled in understanding statistical terms, would understand what was being reported. For the purposes of the present analysis, these explanations had to be translated back into the more technical procedure or statistical index that had been used. To accomplish this objective, each of the 130 stories was read carefully to identify from the verbal explanations exactly what procedures and specific techniques had been employed in the computer analysis of the data used in the story. This translation from prose to procedure required the development of a dictionary that listed and defined each of the techniques that were found.

The dictionary was used as a kind of Rosetta Stone. That is, it permitted the translation of the verbal explanations provided by reporters for their readers back into the more technical and statistical concepts that they had used in their analyses. It worked well as a tool for identifying CAIR techniques and procedures that had been employed in the analyses. (The dictionary appears in Appendix A.)

To explain more fully how the dictionary was used as a tool for translation, the first thing to be understood is how all the many different topics covered in the 130 stories were brought together into a single framework for analysis. To do this, the terms *entities* and *attributes* were used as general concepts within which to review each story. An entity is whatever phenomenon is being investigated—crimes, political contributions, heart surgery, and so on. An *attribute* is any qualitative characteristic of such an entity that appears as a variable in the database. A few selected examples from the dictionary can illustrate the general idea. For example, many stories presented information on some attribute of some entity using an index of central tendency (such as a mode or median). Others contained more complex numerical or statistical information. Some reporters were able to present such ideas in simple and understandable terms. Others did not fare so well. In any case, each of the following examples, using a statistical index from the dictionary shows how such technical concepts can be explained in a news story:

Mode: The story identifies a most frequently occurring value of some attribute of one or more entities.

> *Example:* The most frequently noted high level of rainfall for Spencer County was 3.5 inches, which seemed to occur regularly in August over the last 20 years.

Median: The story identifies a value of some attribute among a set of entities, above (or below) which 50% of the cases were found.

> *Example:* Half of the homes in this affluent middle-class neighborhood were valued at $210,000 or higher.

Matched Comparison: The story compares the values of an attribute between entities selected to be similar on some set of criteria.

> *Example:* The homicide rates of nearby counties with about the same population characteristics were compared to that of Suffolk County to see if it was quite dissimilar. It was much higher.

Simple Association: The story identifies a corelationship between two attributes among a set of entities.

> *Example:* Age at death was generally higher among retirees who had vested pension plans, but lower among those who were living only on social security. In other words, the higher one's income, the longer one tends to live, and vice versa.

Multiple Factor Association: The story identifies a pattern in which two or more attributes appear to be related to another attribute said to be dependent on their values. If these are considered together, they modify the interpretation of a simple association.

> *Example:* Some hospitals have high death rates for bypass heart surgery. Others have much lower rates. This would seem to imply

that those with lower rates have surgeons who have greater skill. However, if a hospital admits more patients who have chronic heart problems (poorer risks for surgery) and if they treat more emergency cases involving heart attacks (also poorer risks for surgery), its rate will go up due to those causes, and not because of a lack of skill by the surgeons. Thus, a given hospital's death rate for heart bypass surgery may not be an indicator of bad performance. It can be a product of several factors.

A total of 24 definitions with examples (drawn in many cases from actual stories) were developed and included in the dictionary. Once the dictionary had been developed, the next step was to read each of the 130 stories again to determine how many of these 24 techniques had been used in each. To assist in this quantitative assessment, a simple form was designed on which to record all 24 specific techniques listed in the dictionary that had been used in the story. The form also provided for the recording of additional information about each of the stories. For example, space was provided to record the following five specific features, or categories of information about, each of the 130 CAIR stories:

1. The *general topic* that the story addressed. Each was classified into one of 11 categories on the basis of whether it was mainly about such issues as politics, crime, education, and so forth.
2. The *level or focus* of the story. These categories refer to whether national, state, or local issues were investigated.
3. The *source* from which the data used in the CAIR analysis had been obtained. These were identified as having been obtained from a federal, state, or local agency.
4. The *general procedure* used in the computer analysis. This referred to whether a tape from an agency was analyzed, a database was developed from paper records, and so on.
5. The *specific analytical techniques* that were used in the analysis (these were the 24 techniques defined and illustrated in the dictionary).

In summary, the dictionary and the form were used to identify, count, and record each specific technique of analysis that had been used in each of the CAIR investigations reported in the 130 stories. Using these data, a SAS file was prepared to permit a numerical analysis of the general topics addressed, their level of focus, the source of the data, procedures followed, and the frequency of use of each of the 24 specific analytical techniques.

FINDINGS FROM THE REVIEW

The results of the review of these 130 CAIR stories are summarized in five tables. These tables are presented with descriptive comments concerning what they revealed. First, Table 5.1 shows the general topics that were emphasized in the 130 CAIR stories. By a considerable margin, politics led the list. Within that broad category, the majority of such stories focused on campaign financing—an area richly deserving of continued monitoring by journalists. Crime and police problems—reflecting a long tradition in journalism—was second. The nature of the former crisis in the savings and loan industry was well represented. However, a number of other topics that were high on the news agenda during the same period, such as medical and health issues, economic concerns, and environmental dangers, were not subjects of many CAIR stories.

As Table 5.2 shows, over 43% of these stories focused on national topics. However, consistent with the community orientation of most newspapers, over one third focused on local issues. Most of the records used in these CAIR analyses came from federal sources (Table 5.3). The two most frequently used databases were from the Federal Elections Commission (campaign contributions) and the Census Bureau (1990 census). A total of 46 stories (about 35%) were developed from these two sources alone. Often, after one newspaper published a story about a specific issue using these

TABLE 5.1
General Topics Emphasized in 130 CAIR Stories

Topic or Issue	Number	Percentage
Politics/Campaign financing	37	28.5
Crime/Police problems	19	14.6
Minority issues/Problems	18	13.8
Savings & loan/Banks	12	9.2
Highway/Airline safety	9	6.9
Medical/Health issues	9	6.9
Income/Economy	6	4.6
Unfairness of taxes	6	4.6
Quality of local community	6	4.6
Environmental dangers	5	3.8
Higher education	3	2.3
Totals	130	100.0

TABLE 5.2
Major Level or Focus of the CAIR Stories

Level	Number	Percentage
National	57	43.8
State	17	13.1
Local	50	38.5
Other	6	4.6
Totals	130	100.0

TABLE 5.3
Source of Records Used to Develop the CAIR Stories

Source	Number	Percentage
Federal agency	82	63.1
State agency	22	16.9
Local agency	22	16.9
Private agency	2	1.5
Other	1	0.8
Not clear	1	0.8
Totals	130	100.0

data, it appeared that a number of other newspapers followed with a similar investigation of their own. Many of these investigated the same topic, but used data collected from their region of the country. For example, several stories examined the changing demographic characteristics of their own state or county as reflected in the 1990 census data. Thus, it is clear that many news organizations found information of interest to their local readers within federal databases. Data from state and local agencies consisted mainly of court records, traffic violations, and criminal prosecutions. Other data sources included the Federal Aviation Administration, the National Highway Transportation Safety Administration, the Federal Bureau of Investigation, and the Federal Deposit Insurance Corporation. Only two of the 130 CAIR analyses used records from a private agency.

Table 5.4 shows that almost three-fourths of these computer-assisted investigations were developed from data on magnetic tape. Less than one third transformed paper documents into electronic information for analysis. At the same time, one in five took the time to develop their own databases from multiple sources.

TABLE 5.4
General Procedures Used to Develop the CAIR Stories

Procedure	Number	Percentage[a]
Analyzed one or more tapes obtained from source	96	73.8
Transformed paper records to electronic form	53	33.1
Developed unique database from multiple sources	26	20.0
Other	6	4.6

[a]Does not add to 130 stories or 100% because some stories used more than one procedure.

TABLE 5.5
Analytical Techniques Used in Developing CAIR Stories

Strategy	Number	Percentage[a]
Assignment to categories	121	93.1
Frequency count	104	80.0
Percent, ratio, fraction	100	76.9
Cross-tabulation	99	76.2
Single value search/Citation	97	74.6
Rank order	82	63.1
Contrast comparison	78	60.0
Numerical variability	59	45.4
Before–After comparison	51	39.2
Numerical trend	45	34.6
Mean/Average	42	32.3
Simple association	27	20.8
Cross-referencing	26	20.0
Median	17	13.1
Matched comparison	7	5.4
Construct index or scale	7	5.4
Select sample	4	3.1
Statistical projection	4	3.1
Multifactor association	3	2.3
Probability of an event	2	1.5
Hypothesis testing	1	0.8
Confidence limits	1	0.8

[a]Does not add to 100 because more than one procedure may have been used.

Finally, Table 5.5 focuses directly on the principal question raised at the beginning of this section; that is, it shows what specific techniques are being used with what frequency by reporters as they make use of electronic records or develop their own databases for analyses. Clearly, the table suggests that most computer-assisted stories are based, at least in part, on the four strategies advocated by Jaspin. Searching, which appears in the table as *single-value search/citation,* is the first of the four strategies discussed earlier. It was used in approximately three fourths of the stories. Counting, noted as *frequency counting* in the table, was found in 80% of the analyses. Sorting, which is the basis of *assignment to categories* listed in Table 5.5, is the most frequently used technique of all, having been employed in over 93% of the stories. Finally, matching by cross-indexing, identified as *cross-referencing* in the table, was used less often, in only 20% of the stories.

The techniques advocated by Meyer as simple first steps in an analysis were cross-tabulation and comparison of means. Comparisons of means were involved in several of the categories listed in Table 5.5 (i.e., in some of the before–after comparisons, in a few of the matched comparisons, and in some of the numerical trends). However, the strategy was seldom used in the statistical sense common in social science or other research, along with a probability interpretation. Finally, such procedures as hypothesis testing, statistical projections, calculating confidence limits of parameters obtained from samples, and others were used by very few.

Although the four procedures advocated by Jaspin were well represented, many of these analyses also employed other procedures. On average, 7.5 of the listed techniques were used in each of the stories. The number of techniques used in the 130 stories ranged from a low of 2 to an impressive high of 14. However, it must be pointed out that some reporters did not do a good job of explaining what had been done. They displayed a poor understanding of statistical terms and concepts, and in a few cases appeared to draw inappropriate conclusions from the data.

IMPLICATIONS OF THE REVIEW

Obviously, no final or definitive conclusions from this set of stories can be projected to the population of CAIR stories published in all newspapers in the United States. Certainly, they did not reveal the existence of a well-developed and standardized CAIR methodology. However, the findings do have several implications.

1. Journalists who have turned to electronic records and computers during the last several years to develop CAIR analyses are pursuing serious goals that fit closely with those that have always characterized investigative journalism. That is, they are probing the performance of public officials and agencies of government at all levels in order to determine if and how well they are performing their missions. The focus of these stories has been on the kinds of issues that have always attracted the attention of the watchdog press—politics, crime, equality, financial misbehavior, and so forth.

2. The most intensive focus of attention of these stories was on national issues (although local issues were well represented). The large number of stories derived from national data may be due to the timing of the release of certain data from federal sources. Such agencies as the U.S. Census Bureau make information available that lends itself to computer analyses of local conditions and trends. Although both state and local data were also analyzed, only one third of the data came from these sources combined.

3. The resource used most often in these analyses was magnetic tape, although many developed databases from paper records. A surprising number constructed their own unique databases from diverse sources to investigate a particular situation.

4. Meyer's concern that the majority of journalists involved in computer-assisted projects are using relatively simple techniques appears to have some basis in fact. By far, the most frequently used techniques in these stories closely resembled those advocated by Jaspin. However, one would expect these basic procedures to be present in higher numbers than the more advanced techniques. On the other hand, only a small number of stories employed additional procedures that made more extensive use of the power of a computer. Almost none used statistical parameters (beyond means and percentages) that computers can readily calculate. Few mentioned probability as a basis for interpreting the significance of findings. It would appear, then, that the "computer cowboy" charge by Meyer has merit.

The results of the review are tentative, but what are the implications of these findings regarding a CAIR methodology? As noted earlier, one clear implication is that a formal and systematic methodology for CAIR analyses needs further development. Many of the specific techniques now being employed by journalists in their computer-assisted investigations can be incorporated into that methodology. A related issue is that relatively few journalists currently seem to go beyond the basics. That is, they appear to fit the "computer cowboy" category identified by Meyer. An important question concerns why; that is, what accounts for the fact that working journalists, who are trying to meet the challenges posed by the computerization of records, are not using a more extended range of analytical strategies in their projects?

One possible explanation is that they simply lack the skills needed for more advanced use of computers. That explanation does not seem particularly consistent with important facts. A number of the CAIR projects summarized earlier in this chapter, and certainly many of those examined in the review of the 130 news stories, were developed by individuals or teams of specialists who demonstrated advanced levels of knowledge.

Another possible explanation is that relatively basic analytic strategies and techniques, such as those listed in the upper half of Table 5.5, represent a level most readily understood by newspaper readers. It may be that reporters are convinced that if they use and try to describe more complex techniques, their readers will be unable to comprehend what the analyses have revealed. There is no answer for this in the present data, but it is commonly perceived that the average newspaper reader has a short attention span, is more interested in entertainment than enlightenment, and cannot be expected to grasp a complex analysis.[7]

In retrospect, however, the reader-limitation explanation does not seem adequate. As the dictionary prepared for this study shows, relatively complex kinds of analyses can be reported in a form that readers can follow. For example, even a multifactor association can be defined and illustrated in ways that nontechnical readers can understand. If reader limitations are leading some journalists to limit their analysis to very simple levels, an important part of the methodology for CAIR should include ways in which relatively complex statistical findings can be explained to nontechnical readers in ways they can understand.

In conclusion, this chapter has shown that journalists currently conducting CAIR analyses are making use of a long list of techniques, procedures, and strategies. In many respects, these include some of the approaches used and advocated by those who pioneered the field. They also include a number of additional analytical techniques. At the same time, the relative frequency with which various techniques and procedures were used in contemporary CAIR stories indicates that the majority are seldom based on the more powerful research and statistical tools that computers can easily handle. However, in defense of contemporary journalists, there are two reasons to suggest that the computer cowboy analogy may be unnecessarily harsh. First, there is a well-established belief among journalists that audiences will have difficulty following a complex analysis. The second is that the procedures currently in use represent a kind of loose collection of techniques and strategies based on common sense and what earlier CAIR pioneers used in their investigations. The implication here, of course, is that contemporary CAIR analysts who limit themselves to basic procedures do so because they do not yet have available a more fully developed formal methodology on which consensus exists to which they can turn when designing their projects. Once such a methodology has been formally stated, debated, and refined, it seems likely that investigative journalists will more easily be able to make use of increasingly standardized and sophisticated techniques and procedures of analysis and widely accepted rules for decision making to achieve their goals. Finally, as investigative reporters improve their ability to analyze computerized databases, they must also develop ways of communicating their procedures and findings so that their readers can understand the conclusions reached from the analysis. In the chapters that follow, some initial steps are taken toward the improvement of both a formal CAIR methodology and a set of guidelines for reporting results to the public.

NOTES AND REFERENCES

1. David Burnham, "Trying to Cover the New York City Crime Scene," paper prepared for a symposium on computer-assisted investigative reporting at the S. I. Newhouse School of Public Communications at Syracuse University, May, 1989.
2. Ruth Walker, "Computer Databases Can Be Valuable Sources," the *Christian Science Monitor,* September 25, 1990, Media Section, p. 14.
3. Elliot Jaspin, "Out With the Paper Chase, In With the Database," speech given to participants of a technology studies seminar at the Freedom Forum Center for Media Studies at Columbia University, March 20, 1989; see also: Elliot Jaspin, "The New Investigative Journalism: Exploring Public Records by Computer," in John V. Pavlik and Everette E. Dennis, *Demystifying Media Technology* (Mountain View, Calif.: Mayfield Publishing Company, 1993), pp. 142–149.
4. Teresa Leonard, "Databases in the Newsroom: Computer-Assisted Reporting," *Online,* Vol. 16, No. 3, p. 62.
5. Philip Meyer, *The New Precision Journalism* (Bloomington: Indiana University Press, 1991), pp. 195–196, 204–205.
6. Philip Meyer, "Reporting in the 21st Century," presentation at AEJMC in Montreal, August, 1992.
7. Herbert J. Gans, *Deciding What's News* (New York: Vintage Books, 1980), pp. 229–342.

6

Analyzing Large-Scale Electronic Records: An Example Using Data From the Federal Courts

This chapter provides an example of a large-scale CAIR project. Although the example focuses on a specific agency—the U.S. Federal Court system—the techniques, procedures, and strategies described can serve as guides for analyses of many other kinds of records. This detailed case study describes the problems and limitations of the raw data received from the agency, the process of converting the raw data to a form suitable for statistical analysis, and comprehensive reviews of the records that enabled the investigator to identify specific issues and goals for analysis. Finally, typical errors and problems that reporters are likely to encounter when using databases of government records are illustrated and explanations are offered as to why these occur and how they pose problems for investigative analyses.

The data used in the example consist of the electronic records of the Federal Court system for the entire United States that accumulated over an 18-year period (1970–1987). In their entirety, they include the records of 5.5 million cases of various kinds that were brought before the courts during the years indicated.

The purpose of the analysis is not so much to reveal the detailed workings of the Federal Courts, but to provide a conceptual understanding of procedures that may be needed to conduct a large-scale computer-assisted investigative inquiry. Therefore, it focuses on steps and processes rather than on a detailed presentation of the computer programming, the statistics used, or the findings of the study. In this way, the chapter adds additional elements to the foundation needed for improving a formal methodology for CAIR.

SELECTING RECORDS FOR STUDY

In 1989, a small research organization called Transactional Records Access Clearinghouse (TRAC) got its start at Syracuse University. The organization was founded by David Burnham, a well-known investigative reporter, and Dr. Susan B. Long, a professor in the School of Management. TRAC's main focus would be the analysis of the computerized records of agencies of the federal government.

Burnham had worked as an investigative reporter for the *New York Times,* UPI, CBS, and *Newsweek.* He had specialized in examining the performance of various kinds of government agencies, such as the New York Police Department, the Nuclear Regulatory Commission, and the National Security Agency. He was completing an investigative book probing the policies and practices of the IRS.[1] For additional information, he turned to Long, an applied statistician and sociologist who had written several articles about taxpayers' compliance with tax laws and the efforts of the IRS to enforce these laws. For years, she had been collecting and analyzing computer records obtained from the IRS.

Their successful collaboration led Burnham and Long to realize the importance of bringing together the skills of journalists and researchers to monitor the performance of government agencies. By obtaining and analyzing the computerized records of other federal agencies, they saw that they could help other reporters and editors to discover how well the resources of government were managed. Using the FOIA, they wanted to acquire the internal administrative files of federal government agencies—files that the agencies develop themselves to monitor their own activities. The information in these records would show whether the agencies are achieving their stated goals, and demonstrate the nature and impact of federal regulatory and enforcement activities.

The computerized files of federal regulatory agencies are often extensive in scope and may include millions of transactions. Managing such massive files to turn the raw data into information useful to investigative reporters or others can require advanced computer technology. Burnham and Long recognized that few newsrooms had either the equipment or personnel with the skills that were needed. However, by using the supercomputing facilities of the university, they proposed to examine the databases of government records and to make the findings available to the press and to the public. The purpose of the organization, in other words, was "to improve the ability of journalists, Congress, academicians, and public interest groups to conduct effective oversight of federal enforcement agencies."[2]

Federal Court Data Become Available

Shortly after TRAC was established, work began on its first project. Burnham, who lived in Washington, DC and frequently consulted with representatives of federal agencies, learned that the Federal Judicial Center planned to make one of its large internal computer databases available to the public. The Federal Judicial Center is a government office that conducts research and educational projects for the U.S. Federal Courts. It developed and manages its computer systems. The Center also compiles and maintains detailed information about every criminal defendant and civil case appearing before a federal court.

Burnham contacted the Center's administrative officers to learn more about the database that was to be released. He learned that the information in the database was used to construct the annual reports summarizing the work load of the federal court system that were presented to Congress each year. Burnham also learned that, other than the agency itself, only a few legal scholars had access to these records.[3] Thus, the computerized files contained a wealth of information that had never been examined by the press. He also learned that it would not be necessary to file a Freedom of Information request with the agency in order to get the database. This meant that lengthy delays that often accompany such requests could be avoided. Burnham and Long thought that the federal judicial records would be an ideal database for TRAC to examine for its first project.

To obtain the records, Burnham and Long purchased several blank nine-track computer tapes and sent them to the Federal Judicial Center. The Center transferred the data to the tapes and returned them to TRAC. By this time, the author of this book had joined the team as Director of the project.[4]

The General Goals of the Investigation

The computerized database received by TRAC contained the records of approximately 5.5 million criminal, civil, and appeals cases covering the entire federal court system for the period of 1970 to 1987. Each individual record contained about 40 variables, for a total of more than 220 million "pieces" of information.

In addition to the records of the 5.5 million federal court cases, TRAC obtained census data covering each state and judicial district. These files contained data from the 1980 census and the 1983 county and city updates. They included detailed information about each state and district, such as the area in square miles, population, ethnicity, income, characteristics of the head of the household, the number of reported crimes, housing, level of education attained, labor force statistics, government finances, and statistics on manufacturers, wholesalers and retailers, the service industries, and agriculture. Population figures from the 1970 census were also included. In all, the census files contained a total of 233 variables recorded on magnetic tape.

When the computer tapes arrived from the Judicial Center, the TRAC team had only a general idea of their actual contents. Because of the massive size and complexity of the court database, a thorough understanding of its structure and contents could not be acquired without extensive examination and review of the files. It was not clear, for example, exactly which variables were recorded on the tapes. Until the files were studied, it was not possible to determine if significant portions of the data were missing or how useful all of the information would be for TRAC's purposes. This meant that only general goals could be formulated for the investigation at this point. Specific research questions could not be addressed until more was known about the database.

The team decided that the overall goal of TRAC's first project would be to evaluate the performance of U.S. Attorneys, the heads of each of the 94 federal judicial districts. Furthermore, the team hoped that the information in the database would reveal how well the Justice Department as a whole was fulfilling its mission of enforcing the criminal and civil laws of the United States.

TRAC was especially interested in the work of the U.S. Attorneys because so little attention had been given to their powerful roles. These prosecutors are extremely influential federal officials whose policy decisions have rarely been examined. As former Attorney General Robert H. Jackson noted: "The prosecutor has more control over life, liberty and reputation than any other person in America. His discretion is tremendous."[5]

The power and discretion of the prosecutors comes from several sources. The Judiciary Act, signed by President Washington in 1789, created a system of circuit and district courts.[6] It also established the office of the Attorney General and set forth the duties and responsibilities of the office. Finally, the act authorized the President to appoint marshals and U.S. Attorneys to carry out litigation duties in each of the federal districts.[7] Over the years, the duties of the Attorney General were expanded to include the supervision of U.S. Attorneys.[8]

At the present time, the litigation of the federal government is carried out for the Attorney General by the Justice Department and 94 U.S. Attorneys. The Justice Department, created in 1870, now employs more than 75,000 people and its budget in the fiscal year 1996 was $16.3 billion.[9]

These U.S. Attorneys, the federal prosecutors in charge of each of the 94 judicial districts, have the power to investigate, obtain documents, arrest individuals, ask federal grand juries for indictments, and bring civil charges. They also have the authority to negotiate settlements. In criminal cases, for example, they can agree to charge an individual with a lesser offense in return for a defendant's guilty plea. Equally important, prosecutors may decide not to investigate or prosecute a case. They may decline a case because evidence is lacking, because the matter is not considered to be important enough, or even for political reasons.[10]

The discretionary authority of U.S. Attorneys appears to have increased in recent years. Because of widespread concern over the great variation in sentences imposed in the federal court system, Congress passed the Sentencing Reform Act of 1984.[11] This act restricted the power of judges to decide the nature and length of sentences. The act required judges to provide reasons for the sentences imposed and to adhere to specific guidelines prepared by the U.S. Sentencing Commission.[12] Critics have argued, however, that the act simply shifts sentencing discretion from judges to the prosecutors.[13] This is because a particular offense may violate several statutes. Under the new guidelines, each statute carries its own (and often different) recommended sentence. When a charge is filed, however, it is the prosecutor who determines the statutory provision under which an individual is charged. This means that, in effect, the prosecutor also plays a role in selecting the sentence.

Although federal prosecutors have considerable authority and discretion, they have rarely been studied. Between 1978 and 1990, for example, the General Accounting Office (GAO) completed only two reports on the role of the prosecutors. The first study found that U.S. Attorneys prosecuted only 38% of the criminal complaints referred to them between 1970 and 1986.[14] The second report concluded that U.S. Attorneys lacked uniform policies to guide the handling of cases.[15] In contrast, the GAO completed more than 100 reports about the IRS.[16]

Only a few legal scholars have examined prosecutorial discretion. A 1972 study, for example, investigated matters referred to prosecutors from federal agencies.[17] A 1977 study examined the decisions of prosecutors within the Antitrust Division of the Justice Department.[18] The actions of U.S. Attorneys during the investigative and charging stages were studied in 1989.[19]

Journalists also have neglected the role of the prosecutors. David Burnham, a working journalist for more than 30 years, concluded that "only rarely have reporters attempted to assess the actual enforcement activities and policies of U.S. Attorneys."[20] He claimed that:

A close reading of the *New York Times,* the *Washington Post,* the *Wall Street Journal,* and other major American papers shows that a large proportion of the articles about federal, state, and local prosecutors actually consist of formal announcements or informal leaks by these offices. The most typical articles concern the indictment of well-known individuals such as Imelda Marcos and Ivan Boesky, or the investigation of some other notorious or powerful person.[21]

It was clear, then, that the public as well as the government would benefit from an in-depth examination of the activities of the U.S. Attorneys. It was appropriate, therefore, that the goal of TRAC's first project was to evaluate the performance of prosecutors in each of the federal judicial districts.

REVIEWING THE RECORDS

It must be kept in mind that the records of any federal agency are compiled year after year over long periods of time. The information in them may be recorded by hundreds of clerks of different skill levels who are located in states, districts, or counties throughout the United States. For example, there are 94 U.S. Federal Court districts that include Guam, Puerto Rico, and the Northern Marianna Islands. The personnel who entered the information in these records include individuals in prosecutors' offices as well as those who kept track of actions and decisions made by judges in federal courtrooms. Throughout the years that the records were kept, there were changes in personnel, in record format, in the kinds of information collected, and in the ways in which the information was recorded. Thus, when the judicial records arrived, they were in many ways an "unknown territory." Although the general contents of the files were known, the database needed to be explored further and studied closely before specific analyses could be designed.

The Initial Examination

The computer tapes contained about 60 files. Each was a collection of similar records. To illustrate, one file contained all of the criminal defendants whose cases terminated during 1970. Another included all the civil cases that were decided in 1970. The appeals cases for the same year were in another file; those cases still pending in another. In other words, there were separate files for each year for each set of criminal, civil, and appeals cases. Furthermore, each of the major types of files—criminal, civil, appeals, and census—had a different set of variables.

The data were received in raw form. This meant that the entire database would have to be converted to software before any significant manipulation or analysis could begin. The first task was to determine exactly what variables the records contained, how those variables were arranged on the tapes, and whether their positions were consistent with the descriptions in the accompanying printed documentation. The purpose of this task was to begin an assessment of the accuracy and completeness of the records.

In more specific terms, an initial assessment of the records was conducted by preparing a printout of about 100 lines of the entries for each file on the tapes. These printouts showed the packed raw numbers as they exist in the files—no variable names, spaces, headings, or anything else. Documents provided by the Judicial Center were consulted to determine where each variable should begin and end. These documents showed what kind of information was supposed to be in each column. This was a check, in other words, of whether the information and position of each variable in each file was consistent with the descriptions in the documentation.

This initial examination confirmed the presence and exact position of each variable in each file. It also revealed a problem. The printouts showed that, in each of the civil files, the names of the presiding judges had been deleted from the tapes. This meant that TRAC would be unable to investigate the performance of the judges. TRAC had hoped that such an investigation could be a part of its project.

The Conversion of EBCDIC Files to SAS Files

The files were received as raw EBCDIC files on magnetic tape. EBCDIC (Extended Binary Coded Decimal Interchange Code) files are encoded in a sort of "base" language—similar in concept to ASCII files for personal computers. This allows EBCDIC files to be moved to other computers and imported into any software. However, the data in the files cannot be analyzed in this form. Thus, the raw files on the federal court tapes had to be transferred to new files in a software format that the mainframe computer could use for statistical calculations and other operations. Essentially, this meant that programs had to be written in a software language. These programs told the computer where to get the data on the tapes to move to disk; they named each of the variables and specified its location, indicated whether each variable was character (composed of letters) or numeric, and specified other needed information. The programs converted the EBCDIC files to SAS software for mainframe computers.

Because they contained not only the original numbers, but the new programming, the resulting SAS files were much larger than the raw EBCDIC files. It quickly became clear that an enormous amount of computer disk space would be needed for this project. First, vast amounts of disk space would be required just to "park" or store the data. The computer would also require additional "thrashing around" space in order to sort and manipulate the data during statistical calculations.

The investigator calculated the minimum amount of additional disk space that would be needed simply to store the files for the project. To say the least, it was very large. The investigator sent a request to the systems administrator for at least an additional 2,000 cylinders of assigned fixed disk space. That individual set back the following reply:

> It is impossible both now and in the foreseeable future to ever give you a 2,000 cylinder minidisk since an entire dedicated volume is not that big! And 2,000 cylinders is about the total available on all 48 volumes [of the super-computer]. I'll give you one of our few remaining contiguous chunks of space (420 cylinders).

One of the first difficult problems encountered, then, was simply to obtain enough storage and disk space to conduct the analysis.

In most mainframe or networked computer environments, disk space is divided up and allocated to a large number of users. There is seldom a lot of surplus remaining. Thus, a user who suddenly needs a huge amount of extra disk space cannot always obtain it. Although the investigator did obtain additional computer space for this project, it was clear that adequate space would always be a problem. In fact, some of the short-term strategies devised by the investigator to find temporary storage resulted in considerable problems that affected the entire computer system. For example, a system manager sent the following message to the investigator after one such attempt:

> We noticed that system space is in a critical situation and getting pretty full in recent days. Further analysis shows that you have sent a total of 1,817,938 records or files in the past few days. Please process the reader files as soon as possible to avoid system crash. We may need to dump your reader files to tape at any time to save the system.

To help remedy the space problem, additional programs were written to compress the data in each file and force it to fit in less space. Although this worked, more space was still needed, and additional solutions were devised. To explain, the computing platform that supported this project was an IBM 3090-150 running a VM/CMS operating system. This supercomputer system allowed the investigator to access unused and unassigned disk space on a temporary basis for up to 24 hours at a time. Furthermore, the investigator "borrowed" unused disk space assigned to others (with their permission, of course). Thus, throughout the project, various structures of assigned, borrowed, and temporary disk space were patched together, often for several hours late at night. This was not always a happy solution—interruptions and fluctuations in the power or the phone lines sometimes caused the loss of a night's work.

A Detailed Examination of the Records

After the raw data had been transferred to software, a more comprehensive check on the nature and the completeness of the entries for each variable in each file was conducted. The first step here was to write programs to provide printouts of the simple *frequencies* of all of the variables and the values within each variable. In the criminal court records, for example, one of the variables in the database was the *filing offense*. This is the most serious offense with which a defendant was charged when the case was originally filed. The frequency distribution for this variable revealed how many defendants had been charged with a particular offense during a year. During the first 6 months of 1987, for example, 57,667 defendants were initially charged with 174 different major offenses. The printout showing the distribution of each filing offense is too lengthy to reproduce here, but it included the information shown in Table 6.1.

The first row in the displayed distribution shows that no filing offense was recorded for 53 of the defendants. The missing information is coded as −8 in the database. The code 0100 in the second row shows that a total of 92 individuals (0.2%) were charged with first-degree murder. In the third row, one person was charged with the first-degree murder of a government official (code 0101), and so on.

The distribution is important for several reasons. The first reason is to discover how completely the information has been recorded. In this case, 53 missing filing offense codes pose no serious problem, because the information is available for 99.9% of the defendants. If the information had been missing for a large number of the defendants, however, it would have been impossible to do any kind of analysis based on the filing offense code.

The printout of the frequency distribution (see Table 6.1) also provides an indication of promising directions for the analysis. The investigator can see at a glance which offenses were committed most (or least) frequently. This might be a starting point for the design of a specific analysis that will pursue the question of "why."

The distribution also allows the investigator to compare each value of a particular variable in the database with the paper documentation provided. In this case, each filing offense code was checked against the documenta-

TABLE 6.1
Filing Offense Code

Cumulative Percentage	Code	Frequency	Percentage	Cumulative Frequency
.	−8	53	.	53
0.1	0100 (1st degree murder)	92	0.2	145
0.3	0101 (1st degree murder of government official)	1	0.0	146
0.3	0200 (2nd degree murder)	46	0.1	192
0.3	0300 (manslaughter)	20	0.0	212
0.4	0301 (manslaughter of government official)	1	0.0	213
0.4	0310 (negligent homicide)	19	0.0	232
0.4	0311 (negligent homicide of government official)	2	0.0	234
0.4	0437 [apparent error]	1	0.0	235
0.4	1100 (bank robbery)	1614	2.8	1849
3.2	1200 (postal robbery)	56	0.1	1905
3.3	1400 (other robbery)	47	0.1	1952
3.4	1500 (aggravated assault)	615	1.1	2567
4.5	1560 (aggravated assault, Fair Housing Law)	2	0.0	2569
4.5	1600 (other aggregated assault)	156	0.3	2725
4.7	1601 (assault of government official)	1	0.0	2726
4.7	2100 (burglary, bank)	15	0.0	2741

(continued)

TABLE 6.1
(Continued)

Cumulative Percentage	Code	Frequency	Percentage	Cumulative Frequency
4.8	2200 (burglary, postal office)	35	0.1	2776
4.8	2300 (burglary, Interstate Commerce)	9	0.0	2785
4.8	2400 (burglary, other)	83	0.1	2868
5.0	3100 (larceny/theft, bank)	236	0.4	3104
5.4	3200 (larceny/theft, postal)	714	1.2	3818
6.6	3300 (larceny/theft, Interstate Commerce)	389	0.7	4207
7.3	3400 (larceny/theft, U.S. Property)	1766	3.1	5973
10.4	3600 (transportation of stolen property)	447	0.8	6420
11.1	3700 (larceny/theft, felony)	208	0.4	6628
11.5	3800 (larceny/theft, misdemeanor)	499	0.9	7127
12.4	4100 (embezzlement/fraud, bank)	1063	1.8	8190
14.2	4200 (embezzlement/fraud, postal)	406	0.7	8596
14.9	4310 (embezzlement/fraud, public money or property)	383	0.7	8979
15.6	4320 (embezzlement/fraud, credit, insurance institution)	358	0.6	9337
16.2	4330 (embezzlement/fraud, by officers of a carrier)	4	0.0	9341

tion. Did the documentation define the meaning of each offense code? Were there "extra" offense codes in the data for which there was no description?

To explain, the distribution indicated that one person was charged with offense 0437. The codebook that came with the database, however, did not list any code 0437. This meant that an error had been discovered, either in the data or in the codebook. A call to the Federal Judicial Center confirmed that there was an error in the data. No such offense code existed and this piece of information had been entered incorrectly. Obviously, if too many errors are present, the variable would be unusable.

This process was repeated for each variable in each of the 60 files. When this step had been completed, a summary chart was constructed from the printouts of the frequency distributions for each of the criminal and civil files. These summary charts listed how completely the information was recorded in each year—whether the information appeared to be complete (C), incomplete (I), or missing entirely (left blank). A portion of the criminal chart, for example, is shown in Table 6.2.

This chart shows at a glance that information on the judicial circuit, district, and office in which the defendant was charged was recorded completely for all of the years. Many other variables were also complete, such as the docket number, filing date, offense code, the interval in months between the filing of the charges and the termination of the case, and the number of months in prison or probation to which a convicted defendant was sentenced. Information on the defendant's counsel, such as whether the defense attorney was a court-appointed attorney, private attorney, or whether the defendant represented himself or herself, was complete except in 1987. Information about the defendant's gender and race was noted sometimes (i.e., incompletely) in 1970, and the years 1973 to 1983; it was missing or mostly missing in the years 1971, 1972, and after 1983. The marital status of the defendants was recorded only during 3 years, and even then much of this information was missing. This meant that it probably would not be possible to do an analysis of the defendants' backgrounds and demographic characteristics. Several other variables had considerable information missing.

In this manner, the completeness of the entire body of records was examined and studied. This was a time-consuming but very important process. Because this was a complex database, the analyses could not begin until the investigator had thorough knowledge of its contents. The investigator also needed to have confidence in the levels of accuracy, validity, and reliability of the data. Only then did the investigator know which kinds of questions could be addressed or answered with confidence using these data.

TABLE 6.2
Criminal Court Records

Variable	Year																	
	70	71	72	73	74	75	76	77	78	79	80	81	82	83	84	85	86	87
Circuit	C	C	C	C	C	C	C	C	C	C	C	C	C	C	C	C	C	C
District	C	C	C	C	C	C	C	C	C	C	C	C	C	C	C	C	C	C
Office	C	C	C	C	C	C	C	C	C	C	C	C	C	C	C	C	C	C
Docket number	C	C	C	C	C	C	C	C	C	C	C	C	C	C	C	C	C	C
Defendant number	C	C	C	C	C	C	C	C	C	C	C	C	C	C	C	C	C	C
Filing date	C	C	C	C	C	C	C	C	C	C	C	C	C	C	C	C	C	C
Proceeding code	C	C	C	C	C	C	C	C	C	C	C	C	C	C	C	C	C	C
Filing offense	C	C	C	C	C	C	C	C	C	C	C	C	C	C	C	C	C	C
Termination date	C	C	C	C	C	C	C	C	C	C	C	C	C	C	C	C	C	C
Interval	C	C	C	C	C	C	C	C	C	C	C	C	C	C	C	C	C	C
Termination offense	C	C	C	C	C	C	C	C	C	C	C	C	C	C	C	C	C	C
Offense disposition	C	C	C	C	C	C	C	C	C	C	C	C	C	C	C	C	C	C
Counsel	C	C	C	C	C	C	C	C	C	C	C	C	C	C	C	C	C	I
Termination judge							C	I	C	I	C	I	I	I	I	I	I	I
Sentence category	I	I	I	I	I	I	I	I	I	I	I	I	I	I	I	I	I	I
Statute	I	I	I	I	I	I	I	I	I	I	I	I	I	I	I	I	I	I

Variable	Year																	
	70	71	72	73	74	75	76	77	78	79	80	81	82	83	84	85	86	87
Sentence type	I	I	I	I	I	I	I	I	C	I	C	I	I	I	I	I	I	I
Prison term	C	C	C	C	C	C	C	C	C	C	C	C	C	C	C	C	C	C
Probation term	C	C	C	C	C	C	C	C	C	C	C	C	C	C	C	C	C	C
Fine	C	C	C	C	C	C	C	C	C	C	C	C	C	C	C	I	I	I
Sex	I	C	C	I	I	I	I	I	I	I	I	I	I	I	I	I	I	
Race	I	C	C	I	I	I	I	I	I	I	I	I	I	I	I			
Birth year	C			I	I	I	I	I	I	I	I	C	I	I	I			
Marital status									I	I	I	I	I	I				
Education												I	I	I				
Presentence inves.	I			I					I	C	C	I	I	C				
Defendant name																		
Filing off. level												C	C	C	C	C	C	C
Termination level												C	C	C	C	C	C	C

Note. C = Information is complete. I = Information is incomplete. Blank spaces = Missing information.

IDENTIFYING SPECIFIC ISSUES FOR ANALYSIS

Selecting the specific objectives of a CAIR analysis is a unique process. CAIR analyses may differ in many ways from other forms of inquiry. In most social science research projects, for example, the goals are stated and defined before data are gathered. These goals usually address the ways in which an antecedent condition influences a dependent situation or outcome. In a project such as the judicial records analysis, in contrast, the data are whatever are on the tape. No further data can be gathered and the objectives must be shaped post facto by what the records contain. Thus, only after the contents of the database are well understood, and their completeness and accuracy assessed, can specific research questions be formulated.

Deciding on the specific goals of a CAIR analysis, however, involves more than computer skills and data manipulation. Selecting the objectives is also a creative activity that depends on the intuitive judgment and the news values of the reporter. All of the insights and skills of the investigative reporter, in other words, are joined with the technical expertise of the computer analyst to produce newsworthy information.

An example of this working relationship is demonstrated by an event that occurred at an early point in the project. The team learned that a U.S. attorney had declared himself a candidate for the office of mayor of New York City. This event created a unique opportunity to provide timely information of interest to the public. The project team saw that they could examine the candidate's actual record of prosecutions while in office and compare this to the candidate's claims during the heat of a campaign.

The Mayoral Race in New York City

In the fall of 1989, Rudolph Giuliani won his party's primary election and became the Republican candidate for mayor of New York City. He ran against David Dinkins, the democratic nominee, in a highly publicized and often bitter campaign.

Early in the campaign, Giuliani declared that "crime, crack, and corruption" were the major issues facing the city. Dinkins intoned that the city needed a mayor who could heal the city's racial divisions and "bring people together." Although the campaign included many harsh attacks on personal integrity and character, these issues remained as dominant concerns.[22]

Rudolph Giuliani knew a lot about "crime, crack, and corruption." Not only was he was born and raised in New York City, but also he had served as an assistant U.S. attorney in the Southern District (the Manhattan area) of New York from 1970 to 1975. Later, he rose to the position of associate Attorney General for the entire United States, the "number three" job in the Justice Department. In this position, he supervised all 94 U.S. Attorneys in the country, including the Southern District's.

In June 1983, Giuliani willingly gave up his high position in the Justice Department to accept President Reagan's appointment to return to the Southern District of New York as the U.S. Attorney. He did this because the Manhattan area is a center for major criminal and civil cases. The U.S. Attorney in this district receives a great deal of attention and publicity. Some people think, therefore, that the appointment is one of the most coveted federal law enforcement jobs in the country.[23] Giuliani held this position from 1983 to 1989, when he decided to enter the mayoral race.

During the campaign, Giuliani proudly stated that he had dramatically increased the prosecution of drug offenses and aggressively pursued cases of white-collar crime, organized crime, and public corruption while he was in office. Critics responded that Giuliani had flooded the courts with low-level drug dealers and neglected more important matters. Others charged that he had focused too much attention on high-profile cases of well-known individuals simply to use them as a stepping stone to a political career. No one, however, had completed a thorough and factual examination of all of the cases he had prosecuted.

Many of the cases Giuliani prosecuted involved drugs, racketeering, and corruption, or so it seemed from news reports. He conducted dramatic "sting" operations and achieved convictions of groups such as electrical inspectors and sewer workers for accepting bribes and other corrupt practices. In his first year as prosecutor, he brought criminal charges against the employees of six law firms, 10 securities firms, one accounting firm, and one printing firm for insider trading. During one 9-month period alone, 22 people were indicted on charges of stock trading based on information not available to the public.[24] Not only were white-collar criminals pursued, but he also concentrated on drug partnerships in lower Manhattan. Following an 18-month investigation, for example, 30 people from two drug-trafficking rings that worked together were arrested and charged with distributing and conspiring to distribute narcotics. These two rings had sold $200 million in heroin and $30 million in cocaine during a 3-month period.[25]

Certainly it was true that Giuliani had prosecuted many well-known individuals in highly publicized cases. For example, he obtained the racketeering indictments of two close associates of Attorney General Edwin Meese as part of the investigation into the Wedtech scandal. Giuliani charged that E. Robert Wallach and W. Franklyn Chinn defrauded Wedtech and its shareholders of money and control of how the money was spent, misrepresented the value and performance of Wedtech stock, and fraudulently sold Wedtech stock to the public.[26] In another case, Giuliani brought charges against three reputed Genovese crime family mobsters for killing a police detective who was investigating their bookmaking and loan-sharking business.[27] In another prominent case, Ivan Boesky, who led Wall Street's biggest insider-trading scandal, pled guilty to criminal charges and was sentenced to 3 years in prison.[28] Giuliani also successfully prosecuted the directors of Drexel Burnham Lambert, the Wall Street investment firm, for securities law violations. The directors pled guilty to six violations and were fined $650 million.[29]

From these highly publicized cases, Giuliani appeared to be an active and successful prosecutor. Certainly, his policies and practices influenced the lives of a very large number of people. Furthermore, the election of the mayor of New York City often generated a lot of interest and media attention around the country. For these reasons, the TRAC project team concluded that an analysis of Giuliani's actual prosecutorial record could be contrasted with his election claims. Such a disclosure would be of interest to the news media and important to the public. Therefore, an examination of the number and kinds of criminal and civil cases that were prosecuted while Giuliani was the U.S. Attorney in the Southern District of New York would be a major focus of the project.

A Comparison of Major Judicial Districts

Although Giuliani's record would receive close attention, it was clear that the project would have to highlight other districts as well. Media groups and individuals who would be interested in Giuliani's record surely would want a standard by which to compare his performance. They would want to know what the U.S. Attorneys in other judicial districts had done during the same time period. How many and what kinds of cases had they prosecuted? Were there differences in the caseload even when the population of the district was considered? Did a heavy emphasis on criminal matters result in little attention to civil cases or the reverse? Or, if particular attention was given to specific criminal matters such as drug offenses, did the prosecution of other criminal offenses such as embezzlement and fraud decrease? Did the picture change when a new U.S. Attorney was appointed within a district?

It was also clear that in order to compare the performance of prosecutors in different districts effectively, the districts would have to be as similar as possible. That is, the composition of the population, the proportion of the people who live in urban or rural areas, and the economic conditions of the districts would have to be substantially alike. Only then would a fair comparison be possible.

Using the computerized census data that TRAC had obtained, the investigator began to determine which districts had similar characteristics. The census tapes contained 233 variables that were converted to a SAS dataset. The data listed the *number* of people who had a particular characteristic, such as those who were female or Hispanic, or who had graduated from high school. To select comparable districts, however, it also was important to know the *percentage* of the population that these numbers represented. The investigator therefore wrote programs to calculate these percentages for all of the relevant variables and for each of the districts. The percentage of families with a female head of household, for example, was obtained by dividing the number of families with a female head by the total number of families and multiplying by 100. The result was coded as a new variable and made a part of the permanent census data file.

Next, a multivariate statistical procedure called *cluster analysis* was performed on census variables to separate the districts into distinct groups.[30] This procedure classifies entities in a data set into relatively homogenous groups. Cluster analysis is most appropriate when the structure of the groupings has not been determined in advance. In this case, it was hoped that the districts that were most alike would "cluster" together.

All 94 of the districts were examined using a lengthy list of demographic and economic indicators. These included age, birth rate, race, educational level, income level, unemployment rate, households and individuals below the poverty level, rate of reported crimes, population density, and the proportion who lived in urban and rural areas. Also included were the percentage of the labor force who were self-employed, or who worked in manufacturing, wholesale/retail, the service industries, health and education, or government. Economic variables included the revenue generated from each of these sectors, revenue received from the state, from property and other taxes, from sales and gross receipts, and the revenue per capita for the district. Finally, per capita spending on education, welfare, health, police protection, and the local government's outstanding debt as a per person share were factored into the cluster analysis.

The results obtained from the cluster analysis were not entirely satisfactory. One of the reasons was that a vast variety of methods have been developed for performing cluster analysis, and the methods often yield inconsistent results.[31] Some methods are based on least-squares, Euclidean distances, or arithmetic averages. Other methods require multivariate normality, equal variances, or are sensitive to outliers or abnormal values. Although there is general agreement that the methods with the best overall performance are average linkage and Ward's minimum variance, experts recommend that more than one method should be used when cluster analysis is employed.[32] Then, if the outcomes from all of the methods are roughly consistent, a case for the groupings can be advanced.[33]

For this analysis, Ward's minimum variance was used along with other methods. As expected, the districts that were classified together differed depending on the method used and, in some cases, the number of clusters specified. In many of the trials, however, a basic "core" of districts emerged that clustered together with the Southern District of New York. Although additional districts included in the cluster changed from one trial to another, the districts in the core group often remained.

In addition to the cluster analysis, another procedure was used to identify similar districts. Again using the census data, each district was ranked from highest to lowest on the demographic and economic variables noted earlier. By sorting each of the variables such as population density and rate of reported crimes, for example, the districts with the highest population density and crime rate were listed first in the printout. In this way it was easy to see which districts ranked closely together repeatedly. In fact, many of the same districts that appeared in the core group of the cluster analysis showed up together in the ranking procedure as well. In other words, the ranking procedure seemed to confirm the selection of similar districts and gave the investigator additional confidence in the results.

Nine federal judicial districts were selected because cluster analysis showed them to be most similar on a variety of economic and demographic characteristics. Two additional districts bordering Giuliani's district were added to this list. Although these two districts were not always found within the core cluster, the project team decided to include them so that the entire New York metropolitan area would be covered. Furthermore, the project team thought that the results would be of increased interest to the news media during the election if Giuliani's neighboring districts were added for comparison. Thus, the final selection of districts resulted from the combined journalistic insights of the reporter and the statistical procedures used by the computer analyst. Each of the 11 districts finally selected included large metropolitan areas that were heavily urbanized. They were the following:

- *Massachusetts* (this district covers the entire state, including the Boston metropolitan area).

- *Connecticut* (this district covers the entire state, including the Hartford area).
- *Eastern New York* (Brooklyn is the major area included in this district).
- *Southern New York* (Manhattan is the major area included in this district).
- *New Jersey* (this district covers the entire state, including the Newark area).
- *Eastern Pennsylvania* (Philadelphia is the major area included in this district).
- *Maryland* (this district covers the entire state, including the Baltimore area).
- *Eastern Michigan* (Detroit is the major area included in this district).
- *Northern Illinois* (Chicago is the major area included in this district).
- *Northern California* (San Francisco is the major area included in this district).
- *Central California* (Los Angeles is the major area included in this district).

These districts, then, would be highlighted in the study. The number of criminal and civil cases that were prosecuted in relation to the population would be assessed. The project would also examine the kinds of cases that were emphasized in each district. The use of multiple districts would allow individuals and groups to make meaningful comparisons between the districts and their prosecutors. Finally, the analysis had to be completed before the mayoral election in New York City, so that the public would have more information about one of the candidates, Rudolph Giuliani, a former prosecutor in the Southern District of New York.

Trends and Patterns for the United States

The similar districts that were selected for analysis represented highly urbanized, major metropolitan areas. Although there are 94 federal districts, these 11 "big city" districts filed almost 25% of all the criminal and civil cases in the United States. This means that the caseload for these districts was higher than the normal load experienced by the remaining districts in the United States. This disparity in work load underscored the need to examine the average caseload for the United States as a whole. Anyone studying the results of the analysis of the 11 districts naturally would want to know how the results compared to the rest of the U.S. Furthermore, if the workload of the "big city" districts differed considerably from the average, might there be other ways in which the 11 districts were significantly different from the rest of the country? Did the prosecutors in the highly urbanized 11 districts emphasize different kinds of criminal and civil cases than elsewhere? Did this picture change over a number of years?

The project team decided, therefore, that all of the statistics that would be presented on the 11 districts must also be presented for the United States as a whole. Furthermore, the statistics would be assembled for a number of years so that any trends or patterns in the districts or the U.S. could be spotted. Because of the enormous amount of data and insufficient disk space to store and process the data, however, the study would not include all of the years for which data were available. The project team decided to emphasize the more recent years 1980 through 1987.

In addition to the number of criminal and civil cases prosecuted in relation to the population and the kinds of cases emphasized in the 11 districts and the United States during the years 1980 through 1987, the project team wanted to investigate other matters of concern. Many authorities, for example, decried the larger caseloads and the use of the federal courts for mundane and trivial matters.[34] Others complained that increased drug use in the country during these years resulted in a vast number of criminal cases that were "clogging" the courts and causing delays in the processing of the cases. If this were so, had prosecutors increased the use of plea bargaining in order to dispose of the growing number of cases? Had drug offenses, as a percentage of all the criminal charges filed, really increased over the years? If so, what specific kinds of drug offenses were responsible for the increase? What percentage of defendants were convicted of the charges filed against them? Had this rate changed over the years?

The project team planned to assemble a report detailing the results of the study. The report would be distributed to newspapers and press groups around the country, the offices of the federal prosecutors in charge of the 11 districts, the Attorney General of the United States, and other interested individuals and groups.

The final report would consist mainly of tables and charts presenting statistics on the 11 districts and the United States. The report would be divided into three major sections: The first section would present statistics on criminal defendants, including the number of defendants per 100,000 population, a breakdown of the kinds of criminal charges filed with a special emphasis on drug offenses, conviction rates for all offenses, and the percentage of defendants whose cases were decided at the completion of a trial. The second section would present statistics on civil cases, including the number of cases filed per 100,000 population with a breakdown of those cases where the United States was the plaintiff in the suit (i.e., the U.S. brought charges against individuals or corporations) or where the United States was the defendant. This portion of the report would also show the prevalence of different kinds of civil suits. The final section of the report would contain additional information that would be helpful in interpreting the statistics, such as population characteristics of the districts and the number of full-time employees in each of the offices of the federal prosecutors.

COPING WITH ERRORS AND PROBLEMS IN GOVERNMENT DATA

The discussion of this project would be incomplete without attention to some of the many problems faced by the investigator while using the data compiled by the Federal Judicial Center. Any individual using government data is likely to discover that the data contain errors and problems. This is especially true with massive computerized databases that cover many geographical regions or collect data over a number of years. These errors and problems will determine the ways in which the data can or cannot be used. Such errors and problems can also affect the reliability of the results.

It is critically important that the investigator understands and is thoroughly acquainted with all aspects of the database. He or she should learn how the data were collected originally and how and when this information was entered into each of the files. The changes that were made to the database over the years should be studied. Finally, the investigator cannot assume that the government agency that maintains and uses the data is aware of all the problems within the database.

Certain kinds of problems may tend to occur frequently in large government databases. The section that follows lists some of the problems encountered in the judicial database and discusses how this affected the analyses. Many of these represent typical problems that any outside user of government data can expect to find.

Why Errors and Problems Occur in Government Records

There are any number of reasons why errors and problems occur in government databases. Some mistakes and inconsistencies are simply the result of human data entry error. Other problems, such as those that result from changes in laws, are generated by external forces and are beyond the control of the agency. The organization and design of the database itself can cause additional difficulties. Furthermore, errors and problems can occur at any point in a complex chain of data collection, data entry, data transfer, or compilation into a single database. For this reason, it is important to understand how the database was generated.

To illustrate, the information on the criminal, civil, and appeals cases contained in the integrated database compiled by the Federal Judicial Center originated in any of several offices within each of the 94 districts.[35] Standard case status forms, such as the JS-5 Filing Report and the JS-6 Termination Report for civil cases and the JS-2 Criminal Case Opening Report and the JS-3 Criminal Case Termination Report, recorded the details of each case. The forms were filled out by hundreds of clerks of different skill levels according to official instructions and manuals prepared by the Administrative Office of the United States Courts.[36]

The personnel who recorded the case information either on paper or in a computer changed considerably throughout the years. Frequent changes in personnel and repetitive data entry tasks are often cited as reasons for error. Errors are introduced for other reasons, too. In its instructions to users, for example, the Federal Judicial Center cautions that errors in data entry sometimes occurred because clerks continued coding a variable in a particular way out of habit, even after the coding practice had been discontinued. Other errors and inconsistencies in data entry occurred because districts sometimes recorded case information on outdated forms.

The instructions for recording information also changed considerably throughout the years. Often this happened because Congress passed new laws or changes in laws that mandated what kinds of information was to be reported. In order to comply with the requirements of the Speedy Trial Act of 1974, for example, significant changes were made in the criminal reporting system. This law instituted new rules for reporting misdemeanors assigned to magistrates and for tracking the amount of time involved in resolving a case. It also changed the rules for the kinds of cases that were to be reported and created new rules for indictments. New forms and instructions were issued to the districts to capture the new information. As a result, substantially different information was collected before and after the law took effect in 1976. This makes it difficult to compare cases completed before and after this period.

Varying modes, times, and origins of data entry are also responsible for problems in the database. By the late 1980s, for example, some of the offices had direct online connections to the main office of the district. Some of the main offices had online access to the Administrative Office of the U.S. Courts, which collected the data from around the country. Even as late as 1990, however, few offices were able to transmit the data directly by computer to the Administrative Office. Much of the information in the integrated database, especially in the earlier years, was copied from paper records passed from one office on to the next. Errors may have been introduced at any step in the process.

The organization of the database itself presented many problems. When a case was terminated, the information was forwarded to the main office of the district. This did not always happen immediately, however. The case folder, for example, may have remained on the desk of an assistant U.S. Attorney for some time before it was passed on. Eventually the records of the case were sent to the Administrative Office of the U.S. Courts. When the information was received by that office, it was entered into its file for that year, regardless of when the case was actually closed. In other words, it was counted as part of that year's work load, even though the case may have ended years before. In fact, a computer analysis showed that each of the annual files in the database contained a number of very old cases. The criminal cases in the 1980 file, for example, actually contained cases filed as early as 1963; the 1981 file had cases from 1954; the 1982 file contained a case from 1913.

An additional problem arose for the investigator because the "year" of the file represented a statistical year, rather than a calendar year. The statistical year in the federal courts runs from July through June. The 1984 file, to illustrate, covered the period of July 1, 1983 through June 30, 1984. Also, the cases were arranged in the database by the termination date, rather than the filing date.

All of these organizational matters—the old cases, the use of a statistical year and inclusion in the database by termination date—posed considerable difficulties for the TRAC project. The project team wanted to evaluate the performance of the federal prosecutors. This meant that each case had to be matched with the prosecutors' tenure in office. This could be done accurately only by converting to a calendar year instead of a statistical year. Next, the old cases needed to be removed from each year's file so that only the cases that were acted on during that year remained. Finally, because prosecutors exercise most of their discretion when a case is filed, the filing date of each case had to be tied to the prosecutor's actual time in office. To avoid inaccuracies, therefore, the entire database had to be reorganized by calendar year and filing date rather than statistical year and termination date.

The reorganization of the entire court database proved to be difficult and took considerable time. All of the files had to be returned to disk from backup tapes. New variables were created by splitting the filing date variable, which was in the form of YYMMDD, and extracting the year portion to tie the cases to a calendar year. Then, the millions of records were sorted and reorganized so that the cases that were filed during a particular year were placed into that year's datafile.

These problems that required a complete reorganization of the entire database illustrate an important point: Government databases, such as this, are designed for the agency's use and needs—not for reporters or other outside users. The use of a statistical year posed no problem for the agency; it was the same as their fiscal year and matched the way the agency accounted for all resources. Moreover, counting cases that were received late as part of the year's work load was efficient and prevented the agency from constantly having to reopen old files from previous years. The critical lesson is that outside users should not expect that an agency's database will be problem free for their purposes.

In summary, then, the errors and problems that are present in large databases, such as the judicial records in this example, are due to several factors:

1. Clerks of all skill levels, not just "rocket scientists," enter the data. They make errors, use outdated forms, and make some errors out of habit.
2. Varying modes, times, and origins of entry cause additional problems as the information is transmitted from one office to the next.
3. New laws are passed that change what information is to be collected.
4. Databases are designed for the agency's use, not for outsiders. Government agencies have specific requirements for reporting information, and data are collected to fit these requirements. In other words, some of the characteristics of the records may be "problems" only for outside users.

Examples of Typical Problems in Databases

Several kinds of problems may be found in government records and may occur frequently within the same database. Six such problems are illustrated here with examples from the federal judicial database. These problems concern the completeness of the variables and the consistency in the ways the information was recorded.

Are Values Recorded for Every Variable?   In the federal court database, the presence of each variable was indicated by numbers or letters. To indicate the type of counsel used by the defendant, for example, the number 2 meant that the defendant hired a private attorney; the number 3 meant that the defendant waived his or her right to an attorney; a 4 indicated that the defendant served as her or his own attorney; and a 6 showed that the defendant was represented by a public defender.

The information for some variables, however, was completely missing. Although present for the civil cases, the name of the defendant in the criminal records was erased before the database was released for public use. This was expected because privacy laws restrict the kind of information that can be released about individuals in criminal matters. Furthermore, the FOIA exempts from disclosure those records or information compiled for law enforcement purposes when the information may interfere with enforcement proceedings, deprive a person of a fair trial or impartial adjudication, or if the information constitutes an unwarranted invasion of personal privacy.[37]

However, all of the judges' names were also missing. The name of the judge presiding over each criminal and civil case in each district in each file was erased by the Federal Judicial Center before the database was released. The deletion of the judges' names was not expected. After all, the name of the presiding judge is part of the public record in criminal and civil cases. There was no legal reason for this information to be withheld.

The TRAC project team had hoped that the performance of the federal judges could be examined, perhaps in a later study. Certainly, federal judges are influential individuals in the court system and an examination of their records is in the public interest. Factual data concerning their performance are rarely seen. Evidently, officials in the Justice Department or the Federal Judicial Center did not want such an examination to be conducted.

Are Variables Complete for All the Years?   Some of the information in the federal judicial database was not recorded every year. Two variables, *filing offense level* and *termination offense level,* are examples of this. The offense level listed the severity of the offense (such as a misdemeanor, a petty offense, or a felony) with which the defendant was charged. The investigator had considered using these two variables as one indicator of plea bargaining. That is, if there was a change in this level between the time the charges were filed and the case was terminated, then a negotiation of the charges had taken place.

However, this information was not collected by the districts until 1982. This meant that these variables were of limited use to the investigator. Trends or patterns in the use of plea bargaining over a number of years could not be assessed with these variables.

Other variables were incomplete or unreliable for some years. A variable that indicated whether an individual was a defendant in more than one case in the same district during a statistical year, for example, was not considered to be reliable by the Federal Judicial Center before the middle of 1985 because of programming errors.

Do the Values of the Variables Always Have the Same Meaning?   One of the most difficult problems faced by the investigator in using the judicial database was the fact that the meaning assigned to the values of each variable changed frequently. During 1982, for example, the value 4 for one variable meant that the charges against the defendant were acquitted after a jury trial. However, in 1983, the same value was used to mean that the defendant was found not guilty by reason of insanity.

In some cases, several values changed meanings within the same variable. For example, the variable that described the outcome or disposition of the case included the following values and changing interpretations:

8—Convicted, by court after trial.
9—Convicted, by jury after trial.
10—NARA Title I and III.
11—Nolle Prosequi (prior to January 7, 1976, this was coded as 1).
12—Pretrial Diversion (prior to January 7, 1976: deferred prosecution).
13—Mistrial (since August 1979).
14—Dismissed without prejudice (prior to July 1, 1983, coded as 1).
15—Not guilty by reason of insanity (prior to July 1, 1983, coded as 3).
16—Dismissed statistically (prior to January 1, 1982, coded as 0).
17—Guilty but insane (effective October 12, 1984).

There were a large number of such changes within specific variables throughout the entire database. For that reason, the Federal Judicial Center warned users of the data:

> The lack of a consistent correspondence between a coded value and a single interpretation is the most serious challenge to multiyear analysis presented by the data and the researcher must be extremely careful to account for value inconsistency when doing analyses of this type.[38]

It was often difficult for the investigator to keep track of all of the different meanings. Nevertheless, it was critical to do so in order to avoid reaching false conclusions. In many cases it was possible to make valid comparisons for only a few years at a time.

Do the Values of the Variables Have More Than One Meaning?   Another problem facing the investigator was the fact that some values seemed to have more than one meaning—at the same time. The multiple meanings added to the difficulties in using the data. For example, one variable categorized the sentence received by a defendant according to imprisonment, probation, and the length of the sentence. The value 1 for this variable meant the following:

1—Prison only, or probation only, or probation and/or fine only, days in prison followed by probation.

The value of another sentence classification variable had this meaning:

0—Sentence suspended, imposition of sentence suspended, or imprisonment 4 days or less; or sentence consists of time already served, or sentence was fine only and was remitted or suspended. (Prior to SY87, this code also included deportation or probation without supervision in the five immigration districts of Southern Texas, Western Texas, Arizona, Southern California, and New Mexico).

The most puzzling occurrence of multiple meanings, however, was for the variable that listed the number of months of imprisonment to which a convicted defendant was sentenced. At first, this seemed clear enough. The code or value simply represented the number of months of the sentence. For example, the code 078 meant that the individual was sentenced to 78 months in prison. But one of the codes, 000, had an unexpected meaning:

000—Death or none. (Prior to SY87 this also included imprisonment of 4 days or less. Prior to January 1982, this included imprisonment of 15 days or less.)

In other words, the code 000 could have at least two drastically different meanings. Either the convicted defendant received a death sentence, or was not sentenced to any prison time! It is difficult to understand why these two penalties were coded in the same way.

Are Aggregate Data Used?   The Criminal Code of the United States lists every crime, offense, or violation of the laws of the nation. An individual can be charged with any number of violations of the titles and sections of the criminal code. The criminal records in the federal judicial database, however, list only the most serious offense with which the defendant was charged. If a defendant were charged with both bank robbery and auto theft, which upon conviction resulted in a 25-year and a 5-year sentence respectively, only the bank robbery would be recorded in the database.

Several sections of the U.S. Code discuss all of the specific actions that can lead to a charge of bank robbery. This is true of all of the criminal offenses. The offense of bribery, for example, includes more than 30 sections listed throughout the U.S. Code.[39] These sections cover such actions as bribery of public officials, bribery of witnesses in order to influence testimony under oath, bribery to affect the outcome of sporting events, and the bribery of inspectors. There are special sections that deal with unlawful compensation to members of Congress, and the payment or receipt of fees, bonuses, or items of value to procure advances, loans, or credit from a Federal Reserve bank. In other words, many kinds of actions performed for different purposes are covered by the one charge of bribery.

In the federal court database, all of these actions are recorded in the same way. Each is listed as bribery, with the same offense code of 7100. However, a reporter or a researcher may be interested in finding out how many defendants were charged only with bribery to influence the outcome of a sports event. It is not possible to separate out these specific cases from the others because all of the bribery cases have been collected together into the same bin, so to speak, and classified in the same way. Additional details that would clarify the specific bribery offense are not recorded in the database.

All the criminal offenses have been classified in a similar manner. Embezzlement and fraud of public money or property, as another example, includes several specific actions such as custodians who misuse public funds, depositories that fail to safeguard deposits, and the use of tools and materials for counterfeiting.[40] All are listed in the database as offense code 4310.

It is inevitable in a massive database or reporting system that similar data will be classified and grouped together. It is a natural way of organizing and making sense of countless details and cases. But it also means that a reporter or other individual may not be able to access the specific kinds of information that he or she may want from the aggregated data. Even the federal judicial database, with all of the criminal, civil, and appeals cases for the United States, is limited in the sense that specific kinds of actions cannot be separated from the general charges or classifications.

Do the Results Make Sense?   The investigator noticed several curious things while examining the records of the federal court system. During an analysis of the drug offenses filed in the 11 "big city" districts and the United States for the years 1980 through 1987, for example, some unexpected findings emerged: The results of the analysis seemed to indicate that a major change in drug habits and preferences had occurred in the United States around the year 1985. Suddenly, the number of individuals charged with heroin and cocaine offenses decreased sharply and the number of individuals charged with "other" kinds of narcotics offenses climbed dramatically. For the years prior to 1985, the offense category of "other narcotics" represented no more than 1% of all criminal charges filed in the United States. After 1985, the category of "other narcotics" represented 18% of all criminal charges filed in the United States.

An even more dramatic change took place in the 11 districts under intensive study. In the district of Eastern New York (Brooklyn area), for example, the percentage of defendants charged with "other" narcotics offenses averaged about 3% of all criminal charges before 1985. After 1985, other narcotics offenses jumped to 40%, and then to 49%—virtually half of all the criminal charges filed in the district. By 1987, other narcotics offenses totaled 43% of all criminal charges in the district of Southern New York (Manhattan). In addition, cocaine offenses in the United States dropped after 1985 to one fifth of their previous levels. In the district of Massachusetts, cocaine offenses decreased from a high of 22% of all criminal charges filed to only 1% in 1986. In the district of Connecticut, cocaine offenses represented 35% of all criminal charges filed in 1985; 1 year later, in 1986, cocaine offenses were only 3% of all the criminal charges filed in the district.

These findings did not make sense. Certainly they did not agree with media accounts or other published reports of the drug scene in the United States at that time. Such reports indicated that the amount of cocaine flooding the country was still increasing and that cocaine was the "all-American drug" of choice.[41] "Crack" cocaine, first created by a Los Angeles basement chemist, was common in southern California by the end of 1984. It was prevalent and use was growing in New York, Miami, New Orleans, and Philadelphia in the middle of 1985.[42] The investigator was therefore suspicious of the results, especially those showing steep declines in cocaine offenses.

To verify the results, the investigator called researchers at the Federal Judicial Center and asked for confirmation and an explanation for these findings. At first, the officials were reluctant to believe the findings and suggested that the investgator check her work more carefully. That was done, but the results were the same. Finally, after further prodding, the officials conducted their own analysis of the drug cases. They obtained same results.

At first, the researchers at the Federal Judicial Center had no explanation for the unexpected results. Later, they determined that a coding change in the drug categories had occurred in 1985, but the Center had not been informed of the changes. All of the districts were using new code numbers to describe drug offenses. In other words, what previously had been listed as cocaine distribution or possession, for example, was now something much different—but the Center was still using the old codes. Notification of any coding changes is an important issue because the Federal Judicial Center maintains the database and analyzes the data for the Justice Department. The Justice Department and the Attorney General use these data, in part, to make policy decisions that affect the entire nation.

This example points out how important it is that reporters and other users of government data do not take the data for granted. As always, results must be checked and confirmed, and suspicious findings must be questioned. The example also shows that the agency itself may not be aware of all of the problems or errors within its own databases. Officials at the Federal Judicial Center acknowledged to the investigator that their use of the database mainly consists of analyzing national trends for the Justice Department. They do not usually explore trends within the districts or analyze the data for the individual districts in depth. It is therefore quite possible that some problems or errors would remain concealed, especially in a database as massive and complex as the federal court database.

In summary, then, the process of obtaining and analyzing government records can be a difficult and complex task. The analysis of government records in CAIR depends on the combined creative and technical skills of the reporter and the computer analyst. Records that are received in raw form must first be converted and transferred to software for statistical analysis. Massive amounts of disk space may be needed for storage and manipulation. A detailed examination of the records must be conducted to determine exactly what the records contain as well as to ascertain the accuracy and completeness of the records. Only after the nature, contents, and format of the records are understood can specific issues for analysis be identified.

It is inevitable that errors and problems will be present in large databases, especially those that have been collected over a number of years and cover many regions of the country. This may be the result of data entry errors, changes in laws that mandate what information is to be collected, the use of outdated forms or procedures, and varying modes, times, and origins of data entry. Furthermore, additional problems for outside users occur because the database has been designed for the agency's internal use, and it is not always amenable to the needs of others. Finally, certain kinds of problems are typicaly found in large government databases. It is critically important that reporters and other outside users of computerized government records are aware of and understand the problems inherent in such databases. They must be thoroughly acquainted with all aspects of the database. The validity of their results depends on this.

NOTES AND REFERENCES

1. See: David Burnham, *A Law Unto Itself: Power, Politics, and the IRS* (New York: Random House, 1989).
2. Printed announcement of Transactional Records Access Clearinghouse, April, 1990.
3. At that time, only one article was located that made use of the database. See: Terence Dungworth, "A Statistical Overview of Judicial Personnel, Filings and Terminations in Federal Courts," The Rand Corporation: The Institute For Civil Justice (no publication date listed). This document was based, in part, on data from the Integrated Federal Courts Data Base (IFCDB), compiled by the Federal Judicial Center in Washington, D.C.
4. Margaret H. DeFleur was named the Director of the Judicial Records Project for Transactional Records Access Clearinghouse in 1989. DeFleur directed the investigation and completed the computer analyses for the project.
5. Otto G. Obermaier, "White Collar Crime: What United States Attorneys Prosecute," *New York Law Journal,* July 3, 1989, p. 3.
6. The Judiciary Act was signed on September 24, 1789; 1 Stat. 73.
7. Russell R. Wheeler and Cynthia Harrison, "Creating the Federal Judicial System," a publication of the Federal Judicial Center, Washington, D.C., 1989, pp. 4–6.
8. Susan B. Long, David Burnham, and Margaret H. DeFleur, "Federal Prosecutorial Discretion: A Comparative Analysis," paper presented at the annual meeting of the Law and Society Association in Berkeley, California, May 31, 1990. For a discussion of the establishment and powers of the office of the Attorney General and the Justice Department, see also: Daniel J. Meador, "The President, the Attorney General, and the Department of Justice," published in *Proceedings of the Conference on the President, the Attorney General, and the Department of Justice,* the University of Virginia, 1980.
9. Hearing of the Commerce, Justice, State and Judiciary Subcommittee of the Senate Appropriations Committee, on the subject of the budget for the Justice Department, *Federal News Service,* May 2, 1996; See also: Stephen Barr, Thomas W. Lippman, and Bill McAllister, "The 1996 Budget: Winners and Losers," *The Washington Post,* April 29, 1996, p. A15.
10. Susan B. Long, David Burnham, and Margaret H. DeFleur, *op. cit.,* pp. 3–10.
11. Public Law No. 19-473, 98 Stat. 1987; The Sentencing Reform Act of 1984 took effect on November 1, 1987.
12. Judiciary Committee memo to Rep. Charles E. Schumer from Tom Hutchison, January 3, 1990. The memo provided background information on federal sentencing practices and the U.S. Sentencing Commission.
13. See, for example, November 16, 1989 decision in *United States of America v. Stephaney Roberts and Others* (Criminal Nos. 89-0033, 89-0074, 89-0319, 89-0342 in USDC, DC).

See also: January 11, 1990 decision of U.S. District Judge Harold H. Greene in *U.S.A. v. Vernon Holland* and *U.S.A. v. Lamar Harris* (Criminal Nos. 89-0342 and 89-0036 in USDC, DC).

14. U.S. General Accounting Office, "U.S. Attorneys Do Not Prosecute Many Suspected Violators of Federal Laws," Report to the Congress (GGD-77-86), February 27, 1978.

15. U.S. General Accounting Office, "Greater Oversight and Uniformity Needed in U.S. Attorneys' Prosecutive Roles," Report to Senator Max Baucus (GGD-83-11), October, 1982.

16. Susan B. Long, David Burnham, and Margaret H. DeFleur, *op. cit.,* p. 7.

17. Robert Rabin, "Agency Referrals in the Federal System: An Empirical Study of Prosecutorial Discretion," 24 *Stanford Law Review* 1036 (1972).

18. Suzanne Weaver, *Decision to Prosecute: Organization and Public Policy in the Antitrust Division* (Cambridge, Mass.: MIT Press, 1977).

19. John C. Coffee, Jr., Richard Gruner, John J. Hanson, and Monte Fisher, "What Do U.S. Attorneys Prosecute?: An Initial Statistical Profile of Federal Prosecutorial Behavior at the Investigative and Charging Stage," unpublished working paper, Columbia Law School and Whittier College School of Law, April 14, 1989.

20. Susan B. Long, David Burnham, and Margaret H. DeFleur, *op. cit.,* p. 7.

21. *Ibid.,* p. 7.

22. Richard C. Wade, "Tomorrow's New York," the *New York Times,* September 30, 1989, Section 1, p. 23; See also: Sam Roberts, "Free-for-All Mayoral Encounter Displays Rivals' Temperaments," the *New York Times,* November 6, 1989, Section A, p. 1.

23. Selwyn Raab, "U.S. Attorney Steering Office in New Directions," the *New York Times,* January 9, 1984, Section B, p. 1.

24. Michael Blumstein, "Eight Men Are Indicted in Insider-Trading Case," the *New York Times,* September 20, 1984, Section D, p. 8.

25. William R. Greer, "U.S. Reports Breaking up 2 Drug Rings in Manhattan," the *New York Times,* September 7, 1984, Section B, p. 3.

26. "2 Meese Associates Are Indicted," the *Chicago Tribune,* News Section, p. 4.

27. Richard Esposito, "3 Reputed Mobsters Charged in Racketeering Conspiracy," *Newsday,* December 22, 1988, News Section, p. 36.

28. Associated Press, "Boesky Gets 3-Year Prison Term for Insider Trading," the *Los Angeles Times,* Part 1, p. 1.

29. James Warren, "Drexel Plea Bargain Called `Right Result' U.S. Had Strong Case, Writer on Firm Says," the *Chicago Tribune,* Business Section, p. 2; "Deal May Be Good for Drexel, But It's Bad for Public," *Newsday,* Viewpoints Section, p. 38.

30. For an explanation of cluster analysis, see: Mark S. Aldenderfer and Roger K. Blashfield, *Cluster Analysis* (Newbury Park, Calif., Sage Publications, 1984), Series 07-044.

31. *Ibid.,* pp. 14–16; For a review of clustering methods, see also: G.W. Milligan, "A Review of Monte Carlo Tests of Cluster Analysis," *Multivariate Behavioral Research,* 1983, Vol. 16, pp. 379–407.

32. See: *The SAS User's Guide: Statistics,* version 5 edition (Cary, N.C., the SAS Institute, 1985) pp. 45–67, 255–267.

33. Richard A. Johnson and Dean W. Wichern, *Applied Multivariate Statistical Analysis,* 2nd edition (Englewood Cliffs, New Jersey: Prentice-Hall, Inc., 1988), p. 566.

34. See, for example, the remarks of Justice Antonin Scalia to the Fellows of the American Bar Foundation and the National Council of Bar Presidents in New Orleans, La., February

15, 1987, and quoted in Marc Galanter, "The Life and Times of the Big Six; Or, the Federal Courts Since the Good Old Days," the *Wisconsin Law Review*, November/December 1988, pp. 921–954.

35. Each federal judicial district contains several offices. For example, the Southern District of New York, a part of the second circuit, contains eight offices: New York City, Warwick, Kingston, Poughkeepsie, Yonkers, Mamaroneck, White Plains, and Middletown. The Northern and Western Districts of New York are made up of nine offices; the Eastern District of New York contains 10 offices.

36. Information about how the judicial database was generated was obtained from the Civil and Criminal Codebooks for the integrated database prepared by the Federal Judicial Center, August, 1988 and from conversations with Patricia Lombard and Joe Cecil of the Federal Judicial Center.

37. See section 1802 of the Freedom of Information Reform Act of 1986.

38. The Criminal Codebook for the Integrated Database, prepared by the Federal Judicial Center, August 26, 1988, p. 2.

39. The general offense of bribery, listed as code 7100 in the federal judicial database, is covered by the following titles and sections of the U.S. Code: *18*:2, 3, 13, 201(a-i), 203-205, 207(b-c), 208, 209(a), 210, 211-215, 224, 371, 663, 666(c); *21*:622, 1962; *22D*:103, 701-704; *26*:7214(a); *42*:1395NN (b1) (b2), 396H(b) (b1) (b2); *46*:239(i); *49*:10(4), 917(b), 1472(d).

40. The offense of embezzlement and fraud of public money or property, listed as offense code 4310 in the federal judicial database, includes the following sections of the U.S. Code: *18*:2, 3, 13, 371, 641-644, 647-653.

41. For example, see: "Drug War Gets Even More Vicious," *U.S. News & World Report*, March 18, 1985, p.13; James A. Inciardi, *The War on Drugs* (Palo Alto, Calif., Mayfield Publishing Company, 1986), pp. 79–86.

42. James A. Inciardi, *ibid.*, p. 82; see also: Jane Gross, "A New, Purified Form of Cocaine Causes Alarm As Abuse Increases," the *New York Times*, November 29, 1985, Section A, p. 1.

7

CAIR Analyses and the Press: Problems of Reporting on Disclosures

This chapter summarizes the reaction of the news community to a detailed report provided to reporters on selected statistical results from the analysis of the electronic records of the Federal Court system. It also discusses responses to the report by certain federal agencies and other groups. A central purpose of the chapter is to point out and discuss some of the problems and limitations experienced by the news community in dealing with detailed numerical findings from a project such as the analysis of the Federal Courts. In addition, the chapter includes a brief discussion of additional projects that resulted from the case study.

The reason a review of the reaction of the press is necessary is that an important part of a formal methodology specifically developed for CAIR is that it must include guidelines regarding ways in which results from such an analysis can effectively be reported to the public. Thus, a look at how reporters disclosed the findings of the court analysis to the public, based on a detailed report that they were provided, offers an additional and important part of the foundation needed for developing a methodology specifically designed for CAIR.

To illustrate the kinds of insights obtained from the analysis and the ways in which the press approached its disclosures, specific findings are presented regarding the functioning of the courts and federal prosecutors in selected districts. For example, the chapter compares New York City mayoral candidate Rudolph Giuliani's claims during his election campaign regarding his accomplishments as a federal prosecutor to his actual record. The results that are presented in the chapter also include information about the criminal and civil work load of federal prosecutors based in Boston, Hartford, Manhattan, Brooklyn, Newark, Baltimore, Philadelphia, Detroit,

Chicago, Los Angeles, and San Francisco. National trends and selected information about the operation of the Justice Department are also discussed in the chapter.

More important than the specific findings, however, is an examination of how the study was used by the press. After reviewing the results, reporters interviewed the prosecutors and prepared news stories. Reporters discovered that, rather than providing answers to all of their questions, the results helped them to see what additional questions needed to be asked. In other words, the findings were only a starting point for journalists. Some reporters related that they had problems using and interpreting the findings. These problems are also discussed in this chapter.

The selected findings illustrate the value of CAIR analyses. They show that the existence of computer files, recording the facts of many thousands or millions of transactions by a federal agency, leave a trail of solid evidence depicting the agency's actual performance. That record can be compared with both the mandated goals of the agency or claims regarding its accomplishments made by officials who carry out its functions. Thus, CAIR analyses provide the basis for effective journalistic oversight and the investigation of questions concerning accountability—the basic functions of a watchdog press.

The final report released by the investigators consisted of 189 pages of statistical summaries, tables, charts, maps, and graphs. Illustrations have been selected that reveal some of the conclusions that emerged about the functioning of federal prosecutors and the courts, or that focus on other issues that are significant for the main goals of this chapter.

SELECTED FINDINGS FROM THE COURT ANALYSIS

As stated in the previous chapter, the overall goal of the analysis was to evaluate the performance of federal prosecutors. The study emphasized three major areas for analysis: First, the study included a special examination of the Southern District of New York while Rudolph Giuliani was prosecutor. (He served in that post from the middle of 1983 until 1989.) His record concerning his performance in that important post was compared to the claims he made during the election campaign. Second, a comparison of the criminal and civil work load of 11 similar metropolitan judicial districts was completed. Finally, the average criminal and civil work load for the United States as a whole was determined. In each of these analyses, the number of criminal and civil cases that were prosecuted in relation to the population was assessed. The project also examined the kinds of cases that were emphasized in each district and the United States as a whole. Of special interest was the use of plea bargaining by prosecutors and the amount of attention they paid to drug offenses.

The Mayoral Race in New York City

Rudolph Giuliani did not win this election for mayor of New York City (although he did win the next). Early in November 1989, voters elected David Dinkins by a narrow margin of only two percentage points. The morning after the election, with all but 3 of the city's 5,243 precincts reporting, Dinkins had received 898,900 votes, or 50%, to Giuliani's 856,450, or 48%. The city's election was the closest in percentages since the turn of the century. At that time, George McClellan, son of the Civil War general, won against his opponent, newspaper publisher William Randolph Hearst, by a mere .6%.[1]

Exit polls indicated that voters chose Dinkins because of his perceived ability to unify the diverse racial and ethnic groups in the city. They felt this was his most important characteristic—more than twice as important as experience in government or leadership qualities. These polls also revealed that Giuliani's negative campaigning, although undoubtedly effective in narrowing the contest, was a double-edged sword. Voters for Dinkins frequently said that the main reason they did not support Giuliani was the nature of his campaign.[2] Giuliani had challenged the character and personal integrity of his opponent. For example, he questioned the sale of stock by Dinkins to his son for $58,000. Dinkins had previously valued the stock at more than $1 million. Giuliani also cited Dinkins' failure to file tax returns in earlier years. Another charge was that he did not list certain paid vacations on financial disclosure forms. Giuliani suggested that Dinkins would be unable to function as mayor because so many questions remained about his personal integrity.[3] During one debate, Dinkins said "We need a mayor, not a prosecutor." Giuliani responded, "I think the people of this town want a mayor who has nothing to fear from a prosecutor."[4]

A great deal of media attention was focused on these character attacks. In fact, they appeared to receive more press attention than the "prime issues" of the campaign, which were characterized as crime, crack, and corruption. However, Giuliani's record as a prosecutor did not escape attention. Some reporters reviewed the findings of the CAIR study and wrote stories that discussed that record, at least in part.

Giuliani's Record as Federal Prosecutor.   Early in the campaign, Giuliani had characterized himself as an aggressive fighter of crime. The results of the court study seemed to support this. During the years 1980 through 1987, more individuals as a percentage of the population had criminal charges filed against them in the Southern District of New York than any of the other 11 metropolitan districts that were under study. On average, the Southern District charged 46 individuals per 100,000 adults with criminal offenses during these years. For the United States as a whole, an average of 31 individuals per 100,000 were charged.

Even more striking was the difference in criminal offenses filed between Giuliani and his predecessor in office. In 1982, the year before Giuliani took office, 39 individuals per 100,000 adults were charged with criminal offenses. In 1984, the year after he became prosecutor, the comparable figure rose to 54—an increase of more than 38%. This level remained fairly constant through 1987, the last year for which data were available at the time of the analysis.

Crime, Crack, and Corruption.   Certainly, the analysis appeared to support Giuliani's claim that he was an aggressive crime fighter. He had stated early in the campaign that crime, crack, and corruption were the major issues facing the city. He placed a special emphasis on these issues during the campaign. The court study indicated that Giuliani had also emphasized these issues while he was prosecutor. For example, in the Southern District of New York during the years 1980 through 1987, drug offenses were filed more frequently than any other category of criminal offenses (Fig. 7.1). On average, drug offenses represented 35% of all criminal charges filed in the district. For the United States as a whole during the same period, drug offenses were 24% of all criminal charges, more than 30% lower.

During Giuliani's portion of those years, he substantially increased the rate of drug prosecutions over that of his predecessor. As noted, he took office in the middle of 1983. In 1982, drug offenses represented 23% of all criminal charges filed in the district. By 1984, with Giuliani having been in office for more than a year, drug offenses totaled 42% of all criminal charges filed—an increase of almost 83%. Two years later, by 1986, drug prosecutions had risen even further, making up 47% of all criminal charges filed in the district (Table 7.1).

Within the drug category, cocaine offenses represented only 4% percent of all criminal charges filed in the district during the year before Giuliani took office. The year after he became the U.S. Attorney, cocaine offenses jumped to 15% of all criminal charges filed. Thus, the analysis seemed to

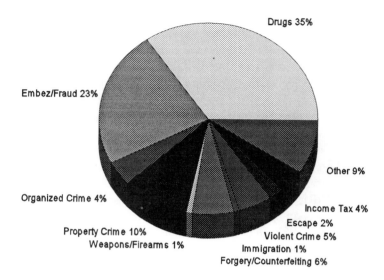

FIG. 7.1. Criminal charges filed against individuals, Southern District of New York (Manhattan), 1980–1987.

show that Giuliani had dramatically increased the prosecution of drug offenses, especially cocaine.

Some critics claimed that these impressive gains were the result of rounding up a large number of low-level street dealers and pushing them through the courts. In fact, Giuliani announced a new policy shortly after he took office of arresting low-level dealers and prosecuting them in federal courts. Previously, federal authorities had concentrated on middle- and high-level traffickers, and left the smaller dealers to the city's police department and the state's criminal courts. Giuliani justified this approach by saying that in order to achieve deterrence and to dispel cynicism about law enforcement, it was necessary to treat everyone alike, whether the individual was a major criminal or a nickel-bag pusher.[5]

Giuliani's critics further stated that the city lacked the resources to prosecute low-level drug offenders, and they claimed that the continuation of this policy would result in less attention to more vital matters. The court study provides some evidence on this issue. Table 7.1 shows that the prosecution of some offenses such as embezzlement and fraud and forgery and counterfeiting suffered decreases in the years after Giuliani took office. The prosecution of violent criminal offenses dropped 50% that year. Supporters might argue that the decreases in other criminal offenses may have

TABLE 7.1

Criminal Charges Filed Against Individuals in the Southern District of New York (Manhattan Area), Percentages of All Charges Filed

Offense	Year								
	80	81	82	83	84	85	86	87	Avg
Drunk driving/Traffic	0%	0%	0%	0%	0%	0%	0%	<1%	0%
Drugs	26	21	23	31	42	41	47	44	35
Embezzlement/Fraud	25	25	31	25	18	21	23	21	23
Escape	2	2	3	3	1	1	1	1	2
Forgery/Counterfeiting	12	5	8	6	3	6	3	4	6
Immigration	1	2	1	1	1	1	<1	1	1
Income tax	5	3	4	2	4	3	6	8	4
National defense	<1	<1	0	<1	<1	<1	<1	<1	<1
Organized crime	1	4	2	3	7	6	3	2	4
Other	10	13	9	9	8	6	7	8	9
Property crime	10	14	9	14	12	9	7	7	10
Violent crime	6	8	8	4	4	5	2	3	5
Weapons/Firearms	2	2	1	1	1	2	1	1	1
Totals	100%	100%	100%	100%	100%	100%	100%	100%	100%

Note. Columns may not total to exactly 100% due to minor rounding errors. Figures for 1987 are for first 6 months only.

resulted from the prosecution of more low-level drug offenders, who often commit other kinds of crime. The data reveal these trends, but cannot always answer why they occurred.

Finally, Giuliani increased the prosecution of organized crime after he assumed responsibility for the Southern District. The year before he took office, only 2% of all criminal offenses involved organized crime. One year after Giuliani took over, the number jumped to 7%, a significant increase. However, in 1986, the prosecution of organized crime dropped back to about where it was earlier.

In conclusion, the findings from the analysis appeared to support Giuliani's claim during the campaign that he was an aggressive crime fighter. The number of individuals per 100,000 adults who were charged with criminal offenses increased substantially during his time in office. He said that crime, crack, and corruption were the major issues facing the city, and his efforts while prosecutor largely reflected these concerns. He made the prosecution of drug offenses, especially cocaine, a priority during his term. Criminal offenses such as organized crime were also targeted. The court study did not specifically address the issue of corruption, because this could include several charges under different categories. For example, it can refer to offenses involving public money or property under embezzlement and fraud, miscellaneous general offenses such as bribery, or bribery involved in transportation or travel in aid of racketeering under the category of organized crime. Yet, although Giuliani's claims about fighting crime and drugs were substantiated, it appeared that during the time he was in charge the prosecution of other categories of offenses such as violent crime and property crime decreased.

A Comparison of 11 Major Judicial Districts

As indicated in the previous chapter, 11 "big city" judicial districts were highlighted in the TRAC study. These districts were selected because of their similarity on a number of demographic and economic indicators. Included were the major metropolitan areas of Boston, Hartford, Brooklyn, Manhattan, Newark, Philadelphia, Baltimore, Detroit, Chicago, Los Angeles, and San Francisco. For each of these districts, the study assessed the number of criminal and civil cases per 100,000 adults filed in federal court. The project also examined the kinds of criminal matters and civil cases that were emphasized in each district. Additional information such as the number of criminal defendants who completed a trial, as well as conviction rates, were calculated. Finally, a special investigation of drug offenses was also completed.

Variations in Criminal Prosecution Rates.   The ability of the government to control crime has long been a central concern of citizens of this country. The federal government's contribution to this effort is relatively small in comparison to the state and local share. State and local agencies employ about 10 times more enforcement and judicial officials than the federal government.[6] Nevertheless, the federal contribution is significant. The federal effort also varies from one district to the next.

Considerable regional variation was observed in the level of criminal enforcement by the 11 federal prosecutors. From 1980 to 1987, when the adult population living in each district is taken into account, the U.S. attorneys in Manhattan and Baltimore charged far more defendants with crimes than the prosecutors in Boston, Hartford, Chicago, Detroit, and Los Angeles (Fig. 7.2).[7] In Boston and Hartford, an average of 15 individuals per 100,000 were charged each year during the period. In Manhattan, an average of 46 individuals per 100,000 were charged annually—more than three times as many. In Baltimore, the average annual rate was 42 individuals per 100,000.

Distinct variations also emerged in the kinds of criminal matters that were emphasized in each district. In most of the districts, drug offenses were prosecuted more frequently than any other category of crime. However, in

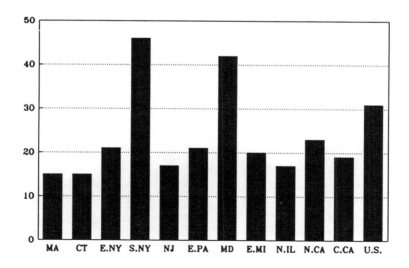

Federal Judicial Districts

FIG. 7.2. *Average number of criminal defendants per 100,000 population, age 18 and over, 1980–1987.*

Newark, Chicago, San Francisco, and Los Angeles, most criminal defendants faced embezzlement and fraud charges. In Baltimore, a surprisingly large number of individuals were charged with drunk driving and traffic offenses. These charges, which averaged only 1% or 2% of all criminal charges filed in the other districts, represented 23% of all criminal charges in Baltimore.

For all federal prosecutors throughout the nation between 1980 and 1987, 24% of all defendants faced drug charges. In Los Angeles, however, only 17% of defendants were charged with drug crimes. In contrast, 40% were charged with drug offenses in Brooklyn—more than twice as many. In 1985 alone, cocaine offenses ranged from 4% to 35% of all criminal charges filed in the 11 districts. Clearly, there were substantial differences among these big-city districts.

Variations in Processing Civil Cases. Most people, if questioned, would probably say that criminal prosecutions are more important than civil suits. However, this is not always true. A civil suit brought against a major corporate polluter or a company that manufactured and sold contaminated food may affect more people and be far more important to the citizens of that district than the prosecution of individuals for such crimes as postal fraud, wagering, or trespassing on timber and government land. Thus, the civil caseload of a prosecutor must be considered along with the criminal work load when assessing a prosecutor's impact on a district. This includes civil cases where the United States is the plaintiff or defendant.

When the United States is the plaintiff, U.S. Attorneys aggressively initiate and pursue suits involving a variety of matters. These range from suing individual students who have defaulted on loans to taking legal action against a huge defense contractor who has overcharged the government. When the United States is the defendant, it is the subject of the suit. Here, individuals or groups bring suits against the government on matters ranging from injuries resulting from tripping on a cracked federal sidewalk to claims by a city that the government has failed to provide adequate protection against the hazards of nuclear waste.[8] The U.S. Attorney must represent and defend the federal government's interests.

Variations in the rates of civil cases filed by the big-city prosecutors were even larger than that observed in the criminal cases. For example, from 1980 to 1987, an average of 9 civil cases (where the United States was the plaintiff) were filed for every 100,000 adults each year in Philadelphia (Fig. 7.3). In contrast, the U.S. Attorney in San Francisco filed an average of 83 civil cases a year for every 100,000 adults—more than nine times as many.

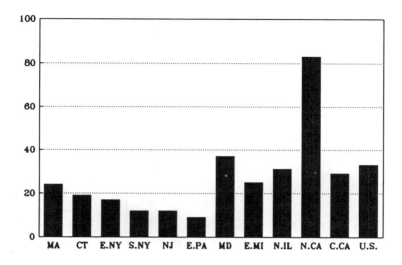

Federal Judicial Districts

FIG. 7.3. *Average number of civil cases filed (U.S. plaintiff) per 100,000 population, age 18 and over, 1980–1987.*

The U.S. Attorneys in Baltimore and Chicago brought 37 and 31 such civil suits per 100,000 individuals, respectively. The number of civil cases filed in which the United States was the defendant ranged from an average of 11 cases (for every 100,000 adults) each year in Boston to 38 cases in Detroit (Fig. 7.4). During the period of 1980 through the first 6 months of 1987, the United States was the plaintiff or defendant in 658,477 civil suits.

Substantial differences also were observed in the kinds of civil cases that were pursued or defended by federal authorities in the districts. In most of the big-city districts, the United States was a plaintiff or defendant most often in suits broadly categorized as "contracts." These include insurance and marine matters, violations of the Miller Act, and negotiable instruments. It includes the recovery of overpayments and enforcement of judgments under Medicare and veterans benefits, and the recovery of defaulted student loans. This category also covers stockholder suits, product liability, and other contract actions.

In the Manhattan area, these contracts disputes represented 16% of all civil cases where the United States was plaintiff or defendant. In Philadelphia, the rate was 19%. However, contracts suits totaled 58% of the civil cases in Chicago and 60% in Baltimore. In San Francisco, 78% of all civil

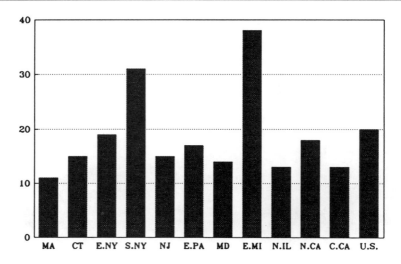

Federal Judicial Districts

FIG. 7.4. *Average number of civil cases filed (U.S. defendant) per 100,000 population, age 18 and over, 1980–1987.*

cases where the United States was plaintiff or defendant involved the contracts category. In other words, these suits ranged from 16% to 78% of such civil cases in the 11 districts, a large range of variability indeed.

Contracts suits were the largest category of civil cases (United States as plaintiff or defendant) in 6 of the 11 districts. In several districts, however, disputes involving social security payments were the most frequent type of civil suit. This category also includes social security disability, black lung, and other related programs. In Brooklyn and Philadelphia, social security suits represented 33% of all civil cases where the United States was plaintiff or defendant. In Detroit, social security cases totaled 47%. These social security suits ranged from 7% to 47% in the districts highlighted in the study.

In Manhattan, statutes suits were the largest category of civil cases in which the United States was a party to the suit. The category of statutes includes energy allocation, interstate commerce, agricultural, antitrust, bankruptcy, securities, commodities, and exchange suits. It covers disputes about the constitutionality of state statutes and state reapportionment. It also includes issues of equal access to justice, deportation, selective service, tax suits, and other matters. In most of the districts, this category made up about 10% of civil cases. However, in Manhattan, statutes represented 25% of the civil cases.

Trends and Patterns for the United States

For all categories of crime, the federal government filed charges against 41,324 individuals throughout the United States in 1980. For the first 6 months of 1987, 28,459 individuals were charged with criminal offenses, or 56,918 when projected for the entire year. Expressed in terms of the number of defendants in relation to the adult population, there were 25 federal defendants for every 100,000 adults in 1980. This had risen to 35 in 1987, representing a growth of 40% in the criminal caseload of the United States for the period.[9]

Drug offenses were prosecuted more frequently than any other category of crime in the United States during each year from 1980 through 1987. On average, 24% of all criminal defendants faced drug charges (Fig. 7.5). Drug offenses include the distribution, importation, manufacture or cultivation, and possession of marijuana, cocaine, heroin, controlled substances, and other narcotics. It also covers illicit drug profits and the laundering of profits from controlled substances. Within this category, more defendants in the United States faced charges involving marijuana than any other drug.

The second largest type of crime prosecuted in the United States was embezzlement and fraud. This category includes the embezzlement of bank, postal, lending, and credit and insurance institutions by officers of a carrier

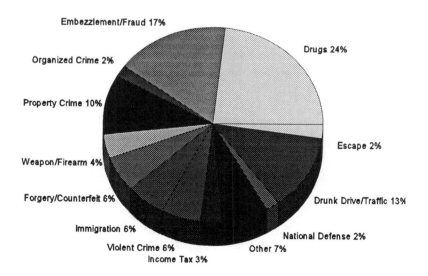

FIG. 7.5. Criminal charges filed against individuals in the entire United States, 1980–1987.

or by officers or employees of the United States. It also includes the fraud of banks, postal facilities, interstate wire communications, lending and credit institutions, securities, marketing agreements and commodity credit, excise, wagering, and other tax fraud.

In 1980, 62,931 civil suits (where the United States was plaintiff or defendant) were filed throughout the country in federal courtrooms. This reached a high of 117,943 suits in 1985. The number of such civil suits filed declined after 1985. A total of 35,681 civil suits were filed during the first 6 months of 1987, or 71,362 when projected for the entire year. Thus, it appears that prosecutors may have deemphasized civil matters in an effort to cope with the increased number of criminal cases in the federal court system.

An average of 48% of all civil cases (in which the United States was a party to the suit) involved the category of contracts (Fig. 7.6). This was the most common type of civil suit filed between 1980 and 1987. Disputes involving social security made up the second largest category.

Perhaps one of the most striking long-term trends observed throughout the United States was the steady decline in the proportion of criminal defendants whose cases were completed at trial. In 1980, the fate of 18% of all defendants was decided at the end of a trial. By 1987, this rate dropped to only 9%—a decline of 50% (Table 7.2). This decline suggested that the cases of a growing number of defendants were being decided by plea bargaining.[10]

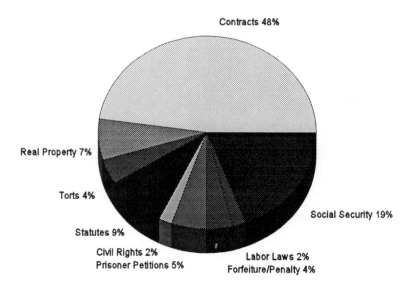

FIG. 7.6. Composition of civil cases in the entire United States (U.S. plaintiff or defendant), 1980–1987.

TABLE 7.2

Percentage of Criminal Defendants in the United States That Completed Trial in Federal Courts

Offense	Year								All Yrs
	80	81	82	83	84	85	86	87	
Drunk driving/Traffic	23%	10%	6%	7%	7%	9%	12%	13%	10%
Drugs	26	22	23	20	20	16	16	10	19
Embezzlement/Fraud	13	13	11	11	9	10	8	4	10
Escape	8	7	9	11	7	6	8	5	8
Forgery/Counterfeiting	10	9	9	9	7	8	5	3	8
Immigration	6	7	6	5	4	5	5	3	5
Income tax	18	20	21	20	19	18	16	3	18
National defense	19	20	19	27	22	24	16	14	21
Organized crime	32	37	32	38	38	38	26	13	35
Other	18	18	16	20	16	16	15	13	17
Property crime	13	12	11	11	11	11	9	7	11
Violent crime	22	22	21	20	19	17	16	11	20
Weapons/Firearms	18	18	16	14	13	14	14	12	15
All categories	18	15	14	14	13	13	12	9	

Note. Defendants whose cases were still pending were excluded. Figures for 1987 are for first 6 months only.

In plea bargaining, a prosecutor may agree not to bring a case to trial in return for a defendant's guilty plea, which is often made to a lesser charge. Therefore, the number of cases decided by trial is one indicator of the incidence of plea bargaining.[11] The increased use of this strategy may reflect growing pressure on prosecutors throughout the United States to dispose of a larger number of criminal cases in the federal system.

Overall, perhaps the most striking aspect of the findings of the court study was the wide variation in the ways federal laws are enforced throughout the country, especially in the 11 similar districts. The numbers and kinds of criminal and civil matters that were emphasized in each district often showed very different patterns. Even geographically adjacent districts such as Manhattan and Brooklyn showed substantial differences in the rate in which criminal and civil cases were filed, and in the composition of those cases. As indicated, the Manhattan district filed criminal charges against more than twice as many defendants as the Brooklyn district (46 vs. 21 per 100,000 adults), whereas Brooklyn filed about 40% more civil cases. Statute cases were the most common type of civil suit in Brooklyn, but contracts cases made up the largest category of civil suits in Manhattan.

Even within a district, significant changes sometimes occurred when a new prosecutor took office. For example, from 1980 to 1987, the Southern District of New York had two U.S. Attorneys. John S. Martin served from 1980 to 1983, and Rudolph W. Giuliani was the prosecutor from mid-1983 to 1989. When Martin was in charge, his office filed criminal charges against approximately 40 individuals for every 100,000 adults in the district. When Giuliani took over, this rate jumped immediately to 54 per 100,000 and remained at this level. During Martin's term, drug cases represented between 20% and 30% of all criminal charges filed in the district. During Giuliani's tenure in office, the percentage of drug cases grew to over 40% of all criminal prosecutions.[12] Table 7.3 shows the details.

TABLE 7.3
Comparative Rates of Filing Criminal and Drug Charges by Successive
Prosecutors in the Southern District of New York, 1980–1987

	John S. Martin				*Rudolph W. Giuliani*			
	80	*81*	*82*	*83*	*84*	*85*	*86*	*87*
Criminal prosecutions (per 100,000 adults)	36	41	39	39	54	54	53	52
Drug charges (% of all charges)	26	21	23	31	42	41	47	44

Similarly, the appointment of a new prosecutor appeared to signal a change in enforcement policy in the District of Massachusetts. Edward Harrington was the U.S. Attorney from 1977 to 1981, William Weld from 1981 to 1986, and Robert Mueller was in office in 1986 and 1987. Shortly after the appointment of Weld, drug prosecutions increased sharply. When Mueller took over, drug prosecutions dropped back again.[13]

It is difficult to account for many of the differences between the districts in the nation. In a country as large and diverse as the United States, some variation in the enforcement of federal law is to be expected, of course. Furthermore, under the laws and customs of the United States, the Attorney General rarely exercises strict control of all of the U.S. Attorneys. Each federal prosecutor has a major voice in setting his or her own enforcement agenda. It seems clear that the differing goals, strategies, and policy decisions adopted by each prosecutor explain some of the variations in the districts. On the other hand, federal laws apply equally in all parts of the country. From this standpoint, wide or erratic variations in the administration of federal laws from one judicial district to another may be contrary to the principle of uniform justice, which this nation values dearly.

THE NEWS IMPACT OF THE PROJECT'S REPORT

The report of the findings prepared for the press and other users cautioned that great care must be taken when interpreting the results. Despite the fact that census data showed that the 11 big-city districts had many similarities, it is clear that many economic, demographic, and cultural differences separate them. Unique conditions and problems exist in each district. The allocation of resources by the Justice Department also varied from one district to another. For example, Manhattan had one staff member for every 16,000 people in the district, whereas Boston had only one for every 81,000 people. Thus, variations in results may come from many sources other than the policies and practices of particular prosecutors. Finally, the statistics presented in the report can sometimes be interpreted in more than one way. For example, a high conviction rate may mean that a particular prosecutor has been unusually skillful and active, but it also may mean that less difficult cases were selected for prosecution.

Despite these and other problems, the statistical presentation of the findings had considerable value. Journalists and other interested users had hard facts concerning the performance of the U.S. Attorneys and the wide discretion they have when enforcing the federal laws of the nation. Rather than a detailed presentation of those findings, however, perhaps it is more important to examine the response of the press and others to the study. The following section discusses the ways in which reporters used the data and the problems they encountered.

The Release of the Report to the Press

The final report of the federal court study was titled, "The Prosecutors: Criminal and Civil Cases Brought in Federal Court by the Offices of Eleven United States Attorneys from 1980 to 1987." The document consisted of 189 pages of statistical summaries, tables, maps, charts, and graphs for the 11 districts and the United States. It also included a nine-page introduction that briefly discussed some of the major findings of the study. No other comments or interpretation of the results were provided.

The report was issued to the press on October 21, 1989—2 weeks before the election for mayor in New York City. The project team believed that the 2-week period would be sufficient time for reporters to go over the report, interview prosecutors and other officials, and prepare news stories before election day. The report was also sent to the offices of the 11 U.S. Attorneys whose districts were highlighted in the study, to the Attorney General of the United States, and to the newspapers in the 11 districts. It also was sent to several members of Congress and to 20 news organizations.

Newspapers Publish Stories.   Reporters for a number of newspapers wrote stories based on the study. Each reporter used the information provided in a different way. For example, Dennis Bell of his paper's Washington bureau wrote a story published in New York *Newsday* on October 29, 1989.[14] The story, "Manhattan Feds Saw More Crime Than Brooklyn's," correctly stated that prosecutors in Manhattan filed more than twice as many criminal cases than their counterparts in Brooklyn, but only two thirds as many civil cases. The story quoted several experts who, although they had not seen the study, provided reasons for the disparities between the neighboring districts. The second page of the article, "Figures: Rudy Staff Busier," showed the increase in the number of criminal charges filed in the district after Rudolph Giuliani took office.

William Glaberson of the *New York Times* focused on a different issue.[15] His article, "Study Sees More U.S. Plea Bargains," highlighted the rise in drug cases in the nation and the increased use of plea bargaining throughout the federal court system. It mentioned that the Southern District of New York prosecuted more criminal cases than any of the other districts and that Giuliani had been the district's prosecutor for most of the years studied.

The *Wall Street Journal* also discussed the finding that fewer criminal cases were concluded at trial.[16] It quoted an official from the Justice Department who rejected the implication that this meant that prosecutors were more willing to plea bargain.

Newsweek magazine published a boxed piece based on the court study report in its "Vital Statistics" section. It showed the number of criminal defendants per 100,000 adults and conviction rates for 6 of the 11 districts.[17]

An article in the *Los Angeles Times* by Ronald Ostrow took a more regional focus. It decried the fact that Los Angeles, regarded as the nation's "cocaine warehouse," prosecuted federal narcotics offenders at a lower rate than any of the other districts in the study.[18] The story, "Federal Drug Prosecutions Lag in L.A.," also disclosed that the district had a low prosecution rate for other kinds of criminal offenses as well. The acting U.S. Attorney for the district blamed the low rates on the fact that the district was understaffed and had fewer assistant prosecutors than some of the other offices studied. He claimed that the defense procurement fraud scandal and the savings and loan crisis produced a heavy caseload for the district and prevented the district from giving more attention to other criminal matters.

The *Recorder,* the official newspaper for the U.S. District Court of Northern California and the city, county, and municipal courts of San Francisco, emphasized the national trend in the rise of plea bargaining.[19] The Northern District of California reflected that trend and, furthermore, had the third lowest conviction rate of the districts studied. The article, "Study Finds Plea Bargain Rise," noted that the San Francisco office brought the highest number of civil suits. A large number of these involved the recovery of overpayments of veterans' benefits.

A story in the *Chicago Tribune,* "Prosecutors Here Not Into Numbers," also emphasized their district. The story centered around the fact that prosecutors in Chicago brought criminal charges against relatively fewer people than the other big-city prosecutors, but maintained a higher than average conviction rate.[20] U.S. Attorney Anton Valukas confirmed the findings and said that his policy had been to focus on more significant and sophisticated types of criminal cases rather than going for a high volume.

As a result of this project and the attention it received in various news reports, the organization itself became the subject of articles. For example, the *Columbia Journalism Review* discussed TRAC's mission, its importance to the press, and the nature of its first study.[21] TRAC and its "pioneering work," which was said to add "a new dimension to the investigative process," were the subject of a favorable editorial in the Syracuse *Post Standard.*[22] Finally, the *IRE Journal* (an official periodical of the Investigative Reporters and Editors professional organization) also published an article describing TRAC and its first project.[23]

The Attorney General's Office Responds. Two weeks before the public release of the final report, TRAC's codirector, David Burnham, requested an interview with the director of the Executive Office for the United States Attorneys in order to discuss the findings of the analysis. The interview was not granted.

After studying the final report, several journalists contacted officials at the Justice Department for their comments and response to the report. It appeared that the Department was not so pleased with the investigative team's efforts. The press spokesman told reporters that TRAC's numbers were "skewed." Ronald Ostrow of the *Los Angeles Times* received a 15-page reply prepared by the Justice Department that challenged several aspects of the study. (The Department's commentary included portions of the text from the report that were disputed, along with a single-spaced response below it.) The Department's public affairs office also distributed the printed commentary to other reporters. Ostrow faxed the reply to the investigators.

The investigators were understandably concerned about the charges that the findings were flawed. They carefully considered each of the Department's claims and extensively rechecked the analyses. Essentially, the Justice Department disagreed with many of the statistics presented in the report, such as the proportion of defendants whose cases were completed by trial. However, the Department used entirely different data when comparing their figures with those in the report. They maintained that their data, based on a fiscal year and involving cases that were terminated each year, were not consistent with the report's claims, and therefore the university group's analyses were incorrect. As explained in chapter 4, the analyses were based on a calendar (not fiscal) year and involved cases that were filed (not terminated) each year. It is no wonder that the numbers were different.

At times, it appeared that the Justice Department officials had not read the report very carefully. For example, they claimed that it was not clear if the investigative analysis was based on the government's fiscal year (October 1 to September 30), the Court's fiscal year (July 1 to June 30), or the calendar year. However, the report explicitly stated in three different sections that a calendar year was used. In addition, the Department said it was not clear whether the percentages cited in the report were for a single year or for the whole period under study. In fact, each of the numerous tables and charts was labeled with this information.

Furthermore, the Justice Department contradicted itself in its commentary on the report. The text of the reply used one set of numbers for the number of defendants who where charged with crimes in 1987, but used entirely different numbers in two tables that accompanied the commentary. At another point, Justice officials used statistics from 1988 to challenge the investigative study's figures for the 1980 to 1987 period. These errors surprised the report's authors, who began to speculate about whether the officials were simply throwing out conflicting numbers in an effort to confuse reporters and deter them from publishing news stories with findings that may not have reflected positively on the Justice Department. More likely, the officials who run the Department simply did not like having someone looking over their collective shoulders.

The Department also charged that the investigative analysis should not have included criminal cases that were handled by magistrates rather than judges, because these involved only minor matters or "petty cases." (Petty cases were defined as those calling for a sentence of less than 6 months in prison or a fine of less than $5,000.) However, a further analysis of this issue showed that magistrates in the 11 districts presided over a substantial number of criminal cases, many of which could not be classified as petty. For example, magistrates in Maryland heard almost 36% of all criminal cases; in New Jersey, magistrates heard 25% of the cases.[24] Furthermore, these cases included drug offenses, embezzlement and fraud, forgery and counterfeiting, and even a handful of national security and organized crime cases. The report's authors did not agree that these cases should have been excluded from the analysis.

The investigative team sent a response directly to Richard L. Thornburgh, the Attorney General. Their letter addressed each point made by the Justice Department concerning the report. A copy of the letter was also mailed to reporters.

In addition to the Attorney General of the United States, other federal officials responded to the investigative report. However, these responses were generally favorable. They included a circuit judge for the U.S. Court of Appeals and a Justice of the U.S. Supreme Court. Finally, the Judicial Oversight Committee asked Burnham to testify before the Committee during its hearings concerning the Federal court system.

How Reporters Used the Findings

Almost all organizations have adopted computers to record detailed information about their daily operations. At the same time, the decreasing cost of the technology has contributed to the growth of computers in the newsroom. Federal and state public information laws have established that the information in the computerized records of government agencies must be made public on request. All of this has greatly improved the ability of the press to monitor the actions of government institutions (and other kinds of institutions such as schools and hospitals). Although this means that more thorough and independent examinations of government are possible, many journalists hesitate to make use of such data. Some of the reasons why this is the case need discussion.

Reporters as Stenographers. Former investigative journalist David Burnham claimed that most of the news printed in the last century has been limited to two basic kinds of reports. The largest category of news has consisted of repetitive stories that describe the day's publicly visible events—fires, airplane crashes, hurricanes, floods, murders, and oil spills. However, when it comes to covering the institutions of government, or of major organizations involved in business, culture, and science, the news media have generally limited themselves to reporting what the people who run these organizations *said* was happening. The officials in charge of these groups usually transmit their views to reporters through various kinds of manufactured events—interviews, leaked documents, news conferences, and press releases. Members of the press usually do not probe behind these staged occurences to discover what the organizations actually are doing. In the manner of stenographers, they write down what the officials say and later publish it.[25]

Burnham did not claim that "stenographic articles" reporting what people in power say are unimportant. It is obvious, for example, that a U.S. President's statements about plans for military intervention in a troubled part of the globe are of great concern and significance. Similarly, the public remarks of a prosecutor concerning the policies he or she will pursue in office are newsworthy. Certainly, news organizations must cover such events as presidential news conferences, the statements of candidates running for election, or public claims of officials who are monitoring the clean-up of a major oil spill. However, Burnham believes that news organizations also should set aside a portion of their resources to investigate, discover, and describe the actual activities of the key institutions in our society and the officials that represent them. The analysis of electronic records makes this possible. Burnham pointed out that it also changes the definition of news from what individuals and officials say they are doing to what they actually are doing.

Reporters face a number of barriers when trying to gain access to computerized records systems, including the time, effort, and technical skills necessary to transform the databases into usable formats. However, even when the analysis is performed for journalists and the results are summarized in tables, charts, and graphs, problems may remain.

In the court study report, the press was provided with detailed statistical summaries of the criminal and civil work loads of the districts. However, some reporters complained that they had difficulty interpreting the report's tables and charts. They felt overwhelmed by the numbers and wanted the report's authors to draw their conclusions for them. Ronald Ostrow, the *Los Angeles Times* reporter who wrote a story from the data, admitted that he was uncomfortable with the project's report. Although he is an experienced reporter who has covered the Justice Department for many years, he did not want to make his own interpretations. He summarized his feelings about trying to interpret the numerical information in this way: "*You* [the reporter] have to find out what it means. I like someone who's familiar with the data to say what it means. Then, if someone wants to shoot it down, I'll include it in the story. I feel uneasy making those kinds of judgments myself."[26]

Other reporters seemed to have a similar response when using the project's report. For example, William Glaberson's story in the *New York Times* focused on the increased use of plea bargaining throughout the country. However, only days before his city's mayoral election, his story made only one indirect reference to Rudolph Giuliani. It appears that the reporter may have been unable to isolate Giuliani's record from the tables showing the district's yearly work load from 1980 through 1987.

In Massachusetts, William F. Weld was a candidate for governor of the state. Weld had been the federal prosecutor for the district of Massachusetts from 1981 through 1986. The work load of this district was highlighted in the investigative study. The Massachusetts newspapers published numerous articles about candidate Weld. For example, the *Boston Globe* published a lengthy story about his privileged background, mentioning a few prominent cases he prosecuted.[27] Although the November election was only days away and the newspaper received a copy of the investigative report, nothing was written about the numbers or kinds of cases that Weld prosecuted while in office.

Here again, it appears that some reporters were reluctant to interpret or draw conclusions about a prosecutor's performance from the tables and charts that were presented in the report. Writers for the *Globe* did make use of the report during this time, however. For example, *Globe* reporters wrote a story about Governor Judd Gregg's visit to a local school in New Hampshire to proclaim the last week in October as "Drug-Free Week."[28] In this story, two sentences were written about the report. It mentioned that criminal cases completed at trial had decreased from 18% in 1980 to only

9% in 1987—a statement explicitly made in the report's introduction. Clearly, the reporters received and reviewed the project's report, but hesitated to interpret or integrate its findings.

Burnham attributed the difficulty that many reporters experience in interpreting numerical data and drawing conclusions to several factors, including a lack of training in the uses of statistics. He also believes it is the result of deeply ingrained assumptions about what makes up a "story" and the kinds of information that serve as the foundation for news. Most investigative projects and newspaper articles are based on written documents—letters, memos, transcripts, court decisions, affidavits, Congressional reports, press releases, and so on. In these documents, words, rather than numbers, supply information. He added:

> Give reporters a copy of a J. Edgar Hoover memo serving up his personal version of some particular national conspiracy and they'll write an article. But give reporters a printout listing the number and types of such cases the FBI investigated during each of the past five years and precisely how many times the Justice Department went on to bring an indictment, and reporters usually look the other way.[29]

Numbers Raise Questions; Do Not Always Give Answers.   The tables and charts in the report often raised questions for reporters rather than providing them with definitive answers. For example, the analysis showed that the district of Maryland charged an unusually large number of individuals with drunk driving and traffic offenses—far more than any of the other big-city districts. In the metropolitan areas of Boston, Hartford, Brooklyn, Manhattan, Newark, Philadelphia, Detroit, Chicago, and Los Angeles, defendants charged with drunk driving and traffic offenses never exceeded 1% of the criminal work load in any of the years from 1980 to 1987. In San Francisco, the rate was slightly higher, but even so, this category represented an average of only 6% of all criminal cases in the district. In the Baltimore area, however, drunk driving and traffic offenses were the second largest category of criminal offenses prosecuted in the district. On average, drunk driving and traffic offenses made up 23% of all criminal charges filed. In 1982 alone, drunk driving and traffic offenses totaled 28% of the district's entire work load.

The numbers provided no explanation for this striking difference between Maryland and the other districts. It was tempting to conclude that federal prosecutors there considered prosecuting speeding to be a higher priority than murder or other serious crimes. However, a phone call by a member of the investigative team uncovered the reason for this disparity.

The Baltimore–Washington Parkway, the heavily traveled beltway that connects the two cities, was built on federally owned land. Furthermore, the U.S. Park Police in Maryland are responsible for enforcing the traffic laws on most of the highway. This automatically made a "federal case" out of even simple traffic violations. Thus, the unusual data resulted from land ownership and policing responsibility rather than prosecutorial discretion or choice.

Reporters used the numbers in the investigative report as the foundation of their stories. The numbers pointed the way to other questions that needed to be asked. For example, Rudolph Giuliani substantially increased the number of individuals charged with drug offenses during his tenure in office. But how did he do this? Did he accomplish this by hauling in large numbers of minor nickel-bag pushers? If so, was that a good policy? Did the prosecution of other matters suffer as a result of the attention given to drug crimes? The numbers in the report did not provide answers to such questions. To obtain additional answers, many reporters interviewed the prosecutors, officials in the Justice Department, and experts in criminal and civil law. In other words, they supplemented the numbers with traditional approaches such as the interview. In fact, in most of the stories published, the numbers from the report made up only a small portion of the article. This confirms what has been suggested in previous chapters: Computer-assisted reporting does not replace the traditional tools of the journalist; it adds one more device to the toolbox.

ADDITIONAL NEWS ANALYSES CONDUCTED FOR THE PRESS

In addition to the newspaper articles that were generated from the report, several news organizations approached the investigative group for special research projects. These included the *Boston Globe, Newsday,* the *New York Times, USA Today,* CNN, and the Associated Press.

Special Analyses for Newspapers

Investigative reporters of the *Boston Globe*'s Spotlight Team requested a special analysis of criminal cases involving "public corruption" in the District of Massachusetts and similar districts for the years 1980 through 1987. The Spotlight Team was investigating government officials who were charged with corruption. The general category of *public corruption* includes three major charges: embezzlement of public money or property, embezzlement by an officer or employee of the United States and bribery. Each of these three charges covers a variety of actions, such as the theft or sale without authority of records, vouchers, money, or things of value of any U.S. department or agency; the misuse of public funds by custodians; unlawful compensation to members of Congress, officers, and others in matters affecting the government; or bribery or gifts to inspectors or other officers.

The project's principal investigator identified the specific actions covered by each of the three charges and provided the information to the *Globe*. In addition, the investigator completed an analysis of these charges for the 11 big-city districts as a whole, and for the District of Massachusetts. This analysis included the following:

1. The number of defendants charged with the three offenses.
2. The percentage of defendants who were convicted.
3. Of those who were convicted, the percentage who received a prison sentence.
4. The median prison sentence (in months) of those convicted.
5. Of those convicted, the percentage who received only probation.
6. A printout listing the docket number, filing date, disposition and sentencing information of every defendant in the district of Massachusetts charged with the three offenses during the calendar years 1980 to 1987.

A few weeks later, the Spotlight Team published the results of its probe of political corruption in the state.[30] The article reviewed the state's efforts in curbing corrupt practices and reforming anticorruption legislation. The article concluded that federal prosecutors pursued corruption cases more actively than local prosecutors. Furthermore, the disparity between federal and state sentences increased over the past decade. Public servants who were convicted of corruption in federal court received prison sentences far more often than those who were convicted in state court. The average prison term for defendants convicted in federal court was 2 years, but the "typical" state jail term was 6 months. It is not clear, however, how the investigative analysis was used or incorporated into the story. In fact, some of the figures in the story concerning federal sentences did not agree with the results provided by the investigator.

Another analysis for a newspaper was conducted in connection with President George Bush's (May 1989) nomination of Robert C. Bonner to head the Drug Enforcement Administration. Bonner was a former U.S. Attorney who had served in Los Angeles from early 1984 until mid-1989.

The Bush administration described him as a tough drug prosecutor and a "no-nonsense manager" who would bring a wealth of knowledge to the new job at the DEA.[31] Several stories written about the nomination quoted officials who said that there was a "tremendous expansion" of drug prosecutions during Bonner's tenure in office.[32] A spokesman for the Justice Department praised Bonner for his "extraordinary experience" in drug investigations.[33] All of these stories written about the nomination reflected positively on Bonner.

Associated Press writer Michael J. Sniffen wondered if those characterizations were correct. He had read the court investigation report, which provided certain information about the period when Bonner was in charge of the Los Angeles office. Sniffin wanted more detailed information so that he could compare what government officials and the press were saying about Bonner with his actual performance. He contacted the investigator and asked for additional information about drug prosecutions in Los Angeles when Bonner was the U.S. Attorney. A special analysis was completed for Sniffen within 3 hours of his request, in time for his next deadline.

The analysis revealed a different story than that put out by the White House, the Justice Department, and what was widely reported in the press. A review of his actual record while in office showed that Bonner lagged behind fellow federal prosecutors in bringing drug and narcotics criminal charges. When Bonner was the chief prosecutor, Los Angeles led the nation in federal drug arrests, but Bonner's office prosecuted a smaller percentage of those arrested on drug charges than the nation as a whole. From the beginning of 1984 through the first half of 1987, 19% of federal criminal defendants in Los Angeles faced drug charges. By comparison, federal prosecutors nationwide charged 27% of their defendants with drug offenses during this time. Furthermore, he prosecuted a lower percentage than other big cities that had fewer drug arrests to begin with.

This changed the picture for Bonner's nomination. There appeared to be a considerable difference between what officials said about Bonner and what Bonner had actually accomplished. A number of newspapers carried Sniffen's story about the Bonner analysis.[34] These stories were seen by members of the Senate committee that was responsible for Bonner's confirmation. The court project directors learned that Senator Joseph Biden planned to question Bonner about his performance as prosecutor during the confirmation hearings. However, they later learned that these plans had changed and the questioning would take place "off record." In the end, in spite of the questions raised by the analysis, Bonner's nomination was approved and he took the oath of office in August 1990.

Background Information for Television News

Requests for additional projects by news media were not limited to newspapers. Representatives of the broadcast media also asked for special analyses or data. For example, in 1989, considerable media attention was devoted to the trial and sentencing of Leona Helmsley, the wealthy New York "Hotel Queen" who was charged with income tax evasion and fraud. Helmsley, who reportedly bragged to a maid that "only the little people pay taxes," was accused of avoiding payment of $1.2 million in federal taxes by billing more than $3 million in personal expenses to the Helmsley Hotel chain businesses. These expenses included such items as underwear, a $29 Itty-Bitty Book Light, and renovations to her mansion. Helmsley was convicted and sentenced to 4 years in prison and fined $7.1 million.[35]

The day before the sentencing, CNN requested a special analysis of individuals charged with income tax offenses. CNN wanted background information for a news segment that would discuss Helmsley's sentencing on CNN's *Business Morning* program. The investigator completed the analysis the same day and provided the following information:

1. The number of individuals in the Southern District of New York (the district in which Helmsley's case was filed) and the United States who were charged with income tax offenses in federal court during the years 1980 to 1987.
2. The percentage who completed trial for income tax offenses and the percentage who were convicted.
3. The number and percentage of those convicted of such charges who received no prison time.
4. The median sentence received for income tax offenses in federal court in the Southern District of New York.
5. The maximum sentence received in the Southern District for income tax offenses.

In addition, as soon as CNN learned the nature of Helmsley's sentence, they asked for the number of defendants who had received as severe a sentence as Helmsley. CNN also requested that a representative from the research group appear on the program for an interview.

Other Users of the Court Data

Finally, several representatives of newspapers and government agencies began to ask for specially prepared data sets for their own use and to build data libraries. *USA Today* wanted to purchase tapes containing all criminal and civil cases filed during the years 1980 to 1987. The GAO wanted to buy the entire federal database (criminal, civil, and appeals cases from 1970 through 1987). Although the GAO could have obtained the original files directly from the Federal Judicial Center, the agency apparently preferred the investigative group's version of the data set that had been recreated as a SAS file and reorganized by calendar year and filing date (rather than fiscal year and termination date). The *New York Times* negotiated a contract with the group that would allow it to have the first look at further reports that would be generated and provide for consultations on other data projects. Some newspapers asked the investigators to give them only the cases filed in their district for a period of, say, 5 years. They wanted the information on a diskette in an ASCII file or imported into a spreadsheet and ready to use.

Although several newspapers wanted special analyses or data that could be stored and analyzed in the newsroom, few seemed to understand the true costs in time and money that were involved in completing such tasks. For example, a reporter from one newspaper requested a complex analysis of certain kinds of criminal cases in the reporter's district, the United States, and at least one other comparison district. The analysis would have taken a skilled analyst using a supercomputer several days to complete. Furthermore, the reporter wanted all of the criminal cases in the district downloaded to diskettes and imported into a spreadsheet program for later use by the newspaper. The reporter ended the conversation by adding: "Oh, by the way, if all of this is going to cost more than $50, let me know because I'll have to ask my editor first." A lack of understanding of the time or real costs of these projects was a common problem.

IMPLICATIONS OF THE FEDERAL COURT PROJECT

In retrospect, the statistical presentation of the findings of the federal court project had considerable value to the news community as well as other users of the information. Perhaps for the first time, journalists and other interested parties had hard facts about the performance of the U.S. Attorneys and the wide discretion they have when enforcing the federal laws of the nation. The final report of the TRAC study received a fair amount of media attention. Several newspapers wrote stories based on the study. Background information was provided for broadcast journalists. In addition, the results of the study were reviewed by the Attorney General's office, members of Congress, the GAO, and other officials. As a direct result of the study, media organizations requested additional research or data for their own use in the newsroom.

Reporters welcomed the analysis by an impartial research group. However, many journalists reported that they had problems with the project's written report. Many claimed that they had difficulty interpreting the tables and charts displayed in the report. They wanted all conclusions and findings to be explicitly stated. Even experienced reporters seemed reluctant to draw their own conclusions. Furthermore, the numbers in the report did not always provide definitive answers to all of their questions. Indeed, sometimes the numbers raised more questions than they answered.

Several years have passed since TRAC's first project was completed. Since that time, a large number of computer-assisted projects have been conducted in newsrooms around the country. Some of these investigations resulted in major stories that made a difference and had a substantial impact in the community; others simply duplicated the efforts and stories of other newspapers.

A growing number of reporters and editors are expressing an interest in learning how to use electronic data for investigative purposes. Professional meetings, special conferences, and workshops are increasingly focusing on computer-assisted journalism. Organizations such as the National Institute for Advanced Reporting (NIAR) at Indiana University and the IRE hold annual workshops devoted to computer-assisted reporting. Reporters can travel to the NICAR at the University of Missouri for training in computer-assisted techniques and pay a fee based on the circulation of the newspaper. A handful of other universities have a class or occasional session on computer-assisted reporting.

Many of these conferences and workshops place most of their emphasis on ways in which computers can be used to automate tasks that reporters have always done—such as replacing manual searches of paper records with computerized searches of electronic records—as well as exploring new uses and techniques. Many reporters have attended conferences and workshops and are beginning to work on computer-assisted projects.

NOTES AND REFERENCES

1. Jennifer Preston, "Dinkins R&R: Rest, Regroup: Dave Meets With Aides to Chart Course," *Newsday*, City Edition, November 9, 1989, News Section, p. 7.
2. Mark J. Penn and Douglas E. Schoen, "Don't Minimize the Dinkins Victory," the *New York Times*, November 11, 1989, Section 1, p. 27.
3. Sam Roberts, "Free-for-All Mayoral Encounter Displays Rivals' Temperaments," the *New York Times*, November 6, 1989, Section A, p. 1.
4. *Ibid.*, p. 1.

5. Selwyn Raab, "U.S. Attorney Steering Office in New Directions," the *New York Times,* January 9, 1984, Section B, p. 1.

6. David Burnham and Margaret H. DeFleur, *The Prosecutors: Criminal and Civil Cases Brought in Federal Court by the Offices of Eleven United States Attorneys from 1989 to 1987* (Syracuse, New York: Transactional Records Access Clearinghouse, October 21, 1989), p. 7.

7. *Ibid.,* p.7.

8. *Ibid.,* p. 4.

9. *Ibid.,* p. 2.

10. *Ibid.,* p. 2.

11. The number of criminal cases decided by trial is not a perfect indicator of plea bargaining. In some cases, plea bargaining may take place and the case may still proceed to trial. For example, a prosecutor may drop one charge against a defendant involving the use of a weapon, but continue with the original charge of robbery. Such an instance would not be reflected in this analysis.

12. Susan B. Long, David Burnham, and Margaret H. DeFleur, "Federal Prosecutorial Discretion: A Comparative Analysis," paper presented at the annual meeting of the Law and Society Association in Berkeley, California, May 31, 1990, pp. 21–22.

13. *Ibid.,* pp. 22–23.

14. Dennis Bell, "Manhattan Feds Saw More Crime than Brooklyn's," *New York Newsday,* October 29, 1989, City Edition, News Section, p. 19.

15. William Glaberson, "Study Sees More U.S. Plea Bargains," the *New York Times,* October 29, 1989, p. 35.

16. Melinda Grenier Guiles and Wade Lambert, the *Wall Street Journal,* October 30, 1989, Legal Beat, p. B10.

17. "Crime and Punishment," *Newsweek,* November 27, 1989, Vital Statistics.

18. Ronald J. Ostrow, "Federal Drug Prosecutions Lag in L.A.," the *Los Angeles Times,* November 6, 1989, Home Edition, p. A3.

19. Michael Checchio, "Study Finds Plea Bargain Rise," the *Recorder,* November 1, 1989, p. 1.

20. Bill Grady, Merrill Goozner, and John O'Brien, "Prosecutors Here Not into Numbers," the *Chicago Tribune,* October 31, 1989, Business Section, p. 3.

21. Tracey L. Miller, "Inside TRAC," the *Columbia Journalism Review,* March/April, 1990; See also: Walt Shepperd, "TRACking the Enforcers," the Syracuse *New Times,* April 11, 1990.

22. "New Tool: TRAC, SU's Computer Bloodhound," The Syracuse *Post Standard,* June 6th, 1990, Editorial page, A8.

23. David Burnham and Margaret H. DeFleur, "Storehouse of Stats," the *IRE Journal,* Winter 1990, pp. 12–13.

24. In 6 of the 11 districts, magistrates were involved in less than .5% of nonpetty criminal cases.

25. Memo from David Burnham and Susan Long to David Rubin, dean of the S. I. Newhouse School of Public Communications at Syracuse University, August 17, 1990. The memo discusses the relationship between the Newhouse School and TRAC's goals.

26. Tracey L. Miller, "Inside TRAC," the *Columbia Journalism Review,* March/April 1990, p. 13.

27. For example, see: Curtis Wilkie, "For Weld, Brahmin Roots Are Impolitic," the *Boston Globe,* October 22, 1989, Metro Section, p. 1.

28. John Milne, "Red Ribbons," the *Boston Globe,* November 5, 1989, City Edition, New Hampshire Weekly Section, p. 1.

29. Susan Long and David Burnham, *op. cit.,* memo pp. 7–8.

30. Gerald O'Neill and Dick Lehr, "State Stumbles in Pursuit of Political Corruption," the *Boston Globe,* December 10, 1989, Metro section, p. 1.

31. Michael Isikoff, "DEA Nominee: Mr. No-Nonsense," the *Washington Post,* May 14, 1990, p. A9.

32. Ronald J. Ostrow, "Bush to Name Judge Bonner to Head DEA," the *Los Angeles Times,* May 12, 1990, Section A, p.1.

33. Michael J. Sniffen, "SU Group Tracks Nominee for DEA," the *Post Standard,* May 21, 1990, p. B-2.

34. Several stories were published as a result of the TRAC analysis of Bonner's record of drug prosecutions while he was the federal prosecutor. These include the following: Michael J. Sniffen, "Records Show Drug Chief Nominee Lagged in Drug Prosecutions," the *Associated Press,* May 20, 1990; "Bush's Drug Pick Hit for Trial Record," the *Chicago Tribune,* May 21, 1990, News Section, p. 10; "Study Cites Record of DEA Nominee," the *Los Angeles Times,* May 21, 1990, p. A18; "Drug Arrests Lagged," *Newsday,* News Section, p. 12; "SU Group Tracks Nominee for DEA," the Syracuse *Post Standard,* May 21, 1990, p. B-2.

35. William Glaberson, "Helmsley Gets 4-Year Term for Tax Fraud," the *New York Times,* December 13, 1989, Section B, p. 1; "Spending It," the *New York Times,* December 17, 1989, Section 4, p. 7.

8

Social Science, Precision Journalism, and CAIR: A Conceptual Comparison

When encountering the concept of computer-assisted investigative reporting for the first time, it is easy to assume that it involves the application of social science research methods to the analysis of government data. Such an assumption comes from the obvious facts that some sort of questions guide the inquiry (rather like the use of hypotheses in social science). In addition, computers are used to analyze numerical data and various quantitative indices are computed. Because these procedures are at the heart of social science research, it seems to follow that the two are essentially the same.

A similar assumption can be made that precision journalism and CAIR are essentially the same. Both forms of journalism were initially developed at about the same time. Both approach the task of developing news stories from a quantitative perspective and computer analysis of data plays an important part in each. However, CAIR and precision journalism are not always identical. It is true that they have a number of features in common, and they belong under the same conceptual "roof." To clarify these issues, the central task of both this chapter and the one that follows is to contrast the basic methodology of social science research (and precision journalism) with a methodology for CAIR. To achieve this goal, it is necessary to examine in some detail the principal features of the methodology used by social scientists for conducting and reporting empirical research relevant to their fields. Against this background, the next chapter brings together the techniques, procedures, and strategies that provide a formal methodology for CAIR.

We begin with a summary of the central objectives pursued in empirical social science research, how they developed historically, and what they consist of today. The discussion focuses on these issues within the context of two traditional social sciences—psychology and sociology—that provide a clear methodological model for comparison with CAIR. Additionally, precision journalism is placed within this methodological context.

SELECTING SOCIAL SCIENCE MODELS FOR COMPARISON

There has been a lengthy debate in academic circles concerning which disciplines should properly be called social sciences. That controversy is sidestepped in this discussion. It is on the methods of inquiry of those that have focused on *observable behavior* that this section focuses. Specifically, the comparison with CAIR is narrowed to psychology and sociology. The reason is that these behavioral sciences share a common emphasis on quantitative research. Qualitative studies are also a legitimate part of psychology and sociology. However, the central research traditions of both fields are based on theory development and strategies of empirical observation and quantitative data analysis adapted from the physical and biological sciences.

The development of a model that sets forth in summary the major features of social science methodology requires a review of three distinct topics. One is the goals for which behavioral research is conducted. Another is the methods and techniques used for controlled empirical observation that is at the heart of the research process. A third is the epistemology—the logic of decision making used by scientists to determine whether or not conclusions that seem to flow from their data can be accepted or rejected. Each of these topics can be addressed briefly.

The Goals of Social Science Research

Any discussion of the goals of social science research immediately confronts a very large and complex set of issues and debates. A huge literature of classic and contemporary writings has accumulated on *why* social scientists conduct their inquiries as well as *how* they go about it.[1] Obviously, that entire body of information cannot be reviewed for present purposes. However, in order to compare the goals of CAIR with those of the two sciences, brief references can be made to milestones in the histories of both psychology and sociology that illustrate clearly how their traditional goals came to be defined. Those references show that they are essentially the same in each discipline, although they focus on different features of human behavior.

Setting the Goals of Psychology.   The major goals of psychology were set by a limited number of philosophers, scholars, and researchers who shaped the modern discipline. Actually those goals are contemporary extensions of earlier ones set over several centuries as students of the human mind tried to develop an understanding of its nature and functioning. From Plato to Kant the major issues debated were the true nature of reality, how human beings come to know that reality, and how that internal knowledge about it influences their conduct. Especially important in these debates was the role played by sensory experience and perception. Even after psychology broke from philosophy and adopted a very different method of obtaining evidence, the goal of understanding the way in which people respond to reality and grasp some inner understanding of its workings remained essentially the same. Psychologists are still concerned with mental conceptions that enable people to adjust to, cope with, and respond to the social and physical world around them.

Although centuries of philosophical speculation produced an enormous body of writings with many significant insights, little consensus was achieved as to the psychological nature of human beings. It was not until relatively early in the 19th century that psychology would break away from philosophy to pursue the study of mental processes within the framework of science. Important steps in developing a new approach to the study of how the mind related to reality were taken over several decades by a number of German scholars, including Helmholtz, Weber, Fechner, and Wundt. It was this group that achieved the break with philosophy to establish psychology as an empirical science based on the procedures of the experiment.[2]

The assumption guiding the first experimental research project in psychology was consistent with the principles of the empiricist philosophers. That is, it explored the relationship between the nature of certain features of reality and the way that those features were apprehended through the senses. In the early 1830s, a German physiologist, Ernst H. Weber, conducted experiments on the relationship between certain features of the world of reality and the perceptions of those features in the subjective world of internal experience. It was essentially the same issue that philosophers had been discussing for centuries—the relationship between reality, as it existed outside of human experience, and phenomena; that is, knowing reality subjectively through sensory perception.

Weber chose to study people's perceptions of weight. The focus was on the way in which people perceived differences in subjective sensations created when holding objects of unequal physical weight. His experimental technique was to provide a subject with a "standard" weight in one hand

and "comparison" of similar weight in the other. Most subjects identified them as the same. Then, in repeated trials, the weight of the comparison was slowly increased to a point where it became just noticeably heavier. Weber was able to determine that, regardless of what weight with which one started, the "just noticeable difference" between the two being compared was always a constant proportion of the standard weight with which one had started. That fraction came to be called *Weber's Constant.* Weber also explored other sensory modalities to check visual and tone discrimination and found similar results.[3]

During the late 1850s, Gustav T. Fechner, a German physicist, elaborated the Weber experiments and formulated his confirmation of the results mathematically in what is now called the *Weber–Fechner Law.*[4] This psychophysical regularity was a significant accomplishment and it had profound implications for the mind–reality relationship that had been debated for centuries. In effect, what these efforts showed was that carefully conducted experiments, following the rules of science, could demonstrate a relationship that had repeatedly been argued about by philosophers but never before demonstrated with empirical evidence.

Another classic illustration of an experiment that helped achieve the break with the philosophical roots of psychology was that of Hermann Ebbinghaus. During the 1880s, he devised a technique based on "nonsense syllables," with which he was able to explore regularities in memory—the way a person learned and forgot a series of verbal stimuli over repeated trials. His "curve of forgetting" remains as a basic law in the functioning of human memory.[5]

All during the last part of the 19th century, psychologists devised experiments aimed at understanding the nature of human mental processes. Wilhelm Wundt established the first laboratory of psychology in Leipzig in 1879 and conducted many kinds of experiments on reaction time. Others conducted imaginative experiments with the perception of color, hearing, and other aspects of sensory functioning.

There were many debates about methodology. During the early period, some psychologists remained wary of the experimental method and sought explanations by using various techniques of self-examination called introspection. Some tried repeatedly to identify such features of human mental functioning as the "elements of consciousness" and the "faculties of the mind." These efforts at explaining the human psyche were eventually abandoned.

Another search for explanations not based on experiments came after Darwin's seminal theories became increasingly dominant in biology. Some psychologists to try explain human behavior as a product of inherited *instincts,* such as those that were clearly in evidence among many animals. Shortly after the turn of the 20th century, instinct theories were rejected as inappropriate.[6]

A truly significant change in psychological thinking took place just after the turn of the 20th century. It was the discovery of the importance of the *learning process* in shaping the psychological nature of the human being. In retrospect, that discovery was what Thomas Kuhn would later refer to as a *scientific revolution*—a shift of paradigms that changed the basic assumptions underlying the ways in which some body of events or class of phenomena are explained.

Up to the beginning of the 1900s, psychological explanations were based mainly on assumptions that human beings inherited whatever faculties, attributes, or other features that motivated and guided their patterned behavior. However, there were opposing positions. Some social scientists, especially in anthropology and sociology, were making a different case, that the societal and cultural environment in which individuals were raised was the major factor in shaping their predispositions and psychological nature. However, most psychologists at the turn of the century rejected that idea and stuck with genetic explanations.

Around these differing interpretations of the sources of human nature a considerable controversy arose within the social sciences. It has been characterized as the "nature versus nurture" debate—about the relative dominance of inherited versus environmental influences on human conduct. It was the discovery of ways to study learning with the use of highly controlled experiments that ultimately led contemporary psychology to emphasize the role of learning processes in shaping human cognition and conduct.

Two figures were important in creating the new psychological focus on learning. One was an American, Edward L. Thorndyke, who, as an undergraduate in the late 1890s, began experiments on the way chicks learned to master simple mazes. Later, he studied fish, chickens, cats, dogs, and monkeys. Even though conducted on animals, his experiments and the two fundamental laws of learning he formulated (the *law of effect* and the *law of exercise*) had significant implications for describing the way in which children and adults form new associations and learn new things.[7]

The second pioneer in learning was the Russian physiologist Ivan Pavlov. Conducted in 1905, Pavlov's famous experiments were able to show conclusively that a behavioral response (an automatic reflex) that was normally aroused only by certain fixed events occurring naturally in the animal's environment could be "conditioned" to occur regularly as a response to a completely artificial stimulus controlled by an experimenter. Pavlov's work has become so well known that most people know that he was able to get a dog to salivate at the sound of a bell.[8] It was a remarkable finding and the idea of conditioning as a mode of learning quickly fired the imagination of psychologists all over the world.

These and other pioneering works on learning launched a tidal wave of experiments on both human and animal subjects. The study of learning led to a host of theories that continue to preoccupy psychologists today. In fact, it is no exaggeration to say that learning remains as the central concept of modern psychology.

The preceding illustrations from the development of psychology yield important lessons regarding the goals of that discipline. Underlying the enterprise throughout has been the assumption that human psychological phenomena follow regularities or *laws* that can be uncovered through research. Many such laws have survived from the early days of psychological study—the Weber–Fechner Law, Ebbinghaus' curve of forgetting, Thorndyke's law of effect, and his law of exercise provide classic examples.

Contemporary psychology has gone on to explore a broad range of conditions, concepts, and activities. However, the central goal of psychology has not changed. Then and now it is to identify the order that exists in human conduct, to conduct research on its causes, and to explain the conditions under which various forms of behavior are likely to occur. Because of these historical developments, then, contemporary definitions of the field emphasize three basic ideas: Psychology uses the methods of science; it studies orderly patterns in both animal and human behavior in all its forms; and it focuses on the goal of developing theories that can explain and predict that behavior.[9]

Setting the Goals of Sociology.   The field of sociology has a history of development that to a certain degree parallels that of psychology. Both grew out of philosophy at about the same time. However, the objects of their study are by no means the same. As indicated earlier, psychology focuses on both animal and human behavior and its mental or biological causes at the individual level. In contrast, sociology is much less concerned with what goes on inside people's bodies or minds; it pays little attention to animals and it focuses almost exclusively on patterned relationships among human beings. Thus, sociology looks to factors outside the individual to account for the organization of human groups and societies. It studies processes of societal and group change and it seeks to develop theories that explain how social relationships have influences on the lives and conditions of people who interact with others.

The philosophical fathers of sociology were those writers who attempted to analyze the nature of society, and in particular that kind of society that provided just living conditions for its inhabitants. The contributions of the classic Greeks to the development of thought about the ideal nature of both individuals and society provided a foundation for further analyses by a long list of thinkers whose works accumulated century after century from the time of Rome to the Europe of the 16th century. These writers included such luminaries as Cicero, St. Augustine, and Thomas Aquinas. In the more modern era, social contract theorists developed the intellectual foundations for the modern democratic state. These include such figures as Thomas Hobbes (1558–1679), John Locke (1632–1704), and Jean-Jacques Rousseau (1712–1778). By the middle of the 18th century, a rich set of philosophical theories and interpretations had accumulated that appeared to justify replacing monarchy with more democratic forms of government. This set of ideas became a part of the intellectual foundation of the social and political movements that ultimately culminated in the American and French Revolutions.[10]

It was in the political chaos of France following the Revolution that sociology was born as a scientific field. The point of separation of sociology from philosophy came with the work of August Comte (1789–1857). It was Comte who provided the first statement as to why a field of scientific study he called *sociology* should exist, and for what purposes its practitioners should develop their knowledge. For that reason he is often regarded as the "father" of the discipline. In his major work, *The Positive Philosophy,* completed between 1830 and 1842, Comte outlined sociology as a field of scientific inquiry.[11]

In discussing the research methods of the new field, Comte drew directly from the physical sciences of his time and discussed experiments, rational methods of observation, the study of pathological cases, and comparisons between existing societies. More important for present purposes, however, he saw sociology's ultimate goal as the improvement of human social life. Specifically, he believed that social scientists could study the problems of society using scientific methods, diagnose their causes by explaining their origins, and then design programs of intervention that could be put into place (by government) to alleviate those problems.

As sociology became more firmly established in academic circles during the last part of the 19th century, a number of other writers tried to define its goals and methods.[12] Among them none was more important in shaping the field as one seeking solutions to important human problems through the use of scientific methods than Emile Durkheim (1858–1917). In his 1895 *Rules of the Sociological Method,* he developed the thesis that social behavior can be observed and explained within a scientific perspective as phenomena in the same sense as physical facts.[13] His arguments were that such behavior is orderly; that is, it has regularities that can be discovered and explained (through research), just as is the case with the objects of study in physical sciences.[14] As Durkheim put it, we can "postulate a truly providential and pre-established harmony [in social behavior]."[15] If that postulate of order is accepted, Durkheim maintained, it follows that social behavior is characterized by natural laws that can be discovered and described, just as is the case with the phenomena of the physical and biological worlds. Discovering those natural laws through research is the basis for establishing theories that can reveal what antecedent social conditions lead to or bring about what social consequences. By specifying antecedent social conditions (rather than people's mental states) as the causes of social consequences, he sharply separated sociology from psychology. As Durkheim put it, "The determining cause of a social fact should be sought among the social facts preceding it, and not among the states of individual consciousness."[16]

To demonstrate the value of the rules of science as a means of theory development for sociology, Durkheim undertook what is now seen as one of the most influential sociological research studies of all time. In his 1897 *Suicide,* he assembled factual information, such as death statistics and various kinds of census information, from various countries in Europe.[17] He showed that the likelihood of a person committing suicide was related to the way in which the individual was either socially isolated from or integrated into various kinds of groups. The greater the social isolation, the greater the chance of a death by suicide. Conversely, the stronger the individual's social ties, the less likely was death by suicide.

If the goals that Comte, Durkheim, and other sociological pioneers set for sociology have a certain modern ring, it is because they remain much the same today. Through their research, sociologists develop and test theories that try to explain such matters as the causes of crime, disharmony between unlike people, alcoholism, drug addiction, poverty, family breakdown, and many more of the problematic social conditions that lead away from rather than toward ideal conditions of life and a harmonious society.

Thus, by the beginning of the 20th century, the general outlines of sociology's goals, as well as its empirical and quantitative methodology, had been made clear. They have remained essentially the same today. To quote from a widely used basic text: "Sociology is the scientific study of human society and social behavior."[18] Thus, the discipline assumes that order exists in social behavior, that social activities are observable in the same sense as physical phenomena, and that they can be explained by the development of cause–effect theories that explain social consequences as being brought about by antecedent social conditions.

In overview, then, although they focus on different forms of behavior—individual versus social—the goals of both psychology and sociology are in every respect the same. The ultimate purpose of both fields is to use the scientific method to develop theories that explain order and patterns assumed to exist in the various categories of behavior under study.

Theories and Their Uses

As their ultimate scientific objective, psychologists and sociologists seek to develop theories stated as sets of interrelated "axiomatic" propositions.[19] Following the models developed by such philosophers of (physical) science as Braithwaite and Nagel, an axiomatic theory is a set of formal statements that identify systematic relationships between the concepts that the theory incorporates.[20]

In one sense, a theory is a description. Taken together, its concepts and propositions are constructed as a kind of shorthand representation of whatever aspect of reality the theory tries to reflect. They are formulated at different levels of abstraction. Some describe relationships between very general concepts, such as social class, and division of labor, or learning and overt behavior. Others, at a much lower level of abstraction, describe connections between such concepts as unemployment and divorce or perception and behavioral intention.

Theories provide for explanation. They do so by setting forth relationships of dependency between concepts; that is, they state what *independent* conditions or variables must be present so that certain consequences will occur among others that are *dependent* on their presence or action. In many respects, this is the most pragmatic reason theories are so important in social science. They provide an understanding of how things work—what conditions or factors lead to what effects. Once understood, this offers a potential means for intervention and control. Without explanations of some kind, modifying or addressing social or psychological problems would not be possible.

Well-articulated deductive theories make predictions. These are theorems—derived statements that logically predict certain consequences if the propositions of the theory are true. Such predictions serve as guides to research in that they constitute formal hypotheses about what one should find in the realities to which the theory refers. This kind of hypothesis is a reasoned expectation of what one should be able to observe among the facts that the theory purports to describe and explain. Deductive hypothesis development of this kind is the basis of what philosopher of science Abraham Kaplan called the "logic of discovery."[21] Theories spell out the reasons for entertaining a particular hypothesis rather than other possible candidates that might occur to the researcher as unsystematic hunches or suspicions.

If theories are supported by a body of carefully accumulated evidence obtained through research, they can increasingly be accepted as valid explanations of whatever they describe. If modifications are required, research data suggest where improvements can be made. Thus, there is a reciprocal relationship between theory and research in the social sciences. Theories guide research, and when conducted, such research addresses the degree of validity (or need for improvement) of the theory. Ideally, only those theories that are strongly supported by convincing research evidence are retained. Psychologist Carroll C. Pratt put it very simply in his classic work on the logic of modern psychology: "The most important function of science is the construction of theory, for theories give meaning to facts and also make it possible to know what further facts are necessary."[22]

Even though the social sciences seek to develop and verify such axiomatic (formal and deductive) theories, most are initially stated as tentative descriptions awaiting critical research that will help determine their merits. Nevertheless, the basic idea remains the same. Theories at whatever stage of development are candidate representations that are formulated as clearly and systematically as possible to provide accurate descriptions of, predictions about, and explanations of some feature of psychological or sociological reality.

Well-articulated and formal theories do not just pop into people's heads. Theory development begins when something needs to be explained. Almost always, a theory has been proposed by a social scientist who has conducted extensive research on whatever it is that needs explanation. The investigator usually has reason to believe that certain independent factors may be at work in some specific way to produce conditions that have been under investigation. It is not enough, however, for the researcher to just spin off a theory on the basis of hunches and suspicions. That kind of "theorizing" would not be accepted in the research community. There must be some clearly indicated factual basis for suggesting that a set of concepts may be related systematically within a system of propositions that constitute the initial version of the theory. That factual basis is virtually always a body of prior research focusing on the concepts in question.

Theories, then, are inductively obtained by reasoning from a body of known facts (verified research results that have accumulated) to a set of generalizations that state relationships between the concepts describing those facts. What appear to be the independent and dependent factors can be identified as the theory is put together. At that point, after the theory has been tentatively stated, it becomes a guide for research and the process of testing, improvement, and verification begins. Thus, the inductive development of tentative theories and their functions as sources of hypotheses is inextricably linked to the process of empirical research. Research leads to theory formulation, which leads to hypothesis derivation, which leads to further research, which provides the basis for theory assessment and modification, which leads to further research, and so on.

The theory–research relationships discussed here make it clear that it would be unwise to conclude that social science theories are little more than hunches, suspicions, or guesses that lead an investigator to look for some answer in a set of data. Social scientists would reject a dissertation proposal or an application for a research grant if its author stated that the project was to be pursued because he or she had overheard gossip in the cafeteria that there might be a relationship between concepts. Social science research is not undertaken as a result of an anonymous phone call in the middle of the night, or even because of a tip from an eminent social scientist suggesting that a certain pattern might be found by making appropriate empirical observations. Research proposals and reports are expected to show very clearly the inductive reasoning from prior research or the deductive steps from existing theory that led them to their hypothesis.

Accurate Description as a Secondary Goal

Although the development and testing of theory is the primary goal of social science, accurate description of behavioral regularities can be a related secondary goal. As was discussed in relation to the inductive task of theory development, detailed and accurate description of personal and social behavior is required before theories can be generated to explain or predict the conditions under which it takes place. Therefore, theory development and description are related.

At the same time, there are many practical uses for accurate and detailed descriptions of social and psychological behavior that are not related to either theory development or theory testing. Thus, the study of social trends, public attitudes, political opinions, population changes, modes of personal adjustment to various kinds of environments, and many other kinds of individual and collective conduct are a part of the research activities of social scientists. Many of these have pragmatic applications in the affairs of government, the military, education, business, and so on.

Descriptive research can be either qualitative or quantitative. Often, in the early stages of study of some form of social behavior, the use of quantitative scales, questionnaires, experiments, or other tools of quantitative analysis is not warranted. The descriptions of sensitive observers can often lead the way in uncovering the basic concepts that seem to make a difference. Some descriptions can take quantitative form. Many kinds of statistical indices, describing central tendencies, variability, and association between factors can be calculated to provide interpretive coefficients that sum up large numbers of observations in a single number.

THE POSTULATES OF SOCIAL SCIENCE

In pursuing their goal of developing either theories or accurate descriptions of personal and social behavior, social scientists must make certain broad assumptions about their subject matter before they even begin to conduct research. These are the *postulates* of social science. They are not greatly different from parallel assumptions made by physical scientists. Such postulates are propositions taken as starting points for analysis; they are "givens," and not claims that must be verified in some way. Postulates of this kind are suppositions that one must make about the phenomena being studied and analyzed. Without making these assumptions, there would be little point in conducting research or trying to develop theories.[23]

The first postulate is that behavior is part of the world of *natural events.* This very basic assumption is an expression of the thesis of Durkheim that "social facts" are as natural as the "facts" studied by any other field. Because they are labeled psychological, social, or cultural does not place them outside the methods of science. In other words, social scientists must assume that they are observing, describing, and explaining events that are legitimately a part of the world of reality, just as are the behaviors of whatever is studied in other sciences. If the charge is accepted that human behavior is not subject to systematic study because it is ephemeral, unobservable, spiritual, or otherwise unattainable through observation, there would be little point in conducting research.

A second fundamental assumption is the postulate of *order.* For research efforts to make any sense, it must be assumed that there is what Kaplan called a "uniformity of nature."[24] That is, it must be assumed that human behavior follows patterns—regularities or laws—that can be discovered (through research). If such behavior were merely random and whimsical (following no predictable trends or regularities), there would be no need even to try to uncover such patterns.

A third postulate is the assumption of *cause and effect* relationships. This is the assumption that psychological and social events do not just happen for no reason at all. Physical scientists constantly search for the antecedent conditions of such consequences as earthquakes, epidemics, and environmental deterioration. They assume that such events are brought about by specific sets of independent factors and conditions.[25] However, identifying cause–effect relationships between factors as opposed to mere associations between them can be a complex problem in any branch of science. For example, in January 1992, a study was reported at the annual meetings of the American Heart Association in which it was concluded that short people have more heart attacks, and that with every inch of height, heart disease risk decreased by 3%.[26] Whether short stature actually is an independent condition bringing on heart attacks or whether some other factor associated with both is the cause requires further research. Because of the immense number of factors influencing human behavior, social scientists often have great difficulty in identifying cause–effect relationships and distinguishing them from associations. Nevertheless, they must make the assumption that dependent psychological and social consequences follow from independent antecedent conditions. Otherwise developing explanatory theories about such causes would be a futile exercise.

A fourth postulate is that social science research is *value-free*. This is the assumption that such research is undertaken for the purpose of discovering the factual nature of reality, revealing how behavior is actually caused. Research undertaken for nonscientific reasons, such as to promote private economic interests, or to support political, religious, or ideological convictions, is "tainted," and not to be admitted into the body of scientific findings. The same postulate guides researchers in the physical sciences. For example, in 1992 the Princeton Dental Resource Center released findings in its newsletter that were good news for chocolate lovers. Their research had indicated that "eating chocolate may be as beneficial as an apple a day," and that if enjoyed in moderation, chocolate "might even inhibit cavities."[27] As it turned out, the prestigious-sounding Princeton Center (not associated with the university) was founded by and received $1 million annually from Mars, Inc., the makers of such chocolate products as M&Ms, Mars, Snickers, and Milky Way. Needless to say, the findings were called into question by the dental research community. In the same way, the results of social science research are regarded as "tainted" and must be called into question by the community of colleagues if they are made to conform to the declarations and agendas of value-driven interpretations of social or psychological reality.

Finally, a fifth postulate of *tentative truth* is the basis for the "self-policing" nature of social science. This is the assumption that results obtained from even well-conducted and value-free research, and the descriptions and theories constructed from them, need continuous reexamination to ensure that they accurately reflect reality. It is a "back-to-the-drawing-board" postulate that says descriptions and theories are never proven as final truths. They are always subject to modification, or even rejection, if further data seem to require it. This feature of science is in contrast to other routes to knowledge—such as religious revelation, metaphysical reasoning, and tradition—within which truths are seldom revised or rejected.

SOCIAL SCIENCE METHODS FOR CONTROLLED OBSERVATION

To conduct empirical research within this set of basic assumptions, the social sciences have adopted a relatively uniform set of strategies, techniques, and procedures to make the controlled observations required for accurately describing reality or developing and testing theories. Taken together, along with the criteria used to evaluate findings from research, these constitute their methodology. That methodology has been described and discussed in perhaps hundreds of textbooks on research methods and statistics for the social sciences over a period of many decades.[28] Therefore, the major issues need to be summarized briefly to provide a reasonably concise model against which to compare both precision journalism and CAIR analysis.

Measurement

At the heart of empirical observation, which is the basic process that ultimately distinguished science from philosophy, is the process of measurement. Stated very simply, measurement can be defined as the use of systematic rules to convert subjective sensory experiences into data. The term *data* in this sense refers to empirical observations that have been recorded as symbols. This is a critical feature of science. Data must be "public." That is, in a form that can be understood, examined, and assessed (even repeated if necessary) by other researchers. In qualitative studies the symbols used for recording observations are the words and phrases with which the observer describes what has been seen. In quantitative measurement they are usually numerical indices or coefficients of some sort that locate a person or other unit of observation on a continuum that ranges from low to high.

A host of standardized tests, questionnaires, and scales have been developed to assess and record in quantitative form the behavior of people or groups. Various levels of precision and sophistication in measurement with such instruments are widely understood by social scientists. Nominal, ordinal, interval, and ratio levels refer to distinct features of scales. Each of these levels has either advantages or limitations that make their data more or less amenable to mathematical manipulation.

The range of variables that can be measured by social scientists is impressive. Intelligence tests were pioneered early in the 20th century. Attitude scales were introduced in the 1920s. The list of instruments currently available to measure social or psychological behavior includes such phenomena as alienation, group cohesiveness, occupational prestige, group morale, neighborliness, leadership, marital satisfaction, and literally hundreds more.[29]

Each of the social sciences shares a concern with the precision and trustworthiness of the observation process. Those concerns are often stated in terms of the concepts of validity and reliability. The *validity* of a particular procedure for measurement is the degree to which it actually corresponds to the features of psychological or social reality that it has been designed to assess. A valid intelligence scale, for example, should assess an individual's actual capacity to solve problems effectively, and not something else, like level of education. *Reliability* refers to the consistency of results obtained with a measuring procedure. If it gives one result today but something different tomorrow, it lacks reliability.

Sampling

Regardless of whether the social scientist is studying psychological or social behavior, some specific and limited set of persons or groups have to be selected for observation. It is not practical to study the entire population. The question automatically arises, therefore, as to whether those actually under study are like those in the larger group or population to which the researcher wants to extend his or her results. This is the problem of sampling—how to select a limited and manageable number of persons or groups for study so that the results obtained can be extended to describe the behavior of all similar people.

Various kinds of sampling designs are employed for the selection of representative units on which observations are to be made. Among the formal designs that are frequently used are the simple random sample (the standard for comparison) and various others that approximate its characteristics, such as systematic, multistage random, stratified, cluster, sequential, judgment, and quota samples.[30] The basic rule that such plans try to meet is that each unit in the population under study should have an equal (or at least known) probability of being selected for inclusion in the sample. The selection of samples and the projection of results obtained to larger populations when using different designs is a highly technical aspect of social science research methodology.[31]

Formal Research Designs

Social scientists do not just go about making random observations on samples in the hope that they will accidentally reveal patterns and relationships among the events that they study. Scientific observation is performed under highly controlled conditions. This ensures that what is being observed is the behavior relevant to the theory that guides the research or whatever questions are under study.

The classic research design for science is the experiment. Modeled after procedures developed over centuries in the physical sciences, designs for experiments became the central strategy for controlled observation in psychology during the 19th century. Although the field used many other kinds of research designs, the experiment remains as its procedure of choice today.[32]

Although there are many forms and variations, the logic of the experiment is straightforward. It is a design for observing the results on behavior of some form of "treatment" that those observed experience, controlling for other factors that could influence the outcome. Usually, some form of measurement of a dependent factor under study is completed as a "before" observation on each subject (prior to experiencing the treatment). Then, an experimental condition (the treatment) is experienced by the same subjects. Afterward, the dependent factor under study is assessed again. The question is whether the treatment (independent factor) induced some change in the dependent factor as revealed by the difference between the before and after measurements. There may be several experimental groups, each receiving different values or versions of the treatment. Often, one or more control groups are used. Among the control subjects, the same dependent factor is measured before and after (with no intervening treatment, or some neutral experience). If only the experimental subjects changed, an inference can be drawn that the treatment induced change. Obviously if the control subjects changed in the same manner as the experimental group, no causal inferences can be drawn as to the influence of the independent factor.

Experiments are sometimes conducted outside "laboratory" settings, using entire groups as subjects, such as military units, factory production shifts, or even entire communities. These are usually called field experiments, and they are used for observing subjects systematically without disturbing their normal patterns of life.[33]

The second major research design used in social science is the survey. Because of the nature of their subject matter—usually the social behavior of a large number of people living in a community or society—experiments are not as widely used by sociologists. They do use the field experiment design for some purposes. Also, many kinds of social processes (e.g., jury deliberations) can be simulated in laboratory-type settings and a substantial number of such sociological experiments have been conducted. Nevertheless, the survey is the most widely used research design for sociological research.

The survey is a modern adaptation of the census, which has been in use since ancient times. Rulers often carefully counted the number of their subjects when it came time to build pyramids, raise armies, or collect taxes. Today, the federal government has sufficient power and funds to conduct a nationwide decennial census, but a research enterprise of such a scale is not remotely possible for sociological researchers. Therefore, sampling is a critical feature of survey research.

Systematic observation of respondents in surveys is usually conducted through the use of carefully designed questionnaires carefully administered in interviews or under related conditions. Like other formalized procedures for measurement in social science, survey questionnaires are used to transform researcher's observations to symbols to obtain quantitative data for numerical manipulation.

Opinion polls are essentially surveys in which the behavior under observation usually consists of people's feelings or beliefs about some political issue or candidate. Opinion polls are conducted for the purpose of gaining an accurate description of the orientations of a particular population or some identified category (e.g., voters, adults, residents of a particular community, etc.) at a specific point in time. They are seldom conducted for the purpose of developing or testing a theory—although the data derived from polls can sometimes be used for that purpose. The design of polls, including sampling, questionnaire development, and contact with subjects parallels that of the more general survey design.

CRITERIA FOR MAKING DECISIONS

As already discussed, research in social science is essentially a search for patterns. The discovery of trends, differences, and relationships among the psychological and social factors or conditions under observation provides the basis for constructing theories that may explain those patterns. Thus, an important question always arises when some sort of pattern appears to be revealed by research. Is it really a reflection of reality, or is it just a product of random circumstances? If only chance is at work, the results are relatively meaningless. However, if the pattern found actually resulted because one or more of the factors measured served as an antecedent factor to influence others under study as consequent conditions, then the possibility of a cause–effect sequence is present. But how can one decide?

The answer is that social scientists use the very powerful tool of statistics as criteria in making their judgments. The term *statistics* originated from the concept of "state arithmetic," which from ancient times meant the tabulation of quantitative information about different nations—births, deaths, exports, imports, size of armies, and the like.[34] Today, the term refers to a body of descriptive indices and probability models that serve as tools of analysis and as bases for making decisions about the significance of research results in virtually all of the sciences. Statistics historian James W. Tankard, Jr., summarized the situation succinctly:

> The dominant research paradigm in the social sciences is the use of statistical analysis to study human beings and their society. Basically, this paradigm involves gathering quantitative data and then applying a statistical test that allows the researcher to draw conclusions. This approach is widely used in research in the fields of psychology, sociology [and other social sciences].[35]

Originally, the probability theories on which the field of statistics depends had nothing to do with science. Their development began as far back as the 1400s, when Luca Pacioli and other mathematicians tried to determine the chances of various combinations relevant to games of chance. As time went on, a body of knowledge about probability and applications to various other fields of knowledge accumulated to provide both theoretical foundations and practical applications of modern statistics. Early contributions came from many sources. They included those who studied probabilities at gaming tables, specialists in marine insurance who worried about wrecks and piracy, and astronomers who calculated the curves described by errors made in celestial observations. During the 19th century, a growing number of scholars invented various statistical indices and tests that could be applied in such fields as agronomy, biology, meteorology, and eventually throughout the social sciences.[36] Statistics remains a very lively and constantly developing field today.

The underlying logic of using statistical tests to make decisions about results is basically straightforward. The researcher compares the quantitative pattern found in the data with the probability that such a pattern could have occurred by chance alone. Results obtained from chance alone assume that all the conditions under study had only random influences. If that explanation can be rejected as unlikely (having a very low probability), then an inference can be made that the independent factor or factors under study were responsible for the pattern identified in the dependent factor.

It is a remarkably effective and essentially simple way to make such decisions: Calculate the probability that the pattern among the factors under study could be a product of mere chance. If that probability is sufficient, chance wins! In that case, the hypothesis that there is actually a pattern there in reality producing the findings cannot be accepted. If that is the outcome, the theory from which the hypothesis was obtained does not look all that great. If the probability that only chance were at work is sufficiently low, then the hypothesis that a pattern has been revealed by the data can tentatively be accepted. If that is the case, the theory from which the hypothesis came looks much better.

But what is a "sufficiently low" probability? Social scientists get very conservative at this point. They see their decision-making process as like gambling. (Indeed, as noted earlier, probability theory originated in part from calculations related to gambling.) Social scientists have strong rules against accepting hypotheses without good evidence. Therefore, they design the game so that chance (like the casinos at Las Vegas) is almost always likely to win. They will accept a hypothesis that a pattern exists in their data only if it could occur by chance about 5 times out of 100 or less—which is really a long shot. Sometimes the standard is set even lower, such as 1 time out of 100, or even less, which is an even worse gamble. Thus, when chance is rejected as an explanation of what has been found, the prospects of making a wrong decision are really very limited. Clearly, then, the probability criteria used for decisions about results are conservative, to say the least, and the chances of false readings are very low.

Inferential Statistics

To make these kinds of decisions, pitting hypotheses derived from theory against explanations attributed to chance, the field of inferential statistics was developed. *Inferential statistics* consists of ways to calculate the probabilities of a great many kinds of events. For example, one can easily compute the averages of some factor (like income) for two samples of people. If it is noted that they are different, the question arises as to whether that is a real difference, reflecting the actual condition of life among the two samples, or if it merely represents a chancelike variation that one would expect if one drew many such samples and calculated their averages. To answer this question, a statistical test is performed. It shows the probability of obtaining a difference of that magnitude if a huge number of samples had been drawn and differences had been obtained from repeated comparisons of income averages. If the obtained difference between the two samples has a probability of less than 5 in 100, the hypothesis that it is chancelike can be rejected. The conclusion, then, is that there appears to be a real pattern there, reflecting the actual conditions of life among those studied.

Without detailing calculation procedures or specifics of application, the statistical indices and tests used most widely in social science are the *correlation coefficient* (for the study of associations between factors), the *t test* (for the study of differences between averages of two sets of observations), the *chi-square test* (for comparing observed distributions of data with what would be expected if only chance caused their arrangement) and the *analysis of variance* (a procedure for assessing the variation of the averages of specific groups under study around a general average calculated across all groups that are under study).[37]

Descriptive Statistics

Another category of statistics widely used in research is aimed not at testing hypotheses derived from theories but at accurately describing psychological or social behavior, which was already identified as a secondary goal of the social sciences. Descriptive statistics are indexes and coefficients that can be calculated to "sum up" in a single number the central tendencies, amount of variation, general patterns of association, or overall trends in some body of data. For example, it would be possible to write a sentence that describes accurately how much time most families have their television sets on during a typical day. By specifying the numerical average, however, that statement can be reduced to a single index, such as a mean of 7.2 hours per day. Such indices and coefficients greatly simplify what would otherwise be more cumbersome to describe in words. Thus, a simple statistic, like a mean, sets forth in a single number the value of some measured factor that can be attributed to most of those who were assessed. It does so with a minimum of error for any of those studied. Such an index does not describe accurately any particular family that might have been studied. However, it would truly miss the mark for only a limited number, and it would be a pretty good estimate for the majority. Thus, descriptive statistics are an important means of communicating the characteristics of large numbers of observations.

REPORTING THE RESULTS OF SOCIAL SCIENCE RESEARCH

No social science research project can be regarded as complete until its findings have been reported to other qualified specialists. This is the case because the postulate of tentative truth, noted earlier, provides for self-policing among social scientists. Science is a public enterprise. A researcher may uncover astounding results that could revolutionize the fundamental nature of the discipline, but unless they are published, they never enter the accumulated body of knowledge developed by science. Furthermore, for any research project there is always the question of whether acceptable scientific rules of investigation were followed. This requires examination of the methodology employed as well as what was found in the results. The most qualified individuals to make such judgments are peers who are themselves specialized in the particular area and who understand the rules of methodology. For these reasons, social scientists make use of three procedures to achieve the goal of self-policing.

First, oral reports summarizing the methods and results of recently completed studies are often presented at professional conferences. Others, who are interested in the particular topic, can listen to an account of what was studied and what was found. Reactions by peers to such presentations often provide the investigator with important feedback that can be used in refining the final report.

The second form of self-policing comes just before publication of the report. The results of social science research are normally prepared in the form of an article of one or two dozen pages to be published in a technical journal. There are other outlets, such as government reports, books, and even newsletters put out by research institutes. However, the technical journals are usually the medium of choice for several reasons. One is that they are circulated in a timely manner to a relevant audience of specialists. Another is that they go into a permanent record in the form of library holdings, where they are easily accessed. A third is that abstracts (summaries) or even full text of what appears in each issue of such a journal are entered into computer databases, where researchers can conveniently find out what others have done on a topic.

A report of research must be submitted in manuscript form as a candidate for publication to a technical journal, where it is closely examined and assessed before being accepted. At this point, such manuscripts undergo a process that is standard among the sciences. The editor of the journal receiving the report sends a copy to each of several specialists in the area of the research, who agree to evaluate its merits. Those referees are not given the name of the person who prepared the report and the author does not know the identity of the judges. Only the editor knows. This "blind" process generally works well and reports of research projects that were either done poorly in terms of methodology or that do not add anything significant to the accumulating body of knowledge in the specialty, are rejected. Standards tend to be high, and many social science journals reject as many as 95% of the candidate manuscripts received.

A third form of self-policing takes place after publication. Many specialists in a particular form of psychological or social behavior read the technical journals reporting research in their area. Thus, new results will be scrutinized by many who are able to make judgments about its merits. If a particular researcher feels that flaws are present in the report, a description of the perceived shortcoming is sent to the editor of the journal, who then invites the original author to prepare a reply. These often spirited exchanges are printed in the journal, enabling the community of interested colleagues to make further judgments about the report.

These three features of screening and evaluating research results provide for relatively effective self-policing. They do not absolutely guarantee that research reports are always important, well conducted, and truthful. However, no group outside the scientific community devoted to assembling reliable knowledge referees and scrutinizes its reports as rigorously. Thus, fakery is actually rare in social science (as it is in other sciences). Furthermore, the system makes it difficult for such factors as cronyism and other forms of social ties to influence what gets into the record.

This discussion of social science and its methodology has been presented in some detail to provide a methodological model for comparison with CAIR. Obviously, CAIR is in its infancy, but if it is to develop in the future as a systematic means for generating valid and reliable knowledge for the public about the functioning of their government (or other aspects of society) increasing attention must be paid to its methodological foundation. Over the years ahead, those who use computers for quantitative analysis of electronic records will face many of the issues and problems that were encountered by the social scientists as they developed a formal methodology for their disciplines.

PRECISION JOURNALISM: SOCIAL SCIENCE IN THE NEWSROOM

The second mode of analysis with which CAIR is compared is *precision journalism*. This relatively new approach to journalism makes extensive use of the methods of the social sciences that have been described. To clarify what it is and where it came from, this section of the chapter summarizes briefly the reasons for precision journalism's initial development as well as its major methods and strategies.

The Founding of Precision Journalism

In 1969 Philip Meyer received a grant from the Russell Sage Foundation to produce a manuscript entitled, "The Application of Social Science and Behavioral Science Research Methods to the Practice of Journalism."[38] As it turned out, the title of that proposed manuscript was to become a concise definition of a new approach to fact gathering, analysis, and reporting that Meyer advocated. In searching for a name for the new field, he adopted the term *precision journalism,* which had been suggested by communication scholar Everette Dennis.

The nature of the new approach to journalistic analysis was set forth in 1973 by Meyer in a definitive book entitled *Precision Journalism: A Reporter's Introduction to Social Science Methods.*[39] In this seminal work, he explained the reasons why a new form of journalism was necessary and discussed various methods adopted from the social and behavioral sciences that might be appropriate for use by its practitioners. The book suggested that quantitative techniques, computers, careful conceptualization, statistical reasoning, and research designs from the social sciences could become tools of analysis by which reporters could more adequately perform their roles.

Meyer's reasons for advocating the adoption of quantitative techniques from social science as a means for developing facts for news stories were clear. In many ways, he maintained, journalists and social scientists are on the same mission. Both attempt to develop accurate descriptions of reality; both try to explain how certain events or behaviors occur; and both report their results to a relevant audience. However, traditionally, both groups used different methods to achieve these goals. Most importantly, the methods of the established press often yielded inaccurate accounts of what Walter Lippmann called the "world outside" and news stories inevitably created misrepresentations that distorted the "pictures in our heads."[40]

Why a New Approach Was Needed

As shown in earlier chapters, the development of journalism in the 19th century was very different from that of the social sciences. Fields such as psychology and sociology looked to the quantitative research strategies of the physical sciences as models for conducting their investigations, whereas journalists accumulated their own traditions of inquiry based primarily on qualitative techniques. As discussed earlier, the methods of social science were founded on theory development, measurement, quantitative data analysis, formal research designs, and an probabilistic epistemology. In contrast, Meyer noted, the strategies of journalistic fact gathering and analysis took a different route. Reporters depended mainly on personal intuitions and suspicions to guide their inquiries and relied on spokespersons and anecdotes for evidence. Finally, their findings were interpreted through a filter of personal values. Journalists were also influenced by their own occupational subculture—that is, the "conventional wisdom" about what was worth reporting and how it should be presented to the public with leads, quotes, and human interest accounts.[41] In addition, Meyer noted, journalists "argued with dreary persistence," such issues as whether "objectivity" was possible or desirable.[42] Later, this became a debate over "fairness" in reporting the news. Meyer maintained that these concerns led journalists to emphasize the presentation of both sides of an issue rather than an understanding of its causes and implications. Often, reporters served merely as transmitters of what had been said by various sides, avoiding their own fact gathering, analyses, and interpretations.

Meyer believed that one way to improve the products of reporting was "to push journalism toward science, incorporating both the powerful data-gathering and analysis tools of science and its disciplined search for the verifiable truth."[43] This meant "treating journalism as if it were a science, adopting scientific method, scientific objectivity, and scientific ideals to the entire process of mass communication."[44]

Goals of Precision Journalism

Precision journalism, defined as the application of social and behavioral research methods to the practice of journalism, has gained acceptance in recent years.[45] The findings obtained from research methods such as surveys, polls, field experiments, and content analysis are blended with personal interviews and human interest examples. However, precision journalism differs from social science research in some ways.

In social science, description can be important, but the paramount goal is theory development and verification. In precision journalism, the central objective usually is accurate description. Developing a broad or general explanatory theory is less often the objective. As journalism professors Demers and Nichols stated it:

> Precision journalists are concerned with contemporary social issues; social scientists are more concerned with isolating general principles associated with human behavior or organization. . . . On the whole, precision journalists are less likely to be interested in what causes something than in describing it.[46]

However, Meyer maintained that, quite often, journalists are interested in causation. He pointed out that many important policy issues involve assumptions about causation that journalists can test. For example, in 1967, his *Detroit Free Press* study of riot participants did not support popular theories about the causes of the Detroit riot. Bartlett and Steele's 1972 analysis of court records disproved the prosecutor's claim that lenient judges were the main cause of the release of captured criminals to the streets.[47]

Another relatively obvious difference is that precision journalism seeks a different final product than does social science. The reporter's goal is to produce news stories that can be read and understood by the general public. In contrast, social scientists prepare their reports for journals that are read mainly by other specialists in their field. Moreover, the requirement for rigorous and blind peer review of reports for publication has an enormous advantage for social scientists. Investigators can be reasonably sure that what they report—theoretical considerations, methods used, decisions made, and implications of the findings—will be readily understood by their readers. The self-policing features of scientific publication ensure that findings must survive critical challenges before being added to the accumulating body of knowledge.

Methods and Strategies Advocated

There are a number of techniques, procedures, and strategies that are discussed in available books devoted to precision journalism. The major methods that have been used in precision journalism are surveys and public opinion polls. Other methods such as field experiments and content analysis are also advocated but have been used less frequently. Books devoted to the methods that precision journalism can use include discussions of a list of measuring techniques, research designs, or modes of analysis—such as might be found in any basic text on methodology from the social sciences. For example, in their chapters, Demers and Nichols take their reader through summaries of such topics as the following: levels of measurement, validity, reliability, response rates, questionnaire construction, cross-sectional studies, control groups, sampling design, descriptive and inferential statistics, null hypotheses, bivariate statistics, and multivariate analysis.[48] Each, they feel, can be an important tool.

COMPARING CAIR, SOCIAL SCIENCE, AND PRECISION JOURNALISM

Each of the three approaches to the study of and reporting on human activities—CAIR, social science, and precision journalism—has a distinct history and each has been developed for different purposes. However, although their goals are sometimes different, all incorporate many similar features. Because of this, it can be difficult to identify what is unique to each and what they have in common. The sections that follow attempt to place those similarities and differences into sharper perspective.

CAIR Versus Social Science Research

Social science research and CAIR are similar in many respects. In both cases, the focus is on human behavior and events that affect it. Underlying both are the assumptions that human behavior is part of the world of reality—just as is the case with the physical facts of other disciplines—and can be subjected to systematic study. Furthermore, it is assumed that human behavior follows patterns that are discoverable through systematic analysis.

In social science, detailed and accurate description of social behavior is often an important goal. This objective is shared by CAIR. Thus, the investigation of such phenomena as economic trends, population changes, public attitudes, sentencing patterns in the federal courts, auditing patterns of the IRS, and the description of many other kinds of individual and collective conduct can be part of the research activities of both modes of analysis.

Both social science research and CAIR are essentially quantitative disciplines. Many specific techniques for numerical investigation are used in much the same way by CAIR analysts and social science researchers. These include the calculation of percentages, totals, and descriptive indices, such as means, medians, and modes, or more complex statistical coefficients.

In both fields, the analysis is guided by systematic questions that are to be answered by specific compilations of data, rather than by a random or selective tour through the numbers. The source of those questions may be derivations from theory in the case of social science. In CAIR they are more likely to stem from oversight concerns.

Decisions in social science concerning the meaning of findings are normally made on the basis of a *probabilistic epistemology*; that is, after the relevant observations have been made, carefully formulated statistical hypotheses are accepted or rejected on the basis of probability-based tests. These settle the question as to whether the results could be dismissed as merely chancelike, or whether they appear to depend on the influences of independent factors and variables. This type of decision making is appropriate for CAIR analyses only when statistical indices have been calculated from samples of the available data.

Although the two approaches appear to have those features in common, there are a number of ways in which they differ. To begin with, their overall goals are often not the same. The primary goal of many social science research projects is to develop or verify some cause–effect theory—an explanation of what antecedent conditions lead generally to particular consequences in similar circumstances. The CAIR investigator is typically less concerned with the development, formalization, or verification of explanatory scientific theories. The goal of a CAIR analysis is to seek news—especially that related to oversight and disclosure. Furthermore, in social science, theory building emphasizes concepts, relationships, and cause–effect sequences that are generalizable—that can be used to describe and explain an entire category or class of events under study. In other words, social science seeks principles and laws of individual and social behavior that are widely applicable to various kinds of populations. In contrast, the major focus of most CAIR analyses is usually on a restricted set of events within a specific agency or other setting that are newsworthy.

Social science investigations follow accepted research designs. These include the survey, the experiment, and sample-based content analysis. The purpose of such standard designs is to provide strategies for data gathering in which original empirical observations are made with tight control over extraneous variables. For the most part, current CAIR analyses are rarely based on standard research designs. Also, in many CAIR analyses the observations under study are not gathered firsthand. Many are prerecorded in existing electronic files. In such cases, the investigator has no control over how or why the observations were gathered or the manner in which they were recorded.

In many cases, social scientists seek to project findings from limited observations, such as those obtained by samples, to larger populations. In contrast, many CAIR analyses are based on a complete database combining an entire population of observations rather than a random sample of those records. Thus, current CAIR analyses have made less use of samples, probability distributions, and the inferential statistics needed to estimate population parameters.

Finally, although both modes of analysis report their results to relevant constituencies using established rules and conventions, they do so in diferent ways. Reports of the results of social science research are usually screened by peers in a blind review process before publication. They are read mainly by specialists. In contrast, the results of CAIR analyses are generally reported by a news medium and read by the general public.

CAIR Versus Precision Journalism

There is less confusion about the nature of precision journalism than is the case with CAIR. Books devoted to the methods and techniques used in precision journalism show a close parallel between it and its parent social science disciplines. But what exactly is the relationship between CAIR and precision journalism? Both, after all, have stemmed from the concerns of the press, rather than solely from the traditions of science.

Both CAIR and precision journalism share a number of features. Like social science research, both focus on human behavior and subscribe to the underlying assumptions that human conduct follows patterns that can be discovered through systematic investigation. The primary goal of both is the accurate description of contemporary social behavior related to issues that are newsworthy. Both are quantitative disciplines and use many of the same techniques in their analyses, such as the calculation of percentages, means, median values, and other statistical indices. However, qualitative concerns often play an important role in the sense that the numbers are usually supplemented with interviews and comments of individuals to gain insight and understanding and to help readers relate more easily to the issues.

CAIR Versus "Powerful Browsers"

As noted in chapter 5, Meyer distinguished between journalists who employ complex methods and statistical indices in their analyses and those who use electronic records in the same manner they search paper files. He referred to such journalists as "computer cowboys," or more recently as "powerful browsers."[49] Armed with computers, these individuals read through vast numbers of records for specific newsworthy information, but the strategies they use do not extend beyond those reporters used in the past with paper and pencil. For the most part, they restrict their analyses to the counting, sorting, ranking, and matching procedures that Elliot Jaspin described (chapter 1). Certainly, the "powerful browsers" often uncover striking and critical newsworthy facts, but they leave the majority of the information in the database untouched.

Powerful browsing developed independently from precision journalism.[50] The increased use and diffusion of this form of computer-assisted reporting resulted, in part, from the growing popularity and declining prices of personal computers in the 1980s. Reporters began to buy PCs to use at home for word processing and a few other tasks. As they became more familiar with the machines, they began to see new uses and to understand the power of the computer to manipulate data, not just words. However, most of those journalists did not consider scientific methods as part of the process. Many of their projects consisted mainly of sorting (arranging the data in ascending or descending order) or matching (checking names or information listed in one file or database with information in another), with little use or consideration of statistical procedures.

Summarizing the Conceptual Relationships

In chapter 4, computer-assisted journalism (CAJ) was described as an "umbrella" concept. Some refer to this as computer-assisted reporting (CAR) or database journalism. By whatever label, CAJ includes at least three major ways in which reporters are now using computers to develop news stories. The first involves the searching or use of publicly available or commercially vended online databases, electronic bulletin boards, or the Internet to locate sources or assemble information on a person, topic, or issue. In the second way, CAJ includes the creation or construction of unique "in-house" databases that may contain information collected by reporters from a variety of sources. The third is CAIR, the central focus of this book. In CAIR's most common application, computers and software are used to analyze electronic records in order to conduct oversight investigations and disclose newsworthy findings. Finally, as Meyer notes, other sources of information created or analyzed with a computer could be included in the definition of CAJ or of CAIR. These include survey research data, and the results of public opinion polls, field experiments, or content analyses.

Precision journalism is also an umbrella term. Meyer suggests that the relationship between CAJ and precision journalism can be viewed conceptually as two intersecting circles or categories. In other words, some forms of CAJ can also be classified under the precision journalism umbrella, whereas others cannot. Within this conceptualization, there are four possibilities: A particular analysis can be an example of (a) CAJ but not precision journalism, (b) precision journalism but not CAJ, (c) both CAJ and precision journalism, or (d) neither one.[51]

To illustrate this fourfold conceptualization, the act of searching Lexis/Nexis or a similar commercial database for background information on an individual qualifies as CAJ. But such an act does not use scientific methods and cannot be considered as precision journalism. In a similar fashion, matching a computerized list of drivers' licenses with criminal records to find the state's 10 worst drunk driving offenders qualifies as a form of CAJ but not of precision journalism. On the other hand, the analysis of comparable federal judicial districts reported in earlier chapters, which used census data and multivariate statistical procedures to find districts that were most similar on a number of demographic and economic characteristics, is an example of both precision journalism and CAJ.

Viewed another way, Meyer believes that the conceptual relationship between precision journalism and CAJ can be shown graphically as a 2 × 2 classification, such as that shown in Fig. 8.1.[52]

In this conceptualization, Cell A would include those forms of CAJ that are also examples of precision journalism, such as the case study of the judicial records presented in chapters 6 and 7. Most examples of CAIR would be included here. Cell B would include power browsing, the use of commercial online database searching, and such uses as finding information

PRECISION JOURNALISM

		Present	Absent
COMPUTER-ASSISTED JOURNALISM	Present	A	B
	Absent	C	D

FIG. 8.1. Conceptual relationship between precision journalism and computer-assisted journalism.

on the Internet or on an electronic bulletin board. Cell C might include the more traditionally defined methods of precision journalism, such as surveys, polls, content analyses, and field experiments, or social science methods conducted without the aid of a computer. Cell D would cover the entire domain of conventional journalism.

Another way of conceptualizing the relationship between computer-assisted journalism or reporting and the type of precision journalism discussed by Meyer is as a continuum. It was noted earlier that on one end are those computer-assisted stories that make use of computers for such tasks as sorting and matching, but do not involve social science research designs (power browsing). At the opposite end are more sophisticated precision journalism projects that incorporate standard research designs and statistical analysis strategies from social science. In between are many kinds of projects that in one way or another incorporate some social science methods. Thus, according to Meyer, these are not mutually exclusive boxes, but conceptual categories that merge into each other at various points along a continuum.

In summary, the nature of CAIR can be more adequately understood by comparing it conceptually with both social science and precision journalism. All three share a number of similarities. They are basically quantitative modes of analysis that also make use of qualitative information. Social science is aimed at developing concepts and verifying theories that explain broad categories of similar events and situations. Precision journalism applies the techniques and strategies of social science research to gather and analyze data relevant to a particular news objective. CAIR also makes use of techniques of statistical analysis drawn from social science. Furthermore, unlike social scientists and those practicing precision journalism, CAIR analysts who use agency-generated electronic records have no voice in determining how the data are gathered, for what purposes, or in what format. CAIR is in some respects a unique enterprise—a mode of analysis that in many ways depends on its own rules and methods.

At this time, there has been little effort to formulate systematically a methodology for CAIR. As this book has shown, a variety of specific techniques and strategies have been used by various journalists to analyze records with computers. However, those methods have not been brought together and integrated in a systematic way. In contrast, the methodology of social science (and by extension of precision journalism) has long been formalized and exceedingly well documented. It seems clear that if CAIR is to develop more effectively in the future as a source from which the public can gain trustworthy knowledge about the performance of their government, a formal methodology for CAIR would offer many advantages. It is toward that objective that the next chapter is addressed.

NOTES AND REFERENCES

1. For example, see: James D. Laird and Nicholas S. Thompson, *Psychology* (Boston: Houghton Mifflin Company, 1992), pp. 2–23; James A. Inciardi and Robert A. Rothman, *Sociology: Principles and Applications* (San Diego: Harcourt Brace Jovanovich, 1990), pp. 2–59.
2. For a discussion of the ideas that shaped the discipline of psychology from the 1880s onward, see: Deborah Coon, "Standardizing the Subject: Experimental Psychologists, Introspection, and the Quest for a Technoscientific Ideal," *Technology and Culture,* Vol. 34, No. 4, October, 1993, pp. 757–783.
3. Weber chose to publish his results in Latin, which was not unusual for scientific reports at the time. See: Ernst H. Weber, *De Pulso, Resorpitone, Auditu et Tactu: Annotationes Anotomicae et Physiologicae* (Leipzig: Koehler, 1834).
4. Gustav T. Fechner, *Element der Psychophysik* (Leipzig: Breitkopf and Hartei, 1860). An English version is Gustav T. Fechner, *Elements of Psychophysics,* Vols. I and II (New York: Holt, Rinehart and Winston, 1966).
5. See: Hermann Ebbinghaus, *Memory: A Contribution to Experimental Psychology* (New York: Columbia University Teacher's College, 1913) translated by H. A. Ruger and C. E. Bussenius. First published in Berlin in 1885.
6. See: Louis L. Bernard, *Instinct: A Study in Social Psychology* (New York: Holt, 1926.)
7. See: Harry E. Garrett *Great Experiments in Psychology,* 3rd edition (New York: Appleton-Century-Crofts, Inc., 1951), pp. 40–62.
8. Ivan P. Pavlov, *Conditioned Reflexes* (New York: International Publishers, 1928).
9. Contemporary basic texts in psychology almost uniformly emphasize those three points. Examples are: James W. Kalat, *Introduction to Psychology* (Belmont, Cal.: Wadsworth Publishing Company, 1985) pp. 26–27; John P. Houston, Helen Bee, and David Rimm, *Invitation to Psychology* (New York: Academic Press, 1982) pp. 18–19; and Ernst R. Hilgard, Richard Atkinson, and Rita Atkinson, *Introduction to Psychology* (New York: Harcourt Brace Jovanovich, 1975), pp. 12–13.
10. For an excellent summary of the ideas of these and other writers who contributed to the growing body of writings on the nature of the state, see: William Ebenstein, *Great Political Thinkers* (New York: Rinehart and Company, 1954).
11. August Comte, *The Positive Philosophy,* freely translated and condensed by Harriet Martineau (New York: Calvin Blanchard, 1858). First published in France in six volumes between 1830 and 1842.
12. Important additions to the emerging discipline were made in the late 19th century by Karl Mark, Herbert Spencer, Ferdinand Toennies, Charles Horton Cooley, Georg Simmel, and Vilfredo Pareto. See: Lewis A. Coser, *Masters of Sociological Thought* (New York: Harcourt, Brace Jovanovich, 1971).
13. Emile Durkheim, *The Rules of The Sociological Method,* translated by Sarah A. Solovay and John H. Mueller (London: Collier-Macmillan, 1938). First published as *Les Regles de la Methode Sociologique* (Paris: Felix Alcan, 1895).

14. *Ibid.,* p. 92.

15. *Ibid.,* p. 92.

16. *Ibid.,* p. 110.

17. Emile Durkheim, *Suicide,* translated by John A. Spaulding and George Simpson (New York: The Free Press of Glencoe, Inc., 1949). First published as *Le Suicide: Etude de Sociologie* (Paris: Felix Alcan, 1897).

18. Ian Robertson, *Sociology* (New York: Worth Publishers, 1977), p. 3; Similar definitions can be found in Erich Goode, *Sociology* (Englewood Cliffs, N.J.: Prentice-Hall, 1984), p. 3, and David Popenoe, 3rd ed., *Sociology* (Englewood Cliffs, N.J.: Prentice-Hall, 1980) p. 8.

19. For an exposition of the nature of axiomatic theory in sociology, see: George Caspar Homans, Chapter 25, "Contemporary Theory in Sociology," in Robert E. L. Faris, *Handbook of Modern Sociology* (Chicago: Rand McNally and Company, 1964), pp. 951–977.

20. The most influential work in the philosophy of science influencing the development of social science theory along these lines is: Richard R. Braithwaite, *Scientific Explanation* (Cambridge: Cambridge University Press, 1953). See also: Ernest Nagel, *The Structure of Science* (New York: Harcourt, 1961).

21. Abraham Kaplan, *The Conduct of Inquiry: Methodology for Behavioral Science* (San Francisco: Chandler Publishing Company, 1964), p. 17.

22. Carroll C. Pratt, *The Logic of Modern Psychology* (New York: The Macmillan Company, 1948), p. vii.

23. This discussion of postulates reflects many of the ideas, but is not identical to, the discussion of these issues found in: George A. Lundberg, Ch. 1, "The Postulates of Science and Their Implications for Sociology," *Foundations of Sociology* (New York: The Macmillan Company, 1939), pp. 5–44.

24. Abraham Kaplan, *op. cit.,* p. 20.

25. Kaplan referred to this as an assumption that everything is "causally necessitated." *Ibid.,* p. 21.

26. Syracuse *Herald American,* January 26th, 1992, p. AA3.

27. See: Barry Meier, "Dubious Theory: Chocolate a Cavity Fighter," *New York Times,* April 15, 1992, p. A1.

28. Extensive discussions of the philosophy of science underlying the methodology of the behavioral sciences can be found in: Abraham Kaplan, *The Conduct of Inquiry: Methodology of the Behavioral Sciences* (San Francisco: Chandler Publishing Company, 1964) and Maurice Natanson, *Philosophy of the Social Sciences* (New York: Random House, 1963). Dozens of contemporary texts on research methods and techniques are available. See, for example: Roger D. Wimmer and Joseph R. Dominick, *Mass Media Research,* 3rd ed. (Belmont, Cal.: Wadsworth Publishing Company, 1991), and Kenneth S. Bordens and Bruce B. Abbott, *Research Design and Methods* (Mountain View, Cal.: Mayfield Publishing Company, 1991).

29. For a standard discussion of measuring procedures commonly available, see: Delbert C. Miller, *Handbook of Research Design and Social Measurement,* 5th edition, (Newbury Park, Cal.: Sage, 1991).

30. Classic technical works on sampling are: William G. Cochran, *Sampling Techniques* (New York: John Wiley, 1966), and Leslie Kish, *Survey Sampling* (New York: John Wiley, 1967). For a concise summary of the major characteristics of various designs, see: Russell

L. Ackoff, *The Design of Social Research* (Chicago: University of Chicago Press, 1953), p. 124.

31. Sampling designs used in social science research were derived from and are technically similar to those used in other branches of science.

32. For an excellent contemporary discussion of the use of such experiments in psychology, see: F. J. McGuigan, *Experimental Psychology: Methods of Research* (Englewood Cliffs, N.J.: Prentice-Hall, 1990).

33. The classic example was the early study conducted at Western Electric's Hawthorne plant in Chicago in the 1930s. It yielded data that brought about significant changes in the assumptions of management about the motivation of workers. See: Elton Mayo, *Human Problems of an Industrial Civilization* (New York: Viking, 1966), first published in 1933.

34. The term first appeared in its modern form as *statistik* in the writings of Gottfried Achenwald, an 18th century German political geographer. *Ibid.,* p. 7.

35. James W. Tankard, Jr., *The Statistical Pioneers* (Cambridge, Mass.: Schenkman Publishing Company, Inc., 1984), p. 1.

36. For a summary of the origins of and early contributors to contemporary statistical procedures used in social science, see: James W. Tankard, *Ibid.*

37. *Ibid.,* p. 1.

38. Philip Meyer, *The New Precision Journalism* (Bloomington, Ind.: Indiana University Press, 1991), p. 1 of Preface.

39. See: Philip Meyer, *Precision Journalism: A Reporter's Introduction to Social Science Methods,* second edition (Bloomington, Ind.: Indiana University Press, 1979). The first edition appeared in 1973.

40. For a classic discussion of the ways in which the press distorts reality in its news accounts, see: Walter Lippmann, *Public Opinion* (New York: Macmillan, 1922).

41. *Ibid.,* p. 11.

42. *Ibid.,* p. 6.

43. Philip Meyer, 1991, p. 5.

44. *Ibid.,* p. 6.

45. Bruce T. McIntyre, *Advanced Newsgathering* (New York: Praeger Publishing Company, 1991), pp. 201–213.

46. David Pearce Demers and Suzanne Nichols, *Precision Journalism: A Practical Guide* (Newbury Park, Calif.: Sage Publications, 1987), p. 15.

47. Correspondence to Margaret DeFleur from Philip Meyer, January 22, 1994.

48. Demers and Nichols, *op. cit.*

49. Correspondence to Margaret DeFleur from Philip Meyer, January 22, 1994.

50. Philip Meyer, "Reporting in the 21st Century," Presentation at AEJMC in Montreal, August, 1992.

51. Correspondence to Margaret H. DeFleur from Philip Meyer, March 4, 1994.

52. The author is grateful to Philip Meyer for this conceptualization.

9

A Formal Methodology for CAIR Analyses

The purpose of this final chapter is to describe a formal methodology appropriate for CAIR analyses. That methodology incorporates many of the concepts, principles, definitions, techniques, and procedures that were described in earlier chapters. Thus, it builds in part on the techniques for data analysis currently in use in newsrooms that were described in chapter 5. It also incorporates many of the procedures and strategies presented in chapters 6 and 7, which discussed the conduct and consequences of a large-scale analysis of the records of the U.S. Federal Courts. In short, this chapter brings together the major methodological lessons to be learned from all of the issues, examples, and discussions of CAIR in previous chapters.

As will be seen, a formal methodology for CAIR consists of series of *steps, strategies,* and *responsibilities* for conducting computer-assisted analyses of databases of electronic records in order to develop news stories and present them to the public. Taken together, they constitute a methodology suitable for CAIR that is by no means identical with those used by other fields.

THE MEANING OF METHODOLOGY

The first task in designing a methodology is to clarify just what is meant by that term. In social science, an important distinction is made between the term *methodology* and related terms, such as *techniques,* which are defined more narrowly. This is an important distinction, and it is used as a conceptual framework in developing the discussion of a methodology for CAIR.

In more detail, techniques are specific operations by which one gathers and analyzes data. In social science research they consist of operations such as selecting a sample, using a Likert attitude scale, matching subjects for an experiment, or calculating the probability of a statistical test. These important techniques are a part of the "tool kit" of operational procedures accepted and used in many fields. Philosopher of science Abraham Kaplan clarified the term in this manner:

> Let me call "techniques" the specific procedures used in a given science, or in particular contexts of inquiry in that science. For example, there are certain techniques associated with the use of the Rorschach test, or with a mass opinion survey; there are statistical techniques, like those involved in factor analysis; techniques for conducting an interview or for running a rat through a maze; . . . and so on, endlessly.[1]

Thus, methodology is a very broad concept, whereas techniques are narrowly defined. Philosophers of science define methodology as a set of constructs, shared within a particular field, about how its research should be conducted and reported in order to be regarded as legitimate by its practitioners. For example, Maurice Natanson explained it in the following way:

> By "methodology," I understand the underlying conceptual framework in terms of which concrete studies in history, sociology, economics and the like are carried out, and in terms of which they receive a general rationale. Therefore, I am not concerned here with the nature of specific techniques that social scientists utilize or their evaluation.[2]

Ultimately, then, the term *methodology* refers broadly to the logic of analysis used in a given field. Developing a methodology, whether in social science or in CAIR, requires that the steps used in selecting and studying a problem be described and the justifications for using particular approaches be explained.

One clear implication of this definition of methodology is that there must be considerable consensus within a discipline about the ways to set goals, make systematic observations, reach conclusions, and make public the findings of an analysis of the field's subject matter. A second implication is that there is no single set of methodological standards that prevails uniformly across all disciplines. Each has to work out its own methodology consisting of the investigative standards accepted by its practitioners. Kaplan summarized these points in this way: "The word 'methodology'. . . is one which is used for a certain discipline and for its subject-matter. I mean by *methodology* the study—the description, the explanation, and the justification—of methods, and not the methods themselves.[3]

Following this interpretation of the term, a methodology uniquely suited for CAIR analysis is discussed in the remaining parts of this chapter. This methodology consists of a series of preliminary steps, strategies for analysis, ethical responsibilities, and standards for presenting findings to the public. A requirement of any formal methodology, these are described, explained, and justified.

A METHODOLOGY FOR CAIR

It is clear from the preceding discussion that CAIR methodology need not be the same as those agreed on in psychology, sociology, or indeed any other field. The methodology must be uniquely designed to achieve the goals of its practitioners within a set of constructs that they can agree on and share. In that sense, CAIR methodology begins with a set of preliminary steps taken to ensure a complete understanding of the nature of the electronic records that have been obtained or that have been developed. Once these have been completed, one or more general strategies can be selected that seem likely to meet the overall goals of the investigation. These may be supplemented with additional strategies designed to meet more specific goals if leads are uncovered within the data. Finally, when the analysis phase is complete, a number of ethical responsibilities must be considered as stories are prepared for transmission to the public. Each of these aspects of CAIR methodology are discussed in detail in the sections that follow.

Preliminary Steps

After a set of electronic records has been obtained from a public agency or office, but before the actual data analysis can begin, a number of preliminary steps often must be completed. These initial steps familiarize the analyst with the contents of the database and identify the nature of certain problems that may be contained in the data. They indicate the structure and format of the records and the exact position of each variable. The analyst may need this information to transfer the data to statistical software or to extract a subset of the data and load it into a spreadsheet or other software. Finally, the preliminary steps help the investigator to set specific goals for the project that go beyond the general objectives for which the data set was acquired.

The number or order of the initial steps that the analyst must complete may differ from project to project. This depends on the size, complexity, and format of the database. The following preliminary steps are recommended when tackling a database for the first time—especially one of substantial size.

Set General Objectives for the Investigation.   If a database is large and complex, it may not be possible to identify specific goals for the analysis as a first step. Before that can be done, the analyst must have a thorough knowledge of what the database contains. Furthermore, until the files are studied, the analyst may not know if significant portions of the data are missing or whether all of the information will be useful. All of this information is needed before identifying specific goals.

In some cases, then, only the general objectives of the analysis can be set initially. For example, the records from the federal courts consisted of 60 files containing 5.5 million criminal, civil, and appeals cases covering the entire federal court system for a 17-year period. Each individual record contained about 40 variables, for a total of more than 220 million "pieces" of information. When the computer tapes arrived, the analyst had a general idea of the contents. However, because of the size and complexity of the database, it was impossible to have a thorough knowledge of what the tapes contained. This meant that only a general goal could be set for the project at that point. Because of these conditions, it was decided that the principal objective of the project would be to evaluate the performance of the U.S. Attorneys who were in charge of each federal judicial district. With this general goal in mind, the analyst began to study the records in more detail in order to see which variables could be used to accomplish this objective.

For some projects, the database will present fewer problems. In that case, specific goals may be much easier to identify at the outset. For example, when Elliot Jaspin began to study the school bus accidents that led to the deaths of two children in Rhode Island, he immediately wanted to know whether any of the drivers had a history of prior traffic offenses. He wanted to compare the names of the bus drivers with a database that listed the names of convicted traffic offenders to see if any of the names matched. Thus, the objective of the analysis was highly specific and straightforward from the beginning.

Conduct an Initial Assessment of Raw Records.   Regardless of whether the project or the database is relatively simple or complex, the nature of the records must be examined. One purpose of this step is to confirm the presence and exact position of each variable in the database. A second purpose is to assure that the codebook providing the key to understanding the contents, format, and layout of the tapes agrees with what is actually on the tapes. Because it is likely that the data will be received in raw form, this information may be necessary when transferring the data to software.

One way to accomplish this task is to print 100 or 200 lines of the entries in each file directly from the tape. When this is done, the analyst may see a solid page of numbers and/or letters—with no headings or spaces. Next, start with a date field or some other (such as a name field) that is clearly distinguishable from the solid columns of numbers and letters. Date fields often are in the form of YYMMDD (two-digit specification of year, month, and day) and are easy to pick out. Refer to the codebook and determine whether the field is exactly where the codebook states and contains exactly the number of characters it describes. Work through the printout until every variable is accounted for in this manner. When the presence and position of every variable is confirmed and other format questions have been addressed, then the data can be transferred to software.

It also is a good idea to begin learning about the history of the database. How were the data originally collected? Was the information entered directly into a database, or was it transferred from paper records at a later time? Did data entry occur at one site or did many offices participate? How are the records organized in the database? Does the database contain every record, or were some omitted? All of this information may be helpful later when searching for the sources of errors or problems in the database. Recall that in the case study of the federal court records, each of these factors played a role in the introduction of errors or problems. Records were entered into the database from offices in every district throughout the country over a period of 17 years. During this time, many changes occurred in the specific information that was collected and the way in which the information was recorded. Records were organized by fiscal year and termination date, rather than calendar year and filing date as the investigating team needed. Furthermore, regardless of when the criminal or civil case was actually terminated, the records were included in the file for the year in which it was received at the Federal Judicial Center. In short, it is important that the investigator master every aspect of the database and understand its limitations. Only then can she or he have confidence in the results of the analysis and interpret the results properly.

Transfer the Data to Suitable Software.   The files described in the case study were received as EBCDIC files on magnetic tape. EBCDIC files are similar in concept to ASCII files for personal computers. The data cannot be analyzed in this form, but the files can be moved to other computers and imported into software. How the transfer to software takes place depends on what software will be used. For statistical software, this may mean that programs must be written that specify the location of each file on a tape along with the location and type of each variable in the file. Other format information may be needed, such as whether the data on the tape are stored in blocks of fixed or variable length and the size of the block. This information should be listed in the codebook that accompanies the tape or file. Or, if the analyst plans to import the data into a spreadsheet or database management program on a personal computer, a software program such as Jaspin's Nine-Track Express can be used to extract the data from the tape so that it can then be transferred to the spreadsheet.

Finally, the analyst must determine the size of each file and assess the amount of disk space that will be needed by the computer. The size of the file may be larger after it has been converted to software than it was in the original raw form.

Perform a Detailed Examination of the Records.   After the data have been transferred to software, a more comprehensive check on the consistency and the completeness of the information recorded for each variable should be completed. One way to do this is to prepare frequency tables for the variables and the values within each variable. The distribution for a variable will show all the values of the variable and indicate how often each occurred. For a variable such as criminal offense code, for example, the distribution lists each offense with which a defendant was charged and how often such an offense was listed in the database. The distribution also indicates when the information was not recorded (i.e., was missing). If the information is missing for a large number of records, it may be impossible to do any kind of analysis based on that variable.

A detailed study of the records, then, can reveal whether the information is complete for all of the variables and for all of the years that the database covers. By comparing the information recorded for each variable in the database with the paper documentation, the investigator also may be able to determine whether the values of the variables always have the same meanings, if the meanings change, or if the values have more than one meaning at the same time.

Such an in-depth examination of the records is an important step. The investigator must have confidence in the accuracy and reliability of the data. Only then can the investigator know which kinds of questions can be addressed or answered with confidence when using the data.

Identify Specific Goals for Analysis.   After the investigator has a thorough understanding of the nature of the information recorded in the database and the limitations of that information, specific research questions can be formulated. These are the specific questions that the investigator plans to answer with the data analysis. For example, in the federal court study, the specific goals included a comparison of the numbers and kinds of criminal and civil cases emphasized in 11 similar metropolitan districts. The record of Rudolph Giuliani, a former prosecutor who was a candidate for mayor in New York City, received special attention. His claims during the election period about "crime, crack, and corruption" were compared to the kinds of cases he prosecuted when he was the U.S. Attorney in Manhattan. Plea bargaining and conviction rates throughout the country were also studied. These specific decisions about what to study were not confirmed until the other preliminary steps were completed.

In overview, then, a set of preliminary steps should be completed before the actual data analysis begins. The number and order of the steps that are necessary may depend on the size and complexity of the database. First, the investigator must determine or confirm the general objectives of the analysis for which the database was obtained. It may not be possible to identify specific goals until more is known about the data. Next, the accompanying documentation or codebook that identifies the content and format of the records should be compared with what is found on the tapes or in the files. After the data are transferred to appropriate software, the investigator can check for consistency and completeness of the records. (Do all reporting units record information fully, or do some neglect certain entries? Is each variable coded the same way over the entire span of years? Do the codes always mean the same things?) Finally, the investigator can identify or confirm specific goals for the analysis and design the strategies and techniques that will be used to achieve them.

General Strategies for CAIR Analyses

The dictionary defines the word *strategy* as a "careful plan or method or a clever stratagem." The word *stratagem,* originally a military term, is defined as "a cunning plan to gain an end."[4] A computer-assisted analysis also needs a carefully devised plan (cunning or not) to achieve its goal. Thus, the methodology for CAIR should include strategies that can be used to achieve desired goals. The specific strategy used in a given analysis serves as its overall conceptual framework, outline, or plan that guides the project to its goal.

In chapter 4, the analytical strategies used by CAIR pioneers Burnham and Jaspin for the examination of electronic records were discussed. Burnham set forth a broad conceptual framework or formula that he felt would help him to identify important topics for consideration and topics that he could use when investigating a government or public agency and its officials. He applied this framework to the analysis of the internal computerized records of an agency. In designing a general strategy, Burnham said that two key questions must be asked: (a) What is the stated purpose or mission of the agency? (b) What problems or procedures prevent the agency from achieving its stated purpose or goal? In a broad sense, he used these two general questions as guides to his analysis.

Jaspin carried the conceptualization process to a second step. With a general starting point or question in mind, he wanted to know what must be done with the data to get answers. For example, how can the problems that prevent an agency from accomplishing its mission be found in the computerized data? To answer that question, Jaspin defined four approaches or procedures that can be used when seeking answers in electronic information. These are searching, counting, sorting, and cross-indexing. He described searching as looking for one occurrence of something, such as an individual's address in a database of driver's license records. Counting is described as finding the number of times something occurs, such as the number of convictions obtained by a prosecutor in murder cases. Sorting is defined as ranking facts in ascending or descending order, or finding the largest or smallest of something, such as the amount of overtime pay received by city workers. Cross-indexing is the matching of information in one file or database with information in another. For example, the name of a school bus driver can be matched with the names of traffic offenders in one database, or with the names of convicted criminal offenders in another database.

Finally, Meyer suggested that, as an initial strategy, many stories derived from databases can be developed by comparing groups or subgroups. This can be accomplished by calculating the average value for each group, or by producing tables that divide a group of individuals or things into two or more categories and display the frequency of occurrence. For example, the average annual income of female-headed households can be compared with that of male-headed households within a particular geographical area, or individuals convicted of murder could be categorized by race and then the percentage of each racial group who received a sentence longer than 5 years could be calculated and displayed in a table. Furthermore, Meyer stressed that journalists should consider and incorporate the entire body of social science strategies and techniques into their strategies.

The following sections list 11 additional strategies that can be used to guide CAIR analyses. After a brief explanation, each is illustrated by one or more examples drawn from the 130 CAIR stories reviewed earlier or from the large-scale case study of the federal court records. Many of these strategies are adaptations from those commonly used by social scientists. Moreover, the list is by no means complete. Additional strategies drawn from social science can be added, along with those developed by specialists in the field. In any case, the following are 11 strategies that have already proven to be useful as general guides to CAIR analyses.

Examine Trends Over Time.   One obvious strategy to use when reviewing records containing multiyear data is to discover whether significant trends have occurred over the years. In its simplest form, the analysis of trends involves the laying side-by-side of results from analyses of data that are the same except for their date.[5] In other words, a specific phenomenon of interest is defined, an index of its annual (weekly, monthly) prevalence is devised, and its values period by period are plotted to observe how they change over time. If the results show a clear upward or downward trend, a newsworthy issue may have been discovered. The information can be used in interviews with officials responsible for the phenomenon. They can be asked to justify the trend, or experts can be contacted who may be able to explain what is taking place.

Many of the computer-assisted stories described in chapter 5 examined trends over time. For example, the *Atlanta Journal and Constitution* wanted to demonstrate the ways in which the nation's middle class had changed over the years. Reporters completed the study by analyzing census data for a 40-year period.[6] Statistics such as median family income (measured in 1990 dollars), median home value (in 1990 dollars), percentage of adult women in the labor force, and educational level were calculated and plotted for the years 1950, 1960, 1970, 1980, and 1990. The study also compared the total percentage of annual income spent for food, clothing, housing, education, medical care, and other (consumer) items such as automobile ownership among the suburban population. The resulting multipoint trend analysis of the factors studied showed a picture of a shrinking middle class with stagnant incomes and decreasing opportunities. In the 25 years following World War II, the typical family could count on gaining a higher income each year. However, in later years, since 1970, family income remained relatively flat.

In the study of the federal court records, national data on the percentage of criminal defendants whose cases were completed at trial showed a sharp and steady decline each year from 1980 to 1987. In other words, it appeared that an increasing number of charges were resolved not by trial but by other means, such as plea bargaining. The confirmation of this trend by the analysis generated a number of news stories in newspapers and other media around the country.

Only a few computer-assisted stories were found that compared data over several points in time, such as in the preceding examples. It appears that most stories using time comparisons, at least in the examination of the 130 stories described in chapter 5, made only two-point comparisons. For example, a study of election returns in Georgia for the presidential primary in 1988, and again in 1992, showed a growth in the percentage of voters who voted for the Republican candidate.[7] On the basis of those two points in time, the article concluded that the state was experiencing a shift from its solidly Democratic past and becoming strongly Republican. Even though that trend was confirmed by the national elections of 1994, and although the article used other evidence to support its conclusion, it can be risky to pronounce trends on the basis of data from only 2 years. This is especially true when the two points in time are close together.

Compare Parts With the Whole.   In a database consisting of the records of distinct units, the characteristics or performance of each unit can be compared with similar indices for the whole. If the unit under study departs notably from the whole, this finding provides grounds for asking those in charge to explain the difference. For example, the *Los Angeles Times* calculated the death rates for heart bypass patients for each hospital in California that performed this kind of surgery.[8] The study compared the mortality rates for the individual hospitals to the statewide average for hospitals, after controlling for variations in the age, gender, and race of patients. The study also considered other factors, such as whether a hospital had a high percentage of patients with acute heart attacks or emergency cases. The *Times* concluded that nearly one sixth of the hospitals had significantly higher death rates that were not accounted for by such factors. In fact, at some of the hospitals studied, the percentage of bypass surgery patients who died before leaving the hospital was at least double the statewide average for such cases. Furthermore, most of the hospitals with the highest death rates in bypass surgery performed relatively fewer such operations. Finally, the study found substantial variations in the cost of the procedure.

The database used in the analysis of the records of the federal courts contained information for each judicial district in the United States. Each of these units could be compared with the whole. For the all districts in the United States during the years 1980 through 1987, an average of 48% of all civil cases, where the United States was either the plaintiff or the defendant, involved contract cases. (These include such matters as product liability, insurance, marine matters, overpayment of Medicare or veteran's benefits, and defaulted student loans). In one unit, the Southern District of New York, the comparable figure was only 16%. In another unit, the District of Northern California, the figure was 78%. Such differences can be the basis of probes by reporters trying to understand and account for such variations.

Compare Similar or "Matched" Parts.   In a database that brings together records from numerous units (such as districts), it is sometimes possible to identify and compare those that can be "matched" on selected criteria—such as similar demographic features or economic conditions. This can reveal important differences from one unit to another that cannot easily be explained. Because the units have been matched on demographic and economic features, other conditions or variables are probably responsible for the differences between the units. This opens the inquiry as to whether they are due to differences in administrative procedures, political priorities, staffing levels, or discriminatory practices. All of these provide reporters with leads for interviews with officials who can be asked to explain, especially in situations where there is supposed to be uniform application of laws or policies.

There are many ways to test and assess differences or similarities between parameters in data derived from distinct units. For example, newspapers such as the *New York Times* and the *Atlanta Journal and Constitution* have analyzed government records on mortgage lending.[9] The data included the income and race of individuals applying for mortgages as well as the amount to be borrowed. The analysts matched or grouped applicants within a geographical area according to income level and race. The results showed that minority residents in a community or region are more likely to be turned down for home loans than Whites who have the same level of income. This was true even when other measures of affordability were included, such as the standard that annual income must equal at least 40% of the amount of money to be borrowed. From such matched comparisons, some analysts have concluded that a pattern of racial discrimination exists in the mortgage-lending business in some communities.

In the federal court study, a comparative strategy was to select a number of "big-city" districts that were as similar as possible in order to determine whether federal laws were enforced in a uniform manner in each of the districts. The analyst used census data and statistical procedures to find several districts that were most alike on a number of demographic and economic indicators. Among these similar districts, striking differences were found in the enforcement of the laws. For example, in the Brooklyn district, drug offenses made up 40% of the criminal cases filed by federal prosecutors. The comparable figure for the Los Angeles district was only 17%—less than half as many. It does not seem likely that Los Angeles is far more drug-free than Brooklyn. The same can be said for other demographically and economically comparable cities, such as Manhattan (37%) and Detroit (32%). Thus, it appeared that other factors may have been responsible for these differences. Perhaps there are other unique characteristics in these units, but the priorities of individual federal prosecutors was a good candidate for further investigation. In fact, these differences generated a number of newspaper stories.

Complete a Detailed Analysis of One Unit or Area.   In some cases a very detailed analysis of one region, district, or other geographical unit can be an effective strategy. For example, after data were released from the 1990 decennial census, many newspapers conducted a thorough examination of the numbers for their region. In one such study, the *Los Angeles Times* obtained computer tapes and analyzed all of the socioeconomic data for California.[10] Many factors were included, such as household income, age, education, percentage of income spent on housing, workforce participation, information on the head of the household, and country of birth. The resulting statistical "snapshot" of the state showed that prosperity and poverty grew side by side. The number of households making $75,000 or more annually had increased by 800% over the decade, but the number of children living in poverty grew by 41% and the number of elderly who were poor increased by 21%. More than one in four residents spoke a language other than English in the home and 22% of Californians were born outside the United States.

Another example of this strategy was used to look at a mayoral election in New York City. In 1989, Rudolph Giuliani became a candidate. He had been a federal prosecutor in the Southern District of New York for several years. During his campaign he claimed that he had been "tough on drugs." A detailed analysis of the work load of his district was completed for the period when he had been in office to see if his claim was true. The detailed analysis did show that federal drug prosecutions had increased sharply during the years when he was in charge. However, the prosecution of violent crimes decreased. This kind of information provides valuable leads to reporters to follow up in interviews with such candidates.

Conduct an In-Depth Analysis of a Particular Category of Phenomena.   An effective strategy can be to focus on a particular situation, event, set of phenomena, or group of people. By this means, popular beliefs can sometimes be checked against reality. This strategy is similar to a detailed analysis of a unit or geographical area in that every aspect of the category for which data are in the records is examined. For example, the *Los Angeles Times* analyzed more than 2,200 court cases from across the county in its study of guardianship for the elderly.[11] The investigation examined the characteristics of elderly people who became wards, their guardians, and the court procedures used. The results showed that the average age of those who became wards was 79, and most were women. Hearings were held in most of the cases where an individual petitioned for guardianship of an elderly person. However, the elderly person attended the hearings in only 8% of the cases. Among those elderly, 44% went though the court process without any legal representation. Judges approved 97% of the petitions, and 34% were approved without any doctor's opinion. When a reason for the petition was provided, only 2% were due to Alzheimer's disease. Most of the petitions simply stated that the elderly individuals were unable to care for themselves or handle their household finances. Only 16% of the files contained reports on the conditions of wards after guardianship had been granted. In 48% of the files, annual accountings of money were missing. Such figures offer fertile ground for investigative follow-ups.

In the federal court study, many of the records on civil actions concerned routine administrative matters, such as overpayment of veteran's or Social Security benefits and defaulted student loans. This might suggest that compared to criminal behavior, civil cases concern matters that do not have serious consequences for society. However, that is not always true. Civil cases can involve issues of great concern to the public. Analyses can show that civil cases include corporate pollution, damage to the environment, and workplace safety, to mention only a few possibilities. Obviously, the frequency, location, and disposition of such suits offer many possibilities for newsworthy stories.

Locate and Analyze Deviant Cases.   This strategy can reveal unusual situations that can provide information for good news stories. For example, *USA Today* analyzed fatal accident records from around the nation and found that in New Mexico there are more motor vehicle accident deaths per capita, and more for every mile traveled on highways, than in any other state.[12] The interstate highway in New Mexico's San Miguel County, east of Santa Fe, had the most fatal accidents in the nation. Furthermore, 57% of New Mexico's highway deaths involved alcohol, compared with only 50% nationwide. From this discovery of a deviant pattern, the paper generated a number of stories about the dangers of highways.

Using this strategy in the investigation of the records of the federal courts, the investigator found that nearly 25% of all federal criminal cases filed in the Maryland district involved drunk driving and traffic offenses. This was highly unusual because this category rarely exceeded 1% in other similar districts. It was tempting to conclude that federal prosecutors in the Maryland district considered traffic offenses to be a higher priority than such transgressions as violent crime. On probing further, the investigator learned that the U.S. government is responsible for major highways in the Maryland district that are located on federal land. This automatically made a "federal case" out of all such traffic offenses. Thus, it was not only the zeal of the prosecutor to stamp out drunk driving that accounted for the deviant situation, but an anomaly of land ownership and policing responsibility. Nevertheless, the investigation of deviant cases can often reveal situations that are not so easily explained.

Examine Dramatic Phenomena or Situations.   This   is   a strategy that can reveal what earlier journalists called "man bites dog" situations; that is, certain dramatic and unusual information can come to light that one does not anticipate and that can provide a foundation for an unusual news story. To illustrate, in the analysis of the federal court records several kinds of offenses were found that were entirely unanticipated. One was that offenders are still prosecuted for White slavery. One might be tempted to think that this offense was a phenomenon of opium dens in the early 19th century and that such charges are no longer brought against anyone. However, it is still a federal offense and a limited number of such cases have come before the U.S. courts during the past two decades. Similarly, the offense of sedition also brings to mind an earlier era, when patriots were tried by the Crown for speaking out against government. However, a total of 27 defendants were charged with this offense during the years 1980 through 1987. A third example is threats against the President. One might be tempted to believe that such cases are quite rare. In fact, more than 500 individuals were charged with this offense during the 7 years between 1980 and 1987. Obviously, each of these dramatic phenomena could be followed up and developed into a story.

Provide Background Information for Events Already in the News.   Additional information about items already on the daily news agenda can be discovered in databases, or from databases that are created by news organizations. For example, after carjackers shot and killed four drivers in the Washington, DC area, the *Washington Post* conducted a computer analysis of 218 carjackings that had occurred in the area during an 8-month period.[13] The study showed that the carjackers usually operated at night and almost always used guns. They targeted shopping areas along suburban highways most often and also neighborhoods with high rates of other types of crimes. They also had clear preferences in cars. Nissans were stolen most frequently, but the list also included a substantial number of Jeeps, Blazers, and other four-wheel-drive vehicles. Luxury cars, especially Acuras and Mercedes, were also stolen frequently.

In another application of this strategy, several kinds of information were supplied to the media using the federal court records. When Leona Helmsley, the "hotel queen," was sentenced for income tax fraud, a special analysis was performed for a national news organization concerning the length of sentences normally received for that type of offense. In another example, the same strategy revealed information about the offense of computer fraud. In 1988, Robert Morris released a computer virus that disrupted more than 2,000 computers in the country. A number of cases of computer fraud have been prosecuted in the federal courts. In another example derived from the court data, information was supplied to reporters concerning a nominee to an important federal office. In May 1990, President Bush nominated Robert C. Bonner to head the Drug Enforcement Agency. Press releases from the White House had indicated that Bonner had been especially tough on drugs when he was a federal prosecutor in the Los Angeles district. However, when the investigator conducted an analysis of Bonner's actual record from the federal court database, it revealed that his rate of drug prosecutions was not only below the national average, but also below the rate for comparable districts. This information was followed up by reporters who generated a number of news stories.

Examine the Performance or Claims of Officials.   In some ways, the story about Robert Bonner also illustrates this strategy. However, there are a number of additional examples that can be cited. In several of the 130 CAIR stories examined in chapter 5, the projects were initiated because of claims made by public officials. Reporters wanted to verify or discredit those claims. For example, reporters for the *Los Angeles Times* conducted a computer analysis of 4,400 misconduct complaints filed against Los Angeles police officers from 1987 through mid-1990.[14] These complaints included claims of excessive force, improper tactics, discourtesy, and unbecoming conduct. To illustrate, one charge of improper tactics stated that an officer "inappropriately placed his hands around (the complainant's) throat while assisting him to his feet." Charges of unbecoming conduct included such actions as questioning a rape victim—and then asking her for a date!

The *Times* analysis of the LAPD misconduct complaint records was undertaken after the beating of Black motorist Rodney G. King. Community and civil rights leaders claimed that the beating was symptomatic of the widespread abuse of minority citizens by the police department. In contrast, police Chief Daryl F. Gates stated that the beating was an "aberration," a highly unusual event. To get an objective picture, the *Times* investigated the nature of the complaints and how they were handled by the department, especially when filed by minority individuals.

The analysis showed that complaints against police officers matched the ethnic makeup of the police force. Anglo officers, who were 65% of the force, received 64% of the complaints. Latino officers, 19% of the force, received 21%, and African Americans, who made up 13% of the force, received 13% of the complaints. The records were examined to see what types of misconduct complaints by what categories of citizens were upheld. In all, only 7% were upheld. Complaints by Black citizens had a 5% chance of being upheld by the department compared to 7% filed by Latinos. These figures compare with 9% of those filed by Whites. Excessive force charges against LAPD officers filed by African Americans were slightly more likely to have the charges upheld than when such complaints were filed by Whites or Latinos. However, when Blacks complained about other forms of police misconduct, their complaints were more likely to be turned down. Finally, African American LAPD officers were more likely to disciplined for misconduct than either Latino or White officers.

Make a Before/After (With Intervening Event) Comparison.

This strategy is designed to shed light on a suspected causal sequence. In that sense it is based on the logic of the natural experiment, long used in social science research. The basic strategy is to examine an event or occurrence at one point in time and then look at the same situation at a later date, after an intervening act or set of circumstances has taken place between the two. The goal is to compare the two sets of information to see if it appears that the intervening event had an effect on the outcome in the second period.

A tax situation in New York City can be used to illustrate this strategy. The property tax system had been criticized for more than a decade for placing a heavier burden on less affluent homeowners than on those who were wealthier. Owners of expensive homes often paid lower taxes than those with cheaper properties. Moreover, owners of houses of similar value often paid wildly different taxes. Furthermore, as the values of houses increased for more than a decade, the city seldom revised its assessments. The result was that as market values rose, the tax on more expensive homes was based on a lower and lower percentage of their actual worth. Citizen groups challenged these assessments. In a response to a court decision that would have forced the city to raise taxes on underassessed properties, the Legislature approved a bill that prohibited the city from raising assessments on homes more than 6% a year. Instead, the city reduced excessive tax bills in order to correct the inequities.

Reporters for the *New York Times* gathered reports and data from previous years on home sales, tax assessments, and tax bills. They wanted to compare this to similar data collected *after* the intervening tax reductions had taken place. They conducted a computer analysis of the assessment data and tax reductions. The results showed that although the reductions relieved some overtaxed housing, they failed to lower taxes in many neighborhoods that had suffered the longest. Many of these were Black and Hispanic neighborhoods in poor and working-class sections of the Bronx, Brooklyn, and Queens. The analysis also showed that half the tax cuts went to houses worth at least $200,000. The report concluded that even after ambitious attempts at reform, the property tax system appeared to have become even more inequitable.[15]

In the federal court analysis, this strategy was used to determine if the appointment of a new U.S. Attorney to a district (an intervening condition) made any real difference in the number or kinds of cases that were prosecuted afterward. The investigation compared the records of comparable districts for several years before a new prosecutor was appointed to the records for the same district immediately after the appointment. The results showed that significant changes often occurred when a new official took office. For example, from 1980 to 1987, the Southern District of New York had two U.S. Attorneys. John S. Martin served from 1980 to 1983, and Rudolph Giuliani was in the office from mid-1983 until 1989. When Martin was in charge, his office filed criminal charges against approximately 40 individuals for every 100,000 adults in the district. When Giuliani took over, the rate jumped immediately to 54 per 100,000. During Martin's term, drug cases represented between 21% and 31% of all criminal charges filed in the district. During Giuliani's tenure in office, the percentage of drug cases grew to over 40% of all criminal prosecutions.

Similarly, in Massachusetts, the appointment of a new prosecutor appeared to signal changes in enforcement. Edward Harrington was the U.S. Attorney from 1977 to 1981; William Weld served from 1981 to 1986 and Robert Mueller was in office in 1986 and 1987. Shortly after the appointment of Weld, drug prosecutions increased sharply. As soon as Mueller took over, they dropped back again.

Conduct an Overall "Performance Audit."   The previous sections have described a number of specific strategies—comparing parts with the whole, completing a detailed analysis of one unit or area, analyzing deviant cases, and so on—for accomplishing clearly defined goals. Each of these strategies has been used to develop news stories based on data, or subsets of data, from public or agency records. Each of these strategies can reveal matters of importance that might not otherwise be discovered. These well-focused investigations serve an important role in contemporary journalism and provide opportunities for meeting traditional watchdog responsibilities of the press. In addition, they may be sufficiently limited in scope that they can meet the needs of newsrooms with tight time schedules.

However, there is another, much broader, type of strategy that reviews the entire performance of an agency over time. Rather than focusing on a particular aspect of an agency's performance, or a portion of the available data, every transaction or record is analyzed. The overall purpose here is to assess how efficiently, fairly, and effectively an agency or organization has allocated its resources, efforts, and personnel over a time period for which records are available. The agency's stated mission and goals are compared to its actual achievements.

This was the approach used by David Burnham and Susan Long in the establishment of Transactional Records Access Clearinghouse (TRAC) at Syracuse University. TRAC gathers the internal computer files of federal agencies in order to monitor their performance. It also is the approach used in TRAC's first project, the analysis of the federal court data conducted by the author and described in chapters 6 and 7.

The TRAC study is an example of the performance audit. It was a broad-based review of the records developed by a major government agency over an extended period. It analyzed all of the criminal and civil transactions for the entire United States along with other information recorded by the agency. The study assessed the consistency of the application of federal enforcement policies throughout the nation, the differential treatment of civil versus criminal cases by region, the performance of individual federal prosecutors, the increasing use of plea bargaining, and many other issues. It involved the use of several of the strategies already listed, such as comparisons between matched districts, comparisons of individual judicial districts with averages for the whole United States, and the detailed analysis of particular categories of drug offenses.

Burnham asserts that the performance audit is one of the most powerful tools for fulfilling the watchdog role. He also claims that it is one of the most neglected by journalists. Whereas many reporters may conduct a computer analysis to probe for the answer to a particular question such as which police officer received the most overtime pay, few reporters complete an in-depth examination of an agency's history. Burnham believes that this is especially true at the federal level. Although most newspapers' energies are devoted to regional and local issues, he believes that some resources should be directed toward informing the public how well the federal government is doing its job.

In general, then, the methodology for CAIR includes a number of strategies ranging from simple trend analyses over time to the more extensive performance audit. It also includes those described earlier by Jaspin, Burnham, and Meyer. All of these strategies serve as an overall framework, outline, or plan guiding the types of analyses needed to achieve partciular kinds of goals. Obviously, any analysis requires more than a strategy. Each strategy is implemented by completing specific procedures, such as calculating means, percentages, correlations, or any number of statistical indices or coefficients. In addition, what is found can often be transformed to graphic representations to aid interpretation.

RESPONSIBILITIES IN PREPARING CAIR ANALYSES

Before the results of an analysis are readied for a final report to the public, there are a number of considerations that become important and constitute a set of responsibilities that the investigative journalist must assume. Some derive from the general responsibilities of any form of investigative reporting—whether computers are involved or not. Indeed, some are responsibilities that are recognized by all good journalists who try to provide their readers or viewers with factual accounts of the events or situations on which they are reporting.

Responsibilities in All Investigative Reporting

The fundamental responsibilities of all investigative reporters are threefold. First they have an ethical responsibility to get the facts straight. Second, they have a similar responsibility to reach conclusions from those facts that represent an accurate picture of reality. Third, they have an obligation to report what they have found to the public in such a way that it can be readily understood.

These very basic responsibilities clearly apply to CAIR, but the introduction of unique technologies has often raised new ethical issues for reporters and editors. This was true when the telegraph was first used to transmit stories, when photography became available to the press, and when tape recorders were introduced—to name only a few. Since the appearance of computers in the newsroom, the industry has faced still another set of ethical issues, ranging from the ease with which large quantities of information can be gathered about individuals from various databases to the digital manipulation of photographs. Similarly, the analysis of public records by reporters also brings new concerns and responsibilities.

Unique Responsibilities in Using Computerized Data

In an overall sense, the first responsibility of a journalist conducting a CAIR analysis is to discover, through a detailed look at the records, what the agency or individual under study has been doing and to determine whether this is consistent with what the agency or individual "should" have been doing. If inconsistencies are found, the reporter's second responsibility is to decide whether acceptable norms or standards have been transgressed. Those norms are derived from values governing rational bureaucratic functioning, ethical governance or the mandated missions and goals of the agency. The third responsibility is to describe in an accurate and ethical manner the facts that have been discovered in terms that can be understood by the public. The final responsibility is to disseminate the story as widely as possible so that the public can decide whether or not to insist on change.

In addition to these responsibilities, the analysis of public records by reporters creates a number of special concerns. For example, Thomas J. Moore, a national correspondent for Knight-Ridder who has worked with computer records, identified a set of unique responsibilities for journalists using computerized records.[16] They include verification of the data, the exercise of statistical responsibility and updating of electronic information gathered and used in newsrooms.

Verify All Data Used in the Analysis.   Moore and others have pointed out that because the data are on computer tape or disk does not mean that they are accurate. For example, Moore used a computer tape from the U.S. Department of Transportation for a story on truck safety. However, he quickly discovered that the tape contained reports from 137 states! In an understatement, he said that this was "an obvious indication that there were problems with the data."

In the analysis of the federal courts, the investigator questioned the results of an analysis showing considerable changes in the prosecution of certain drug offenses, such as those associated with marijuana and cocaine. She asked federal officials responsible for the records for an explanation and confirmation of the results. This led to the discovery that the numerical codes for drug offenses had been changed, but the officials had not been informed. Thus, the codebook describing the database still used the old codes. As discussed earlier, it is the responsibility of the reporter to learn as much as possible about the database and how it was generated or compiled. The data, as well as the results, must be checked and confirmed.

Exercise Statistical Responsibility.   In conducting and reporting on CAIR projects, reporters must have a good understanding of any and all statistical procedures used in the analysis. Such responsibility requires that they use appropriate indices or measures and draw correct inferences and conclusions from the data. This means that they also must understand how to interpret the statistical inferences that can be drawn from their findings, such as the implications of the sampling distributions and derived probabilities associated with particular coefficients. Above all, they must avoid common errors, such as attributing causal implications to correlations between variables.

Satisfy Readers That the Data Have Been Used Responsibly. In a CAIR project, conclusions are based on the outcome of a data analysis conducted by a reporter, rather than by independent outside experts. The problem here is that there is no way for readers to know whether the reporter has done the analysis correctly or drawn proper conclusions. Moore suggested several ways to deal with this problem. For example, the reporter could deposit the raw data tape in a library or research facility so that critics or others could examine the data themselves. Another approach would be to provide the data and analysis to outside experts for review prior to publication (such as is the case with refereed articles reporting the results of scientific research). Reporters should also respond to readers who have questions, people who request additional information, or critics who raise objections.

Ensure That Data Are Updated.   News organizations must guard that the data they use are current. Many newspapers are acquiring or building their own data libraries. These include such databases as driver's license records, voter registrations, county tax assessor records, city payroll records, bank mortgage data, hospital admissions, teacher certifications, and census data. News organizations that maintain their own libraries of such records have a responsibility to update them as more recent databases become available. Unless this is done, the risk of error in stories based on old or obsolete data increases. Updating such information requires a continuing commitment of time and other resources.

GUIDELINES FOR REPORTING CAIR STORIES

Another set of responsibilities arises from the need to inform readers about the nature of the data used in a CAIR analysis. They should be told where the records came from, of what they consist, and basically, how they were analyzed. There are ample precedents for developing guidelines for such reporting. A classic example is the set of guidelines developed—and now in common use—for reporting on public opinion polls.

An Example of Guidelines: Reporting on Polls

In 1969, the American Association for Public Opinion Research (AAPOR) adopted disclosure standards for reporting the methodological details of polls. The standards were meant to cover the minimal amount of information that needed to be disclosed to the public so that the nature and limitations of the poll could be readily understood. Included were the following: the identity of the sponsor of the poll or survey, the exact wording of the questions asked, a definition of the population from which the sample was drawn, the sample size, and the response rate. Also included were an indication of the allowance that should be made for sampling error and information regarding which results were based on only part of the sample (such as "probable voters," "those who have heard of the candidate," etc.). Finally, the date when the survey was conducted should be made clear as well as the method of data collection (personal interviews, phone, mail, etc.).[17] AAPOR added that all public opinion researchers were obligated by ethical professional practice "to include, in any report of research results, or to make available when that report is released," the previously mentioned information about how the research was conducted.[18] The purpose of such standards was to prevent poll-takers from concealing vital facts and to help the public to judge the validity of the poll results. Today, such information usually accompanies the results of polls reported by media organizations.

Guidelines for CAIR Analyses

Similarly, news stories based on computer analyses of public records should routinely include certain information about the analysis. However, rather than a rigid set of requirements, the following suggestions are meant as guidelines for reporting the results of a CAIR analysis.

Identify the Source of the Data.   In news writing, it is an accepted policy that information about events not directly observed by the reporter are attributed to the source of the information. Furthermore, direct statements should always be attributed to the person making them. Identification of such sources and individuals helps readers or viewers judge the probable merits of statements, opinions, and conclusions reported in the story. In a computer-assisted story, it is equally important that the source of the data is identified. This may include the unit that collected the data as well as the type of records that were originally prepared, such as census or mortgage information.

Provide a Brief Description of the Data.   It is helpful for the reader or viewer to know what kind of records or information is contained in the database. For example, unless additional information is provided, it may not be clear what is contained in a database such as the "Toxic Release Inventory," or one described as "Finance Department records." A description of the data, along with an identification of their source, can be combined in a simple statement such as the following:

> *New York Newsday* uncovered the existence of the overpayment in a computer study based on the city's own data, obtained from the Finance Department under the New York State Freedom of Information Law. The computer tape contains the complete record of credits for all affected properties in the five boroughs.[19]

> The *Times* study was based on just-released census data for California known as the Public Use Microdata Sample. Provided on four reels of computer tape, the data contain the actual responses of a random sample of 5% of all households completing the detailed "long form" census questionnaire.[20]

> The *Los Angeles Times* began its study of hazardous-material spills in the transportation system by obtaining computer tapes of the U.S. Department of Transportation's Hazardous Material Incident Reporting System. . . . The data detailed episodes involving 2,900 trucking, railroad, air freight and marine freight companies, both common and private carriers. They were

carrying 1,062 different hazardous chemicals and substances for 12,377 shippers nationwide.[21]

Furthermore, any other information about the data that is relevant to the analysis and contributes to an understanding of the project should be stated. This may include such information as the number of records examined or the time period covered by the data. For example, a study that concludes that the nation faces a growing risk of spills of hazardous materials adds that it "examined 67,657 spills reported to the Department of Transportation between January, 1982 and December, 1991."[22] In this case, the information about the years covered is especially important.

Provide a Synopsis of How the Study Was Conducted.
Many computer-assisted stories briefly describe the overall approach used in the study. Usually, this is accomplished in a few sentences, such as the following:

> The computer-assisted study compared the sale price of more than 25,000 one-, two- and three-family homes in all five boroughs with assessor's estimates of values. The sales occurred in 1980 and 1990. The study also looked at sales in neighborhoods, but the numbers in Manhattan neighborhoods and some neighborhoods in the Bronx, Brooklyn and Queens were so small that a local comparison was impossible.[23]

In addition to a general description of the study, certain additional details may be essential for understanding the study and drawing valid conclusions. For example, if a sample or portion of the data was used, rather than the total population of records, that sample should be described along with the criteria used for selection. If certain cases were eliminated from the study, the reasons for this should be included.

Explain or Define Statistical Terms.
Many of the computer-assisted stories examined in various chapters of this book used statistical terms but did not explain or define them. Words such as *correlation* or *median* were used without even a simple explanation, such as "median income is that amount above which half of the group makes more [income] and half of the group makes less."[24]

In addition, many terms were used incorrectly. For example, the word *significant* was used during the presentation of statistical results. However, it was used in a layperson's way to mean important, rather than in its more precise meaning within statistical reasoning. In interpreting a statistical finding, such as a difference between means, the word *significant* indicates that its value is unlikely to have been a product of chance influences alone. Similarly, the word *survey* was used to indicate a computer analysis of records rather than a specific research design based on samples and interviews with people. Some stories showed a lack of understanding and a failure to explain such things as the difference between correlation and causation.

Do Not Let the Numbers Obscure the Human Side of the Story.   Journalists who are experienced with conducting computer-assisted projects stress that the numbers should not overwhelm the story. They say that the story is not finished when the numerical analysis has been completed; it is only a good start. Furthermore, computer-assisted reporting is not a replacement for either good writing or effective interviewing. Good stories, as always, are about people—not just numbers.

SUMMARY AND CONCLUSIONS

As the preceeding chapters have explained, CAIR is an extension of the classic traditions of the watchdog and fourth estate journalism that began when the first newspapers were established. During the 19th century, newspapers came to serve the entire society and not just the affluent elite. Journalists became more aggressive in seeking facts about what was happening in society and reporting their conclusions to their readers. No longer were they mere reporters, passively receiving information in an older meaning of that term. They became investigators actively seeking the truth about what was happening. As investigative reporters they sought to uncover and disclose situations that were unacceptable in view of the norms of the society. That kind of oversight reporting developed more fully toward the end of the 19th century and matured forcefully during the era of the muckrakers, just before World War I.

Shortly after the middle of the 20th century, a major shift took place in the sources of information open to journalists wanting to exercise their oversight function. The digital electronic computer became available to government and agencies began to use the new technology as an efficient means to store their records. A short time later, freedom of information legislation made those electronic records available to all citizens, including members of the press (although sometimes reluctantly). Older paper trails began to disappear and journalists had to master the computer in order to understand what government officials and public agencies had been doing.

Initial attempts were made, with considerable success, to use computers to analyze records of government as early as the 1960s. Today, with computers widely available, and with electronic records of governments at all levels increasingly available, CAIR has become more commonplace. Most CAIR analyses that are routinely reported in newspapers today are based on rather basic techniques that were discussed in earlier chapters. Some, however, can involve massive databases and complex statistical operations, such as those described in the analysis of the federal court data.

But whatever the scope or complexity of the data used, and whatever the level of analysis undertaken, a formal methodology for CAIR may be helpful. As explained, CAIR methodology consists in part of a set of preliminary steps that prepare the data for use and that aid in identifying both general and specific goals for the analysis. It also consists of a set of strategies or logical plans of procedure used by the investigator to achieve those goals. CAIR analytic strategies are implemented by carrying out various kinds of operational procedures and using techniques, such as calculating appropriate statistical indices, determining relevant mathematical values, or preparing graphic presentations of what has been found. Finally, CAIR methodology also includes a set of responsibilities. These pertain to ethical ways of conducting analyses of electronic databases of records and for reporting the results to the public with meticulous accuracy and full disclosure.

In the years ahead, CAIR methodology will continue to improve. Although social science research, precision journalism and CAIR have much in common, some goals, techniques, strategies, and ethical requirements are unique to CAIR. Computer-assisted investigative reporting has, in other words, a methodology in the classic meaning of that term—that is, "a set of constructs, shared within a particular field, about how research should be conducted and reported in order to be regarded as legitimate by its practitioners."

NOTES AND REFERENCES

1. Abraham Kaplan, *The Conduct of Inquiry: Methodology for Behavioral Science* (San Francisco: Chandler Publishing Company, 1964), p. 18.
2. Maurice Natanson, *Philosophy of the Social Sciences* (New York: Random House, 1963), p. 271.
3. Abraham Kaplan, *op. cit.,* p. 19.
4. Philip Babcock Gove, editor in chief, *Webster's Third New International Dictionary,* unabridged version (Springfield, Mass.: Merriam-Webster, Inc., 1986), p. 2256.

5. Guido H. Stempel and Bruce H. Westley, eds., *Research Methods in Mass Communication,* second edition (Englewood Cliffs, N.J.: Prentice Hall, Inc., 1989), p. 255.

6. Carrie Teegardin and Charles Haddad, "Income in America: A Special Report on the Shrinking Middle Class," the *Atlanta Journal and Constitution,* October 2, 1992, Section B, p. 2.

7. Carrie Teegardin, "Ga.'s Shifting Political Landscape," the *Atlanta Journal and Constitution,* November 12, 1992, Section C, p. 1.

8. Robert Steinbrook, "Heart Surgery Death Rates Found High in 1 in 6 Hospitals," the *Los Angeles Times,* July 24, 1988, Section 1, p. 3.

9. Thomas J. Lueck, "Racial Differences in Mortgage Lending: the *New York Times,* July 19, 1992, Section 1, p. 32. See also, Bill Dedman, "The Color of Money," the *Atlanta Journal and Constitution,* May 1-4, 1988.

10. Tom Gorman, "Incomes, Costs Up in San Diego," the *Los Angeles Times,* May 11, 1992, Part A, p. 1.

11. "Computer Analysis Yields Portrait of Elderly Wards," the *Los Angeles Times,* September 27, 1987, Part 1, p. 2.

12. Carolyn Pesce, "USA's Deadliest Roads, *USA Today,* September 4, 1990, News Section, p. 1A.

13. Debbie Wilgoren, "Carjackers Put Drivers on Defensive," the *Washington Post,* August 16, 1992, Section 1, p. A1.

14. Ted Rohrlich and Victor Merina, "Racial Disparities Seen in Complaints to LAPD," the *Los Angeles Times,* May 19, 1991, Part A, p. 1.

15. Alan Finder and Richard Levine, "Unequal Burden: New York City Property Taxes—A Special report: Some of the Rich Pay Less Tax Than Other Homeowners," the *New York Times,* May 29, 1990, Section A, p. 1.

16. John R. Bender, "Ethics and Computers," in John Ullman and Jan Colbert, editors, *The Reporter's Handbook,* second edition (New York: St. Martin's Press, 1991), pp. 56–57.

17. Philip Meyer, 1979, *op. cit.,* pp. 185–186.

18. American Association for Public Opinion Research, "Certificate of Incorporation and By-Laws," March 1986. See also: Philip Meyer and Karen Jurgensen, "Beating Disclosure to Death," *Newspaper Research Journal,* Summer, 1991, p. 5.

19. Penny Loeb, "The City's $275M IOU," *Newsday,* January 7, 1991, News Section, p. 5.

20. Eric Bailey and Richard O'Reilly, "Study Confirms O.C. Anglo-Latino Pay Gap," the *Los Angeles Times,* December 21, 1992, Part A, p. 1.

21. Michael Parrish, "America's Poisons On the Move," the *Los Angeles Times,* September 20, 1992, Part A, p. 1.

22. *Ibid.,* p. 1.

23. Alan Finder Richard Levine, "Unequal Burden: New York's Property Tax," the *New York Times,* July 6, 1991, Section 1, p. 1.

24. Sam Roberts, "Blacks Reach a Milestone in Queens: Income Parity," the *New York Times,* June 8, 1992, Section A, p. 1.

Appendix: Dictionary of Specific Analytic Techniques Used in Review of 130 CAIR Stories (Described in Chapter 5)

DEFINITIONS

1. An *entity* is some phenomenon, such as a person, group, event, action, thing or situation whose characteristics are being investigated and/or described in the story.
2. A *set of entities* is a number of similar phenomena that are conceptually grouped together because they possess one or more similar attributes.
3. An *attribute* is some qualitative characteristic, feature, factor or variable associated with an entity or set of entities that can be assessed in quantitative terms (i.e., with a nominal, ordinal, interval or ratio measure.)

EXPLANATIONS OF SPECIFIC TECHNIQUES

For Searching, Counting, or Sorting

1. *Single Value Search/Citation:* The story identifies a specific value of an attribute for an entity that was obtained by a search of the computerized source materials.

> *Example:* Congressman Smith received $38,123 in PAC contributions from the Howard Corporation.

2. *Assignment to Categories:* The story identifies a set of discrete categories into which a set of entities was classified.

> *Example:* The 3,532 gifts were classified into those that were under $500, those between $501 and $1,000 and those that exceeded this amount.

3. *Frequency Count:* The story identifies tabulated occurrences of an attribute for an entity or set of entities.

> *Example:* Hospital A had 375 heart bypass surgeries, Hospital B had 278, and Hospital C had 317.

4. *Rank Ordering:* The story identifies an ascending or descending order into which entities were sorted on the basis of the value of an attribute.

> *Example:* The amount spent by each of these 10 members of Congress on television commercials was determined. Alan Jones spent over $150,000, followed by Wilbur Smith at $137,000. The others spent the following amounts: (in descending order).

For Using Descriptive Statistics

5. *Mode:* The story identifies a most frequently occurring value of some attribute of one or more entities.

> *Example:* The most frequently noted high level of rainfall for Smith County was 3.5 inches, which seemed to occur regularly in August over the last 20 years.

6. *Median:* The story identifies a value of some attribute among a set of entities, above (or below) which 50% of the cases were found.

> *Example:* Half of the homes in the neighborhood were valued at $178,000 or higher.

7. *Mean or Average:* The story identifies an average value of an attribute that characterizes a set of entities.

> *Example:* On average, juries awarded less than $100,000 to plaintiffs in this type of lawsuit.

8. *Percentage:* The story identifies the number per 100 entities that possessed some attribute.

> *Example:* In the school districts within the city limits, the student body was more than 60% African American.

9. *Numerical Variability:* The story identifies a numerical range or some other quantitative index of scatter regarding the values of some attribute among a set of entities.

> *Example:* Among the unions involved, the salary paid to their presidents ranged from $75,000 to $200,000. Or: The average amount of taxes paid on a typical home in the city was $3,433, but

homeowners paid anywhere from $1,100 to $5,000 for the same type of house.

10. *Simple Association:* The story identifies a corelationship between two attributes among a set of entities.

> *Example:* It was determined that banks that had made few loans to real estate developers were more likely to remain solvent than those who had underwritten such projects. Or: Age at death was generally higher among retirees who had vested pension plans, but lower among those who were living only on social security. In other words, the higher one's income in retirement, the longer one tends to live.

11. *Multiple Factor Association:* The story identifies a pattern in which two or more attributes appear to be related to another attribute said to be dependent on their values. If these are considered together, they modify the interpretation of a simple association.

> *Example:* Some hospitals have high death rates for heart bypass surgery. Others have much lower rates. This would seem to imply that those with lower rates have surgeons who have greater skill. However, if a hospital admits more patients who have chronic heart problems (poorer risks for surgery) and if they treat more emergency cases involving heart attacks (also poorer risks for surgery), its rate will go up due to those causes, and not because of a lack of skill by the surgeons. Thus, a given hospital's death rate for heart bypass surgery may not be an indicator of bad performance. It can be a product of several factors.

For Posing Contrasts, Changes, and Comparisons

12. *Before/After Comparison:* The story identifies a value of an attribute for an entity at one point in time and then contrasts it with the value of that same attribute for the same entity at a later point in time.

> *Example:* In 1980, more than 5 million metric tons of unprocessed logs were shipped to Japan from Washington and Oregon compared to only 3.5 million in 1990.

13. *Contrast Comparison:* The story identifies the value of an attribute for one entity and the value of the same attribute for another entity and then compares the two to provide a contrast.

> *Example:* In 1990, the conviction rate for forgery was twice as high in the District of Manhattan as it was in District of Northern New

York. Or: In 1992, the birth rate for Metropolitan Detroit was 12.8 per each 1,000 residents. The same rate for Metropolitan Cleveland was only 9.9.

14. *Matched Comparison:* The story compares the values of an attribute between entities selected so as to be similar on some set of criteria.
Example: The homicide rates of nearby counties with about the same demographic characteristics were compared to that of Suffolk County to see if it was quite dissimilar.

15. *Numerical Trend:* The story identifies a periodic change in the quantity of an attribute that characterizes an entity or set of entities.
Example: More and more Asians are moving into the neighborhood. Or: Car thefts have risen sharply in the city. Or (more specifically): The amount of taxes paid by citizens in Homeville has risen steadily from $50 per $1,000 of assessed valuation to over $100 in the last 5 years.

16. *Cross-Tabulation:* The story identifies a set of entities that were first sorted into discrete categories and then sorted further into subcategories based on the value of an attribute.
Example: It was determined whether or not each of the NFL football players who had attended a particular college had graduated. Or: For each of the major auto manufacturers, the percentage of vehicle owners who were satisfied or dissatisfied was determined.

17. *Cross-Referencing:* The story identifies a search that was conducted through one set of records to locate the value of an attribute for a specific entity. Then, a second search was conducted through another set of records to determine the value of a different attribute for that same entity.
Example: In a search of the records on driving infractions, it was discovered that school bus driver Donald Powers had been issued two citations for moving violations. In a search of the records on criminal violations, it was discovered that he had also been convicted of a felony.

For Using Inferential Statistics

18. *Sampling:* The story identifies how a limited number of entities were selected for analysis in such a way that they had distributions of attributes that are similar to those prevailing in a larger population of such entities. If

it is claimed that the sample was drawn randomly, the procedure used for selection should have ensured that each entity in the population had an equal chance of being included in the smaller number that was drawn.

> *Example:* A total of 1,250 members of the more than 100,000 who belong to the Association were selected by a random procedure and polled to assess their views about President Clinton's proposal to cap the fees that they can charge for their services.

19. *Confidence Limits:* The story identifies specific values on a scale that are above and below a mean of an attribute of an entity such that the cases falling between the two values include a specified percentage of all such cases in a normal distribution around that mean.

> *Example:* The mean length of sentence in the state for armed robbery is 8.7 years. However, 95% of such sentences are not less than 4.2 or greater than 13.2 years. Another words, the vast majority of the sentences are between 4.2 and 13.2 years.

20. *Hypothesis Testing:* The story identifies a level of chance or probability with which a particular statistical finding, such as a difference between two means of an attribute, is associated. It then explains the implications that could be drawn if only chance were at work to produce such a finding.

> *Example:* The mean annual income of male physicians with 10 years of practice in pediatrics was $156,332. For females in this specialty, with the same years of experience, the figure was only $110,771. Thus, females received $45,561 less per year on average. If only chance were at work as a causal factor, a difference of this size would be found in only 1% of such comparisons. Therefore, chance as an explanation can be rejected and it seems safe to conclude that a difference of this magnitude is due to other causal factors.

21. *Multivariate Analysis:* The story identifies an attribute under examination that is statistically corelated to two or more additional attributes in such a way that if their values are high (or low), the attribute under study is correspondingly high (or low) by specified amounts. This relationship was determined by a specific statistical procedure.

> *Example:* Men with higher incomes tend to live to age 76 on average, 2 years longer than those who are poor. If such males also exercise regularly, they tend to have even longer lives, averaging 78 years at death. If, in addition, they eat a relatively fat-free diet,

they tend to survive an additional 2 years. If they have never smoked, their average age at death is further extended by 2 years (to an average of 80 at death). The reverse is true of poor males. If they fail to exercise, consume a high level of fats, and smoke, such individuals die at 74 years on average. Thus, life expectancy among males is associated in a multiple manner with all four of the factors of income, exercise, diet, and smoking. Each plays a part in determining longevity.

For Other Procedures

22. *Statistical Projection:* The story identifies a forecast in the value or values of an attribute for one or more entities that can be expected in the future because of one or more past trends or present values.

> *Example:* The cost of open heart bypass surgery rose from $10,000 in 1985 to just over $20,113 in 1993, an average of 15% per year. If that trend continues at the same rate, such a procedure will cost over $46,500 by the year 2000.

23. *Probability of an Event:* The story indicates the likelihood of finding a particular value of an attribute, based on a calculation from the data under examination.

> *Example:* On any given day, the likelihood of being a victim of a carjacking is only one in 540,000, based on the number of cars being driven in the city and the frequency of the crime.

24. *Construct Index or Scale:* The story indicates a measure based on some attribute, or a combination of attributes that is used as a basis for rating, ranking, or otherwise arraying entities along some type of continuum.

> *Example:* The index of bank health was based on three factors: The total amounts of the institution's bad commercial real estate loans, repossessed property, and bad consumer loans as a percentage of the bank's capital reserves. If a bank had an index of more than 100%, it was placed on the "troubled" list, due to more bad assets than capital reserves.

Index